Seminars in the Psychiatry of Learning Disabilities

College Seminars Series

Series Editors

Professor Hugh Freeman, Honorary Professor, University of Salford, and Honorary Consultant Psychiatrist, Salford Health Authority

Dr Ian Pullen, Consultant Psychiatrist, Dingleton Hospital, Melrose

Dr George Stein, Consultant Psychiatrist, Farnborough Hospital, and King's College Hospital

Professor Greg Wilkinson, Editor, *British Journal of Psychiatry*, and Professor of Liaison Psychiatry, University of Liverpool

Other books in the series

Seminars in Child and Adolescent Psychiatry. Edited by Dora Black & David Cottrell

Seminars in Basic Neurosciences. Edited by Gethin Morgan & Stuart Butler

Seminars in Psychiatric Genetics. By Peter McGuffin, Michael J. Owen, Michael C. O'Donovan, Anita Thapar & Irving Gottesman

Seminars in Alcohol and Drug Misuse. Edited by Jonathan Chick & Roch Cantwell

Seminars in Psychology and the Social Sciences. Edited by Digby Tantam & Max Birchwood

Seminars in Clinical Psychopharmacology. Edited by David King

Seminars in Practical Forensic Psychiatry. Edited by Derek Chiswick & Rosemarie Cope

Seminars in Liaison Psychiatry. Edited by E. Guthrie and F. Creed

Forthcoming titles

Seminars in Psychosexual Disorders. Edited by R. Haslam

Seminars in General Adult Psychiatry. Edited by George Stein & Greg Wilkinson

Seminars in Psychiatry for the Elderly. Edited by Brice Pitt & Mohsen Naguib

Seminars in the Psychiatry of Learning Disabilities

Edited by
Oliver Russell

GASKELL

British Library Cataloguing-in-Publication Data
A catalogue record for this book is available from the British Library.

ISBN 1-901242-02-1

Distributed in North America
by American Psychiatric Press, Inc.
ISBN 0-88048-590-9

Gaskell is an imprint of the Royal College of Psychiatrists,
17 Belgrave Square, London SW1X 8PG
The Royal College of Psychiatrists is a registered charity, number 228636

The views presented in this book do not necessarily reflect those of the Royal College of Psychiatrists, and the publishers are not responsible for any error of omission or fact. College Seminars are produced by the Publications Department of the College; they should in no way be construed as providing a syllabus or other material for any College examination.

Printed by Bell & Bain Ltd., Thornliebank, Glasgow

Contents

Contributors

Dr T. P. Berney, Consultant Psychiatrist, Prudhoe Hospital, Prudhoe, Northumberland NE42 5NT

Professor Emeritus Joan Bicknell, London University; Farthing Gate Farm, Holnest, Sherborne, Dorset DT9 5PX

Dr Jonathan Bird, Consultant Neuropsychiatrist, Frenchay Healthcare Trust, Burden Neurological Hospital, Stoke Lane, Stapleton, Bristol BS16 1QT

Dr R. A. Collacott, Consultant Psychiatrist and Senior Lecturer, Leicester Frith Hospital, Groby Road, Leicester LE3 9QF

Dr Michael Cooper, Thirlestaine Court, Thirlestaine Road, Cheltenham, Gloucestershire GL53 7AP

Professor Eric Emerson, Hester Adrian Research Centre, University of Manchester, Manchester M13 9PL

Professor W. I. Fraser, University of Wales College of Medicine, Welsh Centre for Learning Disabilities, Meridian Court, North Road, Cardiff CF4 3BL

Dr Tom Fryers, 'Distinguished Lecturer' in Preventive and Community Health, New York Medical College, Lambrigg Foot, Grayrigg, Kendal, Cumbria LA8 9BL

Dr Tony Holland, Section of Developmental Psychiatry, 2nd Floor, Douglas House, 18b Trumpington Road, Cambridge CB2 2AH

Professor Sheila Hollins, Professor of Psychiatry of Learning Disabilities, Department of Psychiatry of Disability, St George's Hospital Medical School, Jenner Wing, Cranmer Terrace, London SW17 0RE

Professor Chris Kiernan, Hester Adrian Research Centre, University of Manchester, Manchester M13 9PL

Dr Mary Lindsey, Consultant Psychiatrist, Trecare NHS Trust, 57 Pydar Street, Truro, Cornwall TR1 2SS

Dr Andrew H. Reid, Consultant Psychiatrist and Honorary Senior Lecturer in Psychiatry, Dundee Healthcare NHS Trust, Royal Dundee Liff Hospital, Dundee DD2 5NF

Dr Oliver Russell, Director, Norah Fry Research Centre, University of Bristol, 3 Priory Road, Bristol BS8 1TX

Dr Stephen Tyrer, Consultant Psychiatrist, Prudhoe Hospital, Department of Psychiatry, Prudhoe, Northumberland NE42 5NT

Dr D. N. Wilson, Department of Learning Disabilities, Floor E – South Block, University Hospital, Queens Medical Centre, Nottingham NG7 2UH

Foreword

Series Editors

The publication of *College Seminars*, a series of textbooks covering the breadth of psychiatry, is very much in line with the Royal College of Psychiatrists' established role in education and in setting professional standards.

College Seminars are intended to help junior doctors during their training years. We hope that trainees will find these books useful, on the ward as well as in preparation for the MRCPsych examination. Separate volumes will cover clinical psychiatry, each of its subspecialities, and also the relevant non-clinical academic disciplines of psychology and sociology.

College Seminars will make a contribution to the continuing professional development of established clinicians.

Psychiatry is concerned primarily with people, and to a lesser extent with disease processes and pathology. The core of the subject is rich in ideas and schools of thought, and no single approach or solution can embrace the variety of problems a psychiatrist meets. For this reason, we have endeavoured to adopt an eclectic approach to practical management throughout the series.

The College can draw on the collective wisdom of many individuals in clinical and academic psychiatry. More than a hundred people have contributed to this series; this reflects how diverse and complex psychiatry has become.

Frequent new editions of books appearing in the series are envisaged, which should allow *College Seminars* to be responsive to readers' suggestions and needs.

Hugh Freeman
Ian Pullen
George Stein
Greg Wilkinson

Preface

This volume aims to provide an overview of the practice of psychiatry as it relates to the needs of people with learning disabilities. The book has two purposes: to provide an up-to-date account of recent research, and to provide a practical guide to the diagnosis and treatment of psychiatric disorder in people with learning disabilities.

The use of the term 'learning disability' in this book rather than 'mental handicap', 'mental defect', or 'mental retardation' is deliberate and reflects changes that have accompanied the wider recognition of the rights and individuality of disabled people. Although 'learning disability' is the term now most widely used in the UK, it is not accepted internationally and indeed in the US the term 'learning disability' refers to pupils with educational problems. To complicate matters further, the main international organisation concerned with this field is called the "International Association for the Scientific Study of Intellectual Disability", but many clinicians and scientists continue to refer to 'mental retardation' or 'developmental disability'.

The most recent definition of mental retardation emerged in the US after an extensive process of consultation (American Association on Mental Retardation, 1992):

(a) Significantly sub-average general intellectual functioning: an IQ of 70 or below on an individually administered IQ test.
(b) Concurrent deficits or impairments in two or more of the following adaptive skill areas: communication, self-care, home living, social skills, community use, self-direction, health and safety, functional academics, leisure and work.
(c) The condition is manifest before the age of 18 years.

Thus a low intelligence quotient is not sufficient on its own for a diagnosis of a learning disability; social functioning must also be impaired and the impairment must have developed before the individual became an adult. For the moment we can use this as a working definition of 'learning disability' in the UK context, although as Fryers discusses in Chapter 2 of this book, we need to be extremely cautious about how we use the many available labels, which are not always interchangeable.

The common characteristic of people with a learning disability is that they have undergone an exceptionally slow intellectual development during childhood. This may be the result of an impairment that has occurred because of a genetic fault, or it may have been brought about by brain damage following an accident or illness, or there may be no obvious reason for the intellectual impairment. There are a vast number of potential causes, and psychiatrists working in this field are expected to be familiar with an ever-expanding database about possible causes of learning disability. In a book like this it is impossible to cover the many scientific developments which are adding to our knowledge. The rapid advances being made in human genetics, the neurosciences, cell biology, developmental psychology, and psychopharmacology cannot all be covered in a single text. In this book we have asked contributors to confine their focus to psychiatric issues. Those who are especially interested in the genetics of learning disability will find that this topic is reviewed in another volume in this series, *Seminars in Psychiatric Genetics* (McGuffin *et al*, 1994).

Doctors who specialise in the psychiatry of learning disabilities need an unusual combination of clinical skills if they are to stay abreast of scientific developments. As physicians we need to have a wide knowledge of medical disorders, sound diagnostic skills and an acute awareness of how symptoms of illness can be detected in those who may be unable to show their feelings of pain and discomfort. As psychiatrists we need to have the sensitivity of the psychotherapist to interpret the symptoms of emotional disorder in those who cannot speak of their distress. As members of community teams we need to have the skills to support professional colleagues and work with them creatively to plan and develop new and better services for our clients.

In writing this book we had to consider what the trainee psychiatrist needed to know about the psychiatry of learning disabilities. The Joint Committee on Higher Specialist Training has laid out an agenda for the trainee, and we tried to keep this in mind as we wrote our contributions for this book.

The aim of postgraduate training is to provide doctors with an education that will fit them for the independent practice of psychiatry in a modern learning disabilities service. The trainee will be expected to acquire:

- Expert knowledge of all forms of psychopathology as they present in people with learning disability.
- Expert knowledge of psychotropic medication and its effects and use in people with learning disability.
- Relevant knowledge of and understanding of the work of relevant co-disciplines, e.g. child psychiatry, forensic psychiatry, neuropsychiatry and rehabilitation.
- Knowledge of particular legal issues for people with learning disabilities, especially consent.
- Ability to communicate effectively with people of all degrees of learning disability.
- Ability to identify factors relevant to the development or maintenance of disturbed behaviour, e.g. abuse, bereavement, and advice on the management of failures in care-giving.

- Ability to assess and manage people with pervasive developmental disorder.
- Ability to manage epilepsy in people with learning disability.
- Ability to identify effects of physical disorders among people with severe learning disability.
- Ability to identify psychopathology within families and carers.
- Ability to work effectively with families, carers and multidisciplinary groups.
- Ability to assess competency to consent.

(Joint Committee on Higher Psychiatric Training, 1996)

This book is not intended to be read on its own but should be used alongside the suggestions for further reading which we have listed at the end of each chapter. We have tried to have an eye for the future and hope that our readers will find stimulus and interest in the chapters which follow.

Oliver Russell
January 1997

References

American Association on Mental Retardation (1992) *Mental Retardation: Definition, Classification, and Systems of Supports.* Washington, DC: American Association on Mental Retardation.

Joint Committee on Higher Psychiatric Training (1996) *Criteria for Award of a Certificate of Completion of Specialist Training (CCST).* London: JCHPT.

McGuffin, P., Owen, M. J., O'Donovan, M. C., *et al* (1994) *Seminars in Psychiatric Genetics.* London: Gaskell.

1 Historical overview: concepts and concerns

Oliver Russell

19th century pioneers ● The 20th century ● Dual diagnosis ●
Challenging behaviour ● Conclusion

> "Medicine has in its hands a powerful method of psychological
> and physical development. Up to a certain point it can blunt or
> sharpen nervous sensitivity and by this means influence man's
> intellect." Jean Marc Itard, 1801 (from Lane, 1976, p. 78)

In this chapter key moments in the history of the psychiatry of learning
disability and some of the concepts and controversies that have marked
the development of this special area of psychiatric practice are examined.

19th century pioneers

Jean Marc Gaspard Itard (1774–1838)

In 1799 a young physician, Jean Itard, was appointed to the staff of the
Institute for the Deaf in Paris. His main task was to study disorders of
hearing and speech and to devise programmes of training for the residents.
Most of those living in the institute were mute as well as deaf. Not long
after he started in his new job, a 12-year-old boy, who had been found
running through the woods of Aveyron in central France, was brought to
him. Subsequently known as Victor, the wild boy of Aveyron, the boy had
been caught by local hunters. A 'feral' or 'wild' child, the boy spoke no
language and uttered inarticulate sounds. He was brought to Paris and
placed in the care of Itard at the Institute for the Deaf.

After carrying out a preliminary assessment Itard sought the opinion of
Phillipe Pinel, the leading psychiatric diagnostician of the day. Pinel saw
Victor in his clinic and prepared a lengthy and very detailed clinical
report. He summarised his findings thus:

> "The child is without speech and without the advantage of making
> himself understood by gestures. The past is for him as if it had
> never existed and we have no other certain source of information;
> we can only be guided by looking for the usual causes that produced
> insanity or idiocy in childhood. Now, excluding from this category
> complications from epilepsy and rickets, the possible causes come

1

down to three: (1) an intense fright suffered by the mother during childbirth; (2) a fright or convulsions occurring in infancy as a result of verminous infection; (3) a painful or tempestuous first or second dentition. Nothing permits us to determine which of these causes might have worked on the child of Aveyron so disastrously to undermine his intellectual faculties ... Do these not assert that the child ought to be categorized among the children suffering from idiocy and insanity, and that there is no hope whatever of obtaining some measure of success through systematic and continued instruction?" Phillippe Pinel, 1799 (in Lane, 1976, p. 69)

Pinel's report is probably the oldest surviving case report of a psychiatric disorder in a person with severe learning disabilities.

Itard believed that it was important for doctors to adopt a psychological approach to the study of their patients and he took a more positive view than Pinel of Victor's potential to develop. Itard wrote:

"Thus psychological man more than physical man has his idiosyncrasies or individual differences; and it is the task of medicine more than any other science to study them and to bring to bear on their correct evaluation and development the resource of knowledge in physiology." Itard, 1800 (in Lane, 1976)

Itard had a strong belief in the value of a close collaboration between doctors and teachers. He embarked upon an ambitious educational programme to help Victor develop language and social skills. He wrote:

"The advantages of education guided by medicine can be expected most dramatically in cases of idiocy. This education could accomplish a great deal with these people, who for the most part are no different from other men save their reduced sensory capacities." Itard, 1800 (in Lane, 1976)

Itard undertook to transform Victor from "savagery to civilisation, from natural life to social life". Although in the end Victor never developed any useful language, he did make remarkable progress during the five years that he was under Itard's supervision. He learned to recognise objects, to identify letters of the alphabet, and to comprehend the meaning of many words. Itard described his behaviour:

"passing suddenly from sadness to anxiety, and from anxiety to fury, he takes a dislike to all his keenest enjoyments; he sighs, sheds tears, utters shrill cries, tears his clothes, and sometimes goes as far as to scratch or bite his governess" (Lane, 1976, p. 158)

Itard's detailed observations of Victor's progress mark the first attempts at the clinical diagnosis and management of a psychiatric disorder in a person with learning disabilities. Itard's skilful blend of education and psychology which characterised his work with Victor established a pattern for others to follow.

Edouard Onesimus Seguin (1812–1880)

Itard's pupil, Edouard Seguin, recognised the importance of his teacher's observations. Seguin was the first to advocate the need for systematic psychological assessments. Nineteenth century psychiatrists claimed that most forms of intellectual impairment were brought about by disease (Berrios, 1994). However, Seguin, who was both an educator and a physician, argued that environmental factors also played a significant role. He opened the first school for children with learning disabilities in Paris in 1839. He put into operation a programme of physical, intellectual and psychological education in his school at the Bicetre and published a major textbook in 1846. His pioneering work attracted much interest among the educators and physicians of the day. He was one of the first exponents of speech therapy.

Johann Jacob Guggenbuhl (1816–1863)

In 1842 Guggenbuhl founded the Abendberg near Interlaken for the cure of cretinism. He takes credit for establishing the first institution in Europe for the treatment of people with learning disabilities. In 1846 the first residential home to be established in the UK was opened in Bath. By this time a shift in philosophy had occurred and the goals of those caring for people with learning disabilities were no longer those of Seguin, "to waken the senses and mind". The new generation of professionals were now more concerned to instil religious and moral values in the minds of their residents (see von Gontard, 1988).

Samuel Gridley Howe (1801–1876)

Seguin's influence extended to the US where Howe, a graduate of Harvard Medical School, took up the challenge. Early in his career Howe had developed an interest in working with blind and deaf children. In 1832 he took a few blind children into his father's house in Boston, Massachusetts. He devised new methods for educating children who had profound sensory handicaps. Following his phenomenal success with one pupil who was both blind and deaf he won international fame. Howe did pioneering work with young people who had sensory impairments and severe learning disabilities. In describing his work he commented: "if so much could be done for idiots who were blind, still more could be done for idiots who were not blind" (quoted by Kanner, 1960).

In 1846 Howe carried out a survey of the Commonwealth of Massachusetts and found over 500 people with learning disabilities, many of whom were neglected and living in appalling conditions. He prepared a report on their medical and psychological condition. The results of this study alerted the state legislature to the dire condition of many of their fellow citizens. Funds were provided for Howe to build a new wing for the Perkins Institution for blind children to enable him to expand his educational programme to include children with intellectual disabilities.

In 1851 Seguin emigrated from France to the US where he joined Howe in his new venture. Seguin organised classes and introduced his methods to the staff of the new school. The experiment flourished and expanded. Ultimately the school moved to another site at Waltham, Massachusetts, where in later years it became the Walter E. Fernald State School (Kanner, 1960; Lane, 1976).

Hervey Backus Wilbur (1820–1883)

Wilbur was another New England physician and pioneering spirit. In 1847 Wilbur took into his home in Barre, Massachusetts, a young boy who had learning disabilities. The boy made progress and Wilbur decided to bring other children into his house where he created an educational programme for them. Like Howe, he based his teaching methods on those of Seguin. Wilbur's programme expanded and he subsequently opened an experimental school at Syracuse. Seguin visited Wilbur's school in Syracuse frequently and worked there as consultant and teacher.

The link from Itard through Seguin to Howe and Wilbur provided inspiration to those who followed them. These pioneers showed what was possible, and using Seguin's methods established the psychiatry of learning disabilities in the US.

The second half of the 19th century

During the second half of the 19th century interest in educational approaches to the management of people with learning disabilities began to wane both in Europe and America. Overcrowding of the institutions and a gradual loss of enthusiasm by both educators and physicians saw psychological approaches replaced by custodial models of care. Physicians retreated from the educational methods of Seguin and Itard. Biological determinism, which held that social and economic differences between human groups arise from inherited, inborn distinctions, was embraced as the guiding principle by the new generation of physicians.

Two themes emerged from this change of focus. The first was a growth of interest in physical anthropology, particularly a fascination with the structure of the brain and the size of the cranium. The second was a concern with creating measures for testing intelligence (see Gould, 1981, for a thorough review of these issues).

Many of the debates about craniometry, or measurement of cranial capacity, were initiated by Paul Broca, professor of clinical surgery in

Paris. Also interested in physical anthropology, Broca founded the Paris anthropological society in 1859. A brilliant anatomist, he amassed an enormous amount of detail about the structure and size of the brain in people from different races and of different backgrounds. Broca and his contemporaries recognised that the frequency of pathological changes in the brain increased with the severity of the learning disability. Although their work laid the foundations for our modern understanding of neuro-anatomy, it contributed little to our knowledge of behavioural and psychiatric aspects of learning disability.

Craniometry also fascinated English physicians. John Langdon Down, who became superintendent of Earlswood in Surrey, carried out post mortem examinations of people with learning disabilities and measured their cranial capacities. His observations led him to his ethnic classification of people with learning disabilities, published in 1887. Down was primarily interested in anatomical differences, and although he did little to apply psychological approaches to the needs of people with learning disabilities he was interested in the mental health of their carers.

The first comprehensive medical text on learning disabilities was published in 1887 by William Wotherspoon Ireland, a physician who had been appointed to be the first superintendent of the Scottish National Institution at Larbert in 1869. He adhered to Langdon Down's ethnic classification system, and although he extended the scheme to include new categories, he gave little consideration to psychiatric matters. However, in France the physician and anatomist D. M. Bourneville showed more interest in psychiatric and educational interventions, and he developed a 'Medico–Pedagogical Institute' at the Bicetre, which emphasised education and training. It was Bourneville who arranged for the re-publication of Itard's and Seguin's books at a time when their ideas were in danger of being forgotten (Scheerenberger, 1983).

The 20th century

Although there was some interest in the relationship between psychiatric disorder and learning disability during the early years of the 20th century, most medical researchers were more concerned with anatomical and pathological changes in the brain. Nevertheless, Tredgold claimed that the same kinds of mental illness found in the normal population also occurred in those with learning disabilities. Kraepelin suggested that some cases of dementia praecox developed as a consequence of a learning disability and, conversely, that some types of learning disability resulted from the early onset of dementia praecox. He referred to such disorders as "schizophrenic psychoses of particularly early onset". Since Kraepelin's time there has been much controversy about whether the different sub-types of major mental disorder can be diagnosed in people with learning disabilities (see Reid, 1982, for a further discussion).

The publication in 1943 by Kanner of his paper 'Autistic disturbances of affective contact' rekindled an interest in the psychopathology of learning disabilities. In this classic account of autism he emphasised the basic problems which such children had in their interactions with others. Kanner's work stimulated new lines of enquiry, not only about autism, but also about the relationship between biological, social and psychological factors in the development of psychiatric disorder in people with learning disabilities.

During the early 1950s psychiatrists became more aware of the need to learn how to diagnose mental illness in people with learning disabilities. This was partly because the newly discovered tranquilliser drugs gave them the means to treat some of the more severely disabled people who had psychotic symptoms and severe behaviour problems, and partly because there was pressure on psychiatrists to develop a more therapeutic and less custodial approach in their professional activity. The use of barbiturates and other heavily sedative drugs was reduced and psychological approaches began to be introduced.

During these post-war years social workers became more aware of the impact of family dynamics on the emotional well-being of the disabled person. Paediatricians began to show greater awareness of the needs of children with learning disabilities, who had often hitherto been excluded from paediatric clinics. Clinical psychologists showed how behavioural approaches could be used to modify unacceptable behaviour. Academic psychologists began to take an increasing interest in researching disorders of mental development. Specialist teachers were trained and recruited to teach children with severe learning disabilities who had previously been declared ineducable.

In 1953 it was discovered that the elimination of phenylalanine from the diet of a child with phenylketonuria could prevent further intellectual deterioration (Bickel *et al*, 1953). This dramatic discovery triggered a determined search by physicians and biochemists for other inborn errors of metabolism which might show a similar response to dietary manipulation. Here was an example of a metabolic condition that could not be treated in the conventional sense, but where the psychiatric and behavioural effects could be eliminated by dietary means.

The recognition by Lejeune in 1959 of the chromosome constitution of people with Down's syndrome opened up the possibility that the genetic information carried on chromosomes might one day be decoded and used to assist the recovery of brain function which had been lost.

Improvements in antenatal and obstetric care led to hopes that neonatal brain damage could be reduced or eliminated. The introduction of neonatal intensive care greatly improved the outlook for prematurely delivered infants.

The 1960s: a new era in the UK

The 1959 Mental Health Act heralded a new era for people with learning disabilities. Those who were resident in long-stay hospitals were no longer subject to the legal constraints of the 1913 Mental Deficiency Act and were free to move out if they wished, provided somewhere could be found for them to live. For those who had never been in hospital but had always lived with their families, 'care in the community' became a realistic option. Local authorities built adult training centres, invested in training programmes and provided residential care.

The psychological needs of people with learning disabilities also began to be more clearly recognised. Tizard (1964) and Clarke & Clarke (1984) had shown that education and training were of prime importance to adults, and by the mid-1960s their views had made a major impact on the pattern of services being developed. Active programmes of education and training were introduced into hospital workshops and day centres. Tizard's research on residential care for children at Brooklands showed that small group settings could provide better learning environments for children who had severe learning disabilities (Tizard, 1964). Parental pressure became an important influence in the drive for better educational provision, and the 1970 Education Act legislated that education should be provided for all children, no matter how severe their disability.

Epidemiological studies

In 1964 Rutter and colleagues began a series of epidemiological studies of educational, psychiatric and physical disorders among children aged 9–11 living on the Isle of Wight (Rutter *et al*, 1970, 1975, 1976). Intellectual retardation (as defined in terms of an IQ of two standard deviations below the mean) was present in 2.5% of children. Severe learning disabilities (equivalent to an IQ of less than 50) were found in three children in every 1000. These studies enabled researchers to examine for the first time the interrelationship between neurological damage and psychiatric disorder. A third of the intellectually retarded children showed signs of a definite neurological abnormality. Intellectual impairment was particularly frequent in the children of unskilled and semi-skilled workers. The rate of psychiatric disorder was greatly raised in children with epilepsy and in children with cerebral palsy.

Using the same epidemiological methods, studies of reading difficulties and psychiatric disorder were repeated among 10-year-old children in an inner London Borough. It was found that behavioural deviance, psychiatric disorder and specific reading retardation were all twice as common in London as in the Isle of Wight (Rutter *et al*, 1975). The results of these studies were very influential and shaped our understanding of the origins and nature of psychiatric disorder in people with a learning disability. The research showed that the main reason why the rates of reading problems, behavioural deviance and psychiatric disorder were high in inner London children compared with the Isle of Wight was that so many children came from disadvantaged families or attended disadvantaged schools.

A new role for the psychiatrist

In a lecture given in 1973 to the Royal College of Psychiatrists, Sir George Godber (at that time Chief Medical Officer at the Department of Health) spoke of the responsibilities of doctors who worked with people with learning disabilities. He suggested that with the expansion of community care the contribution made by psychologists and educationalists would increase and there might, perhaps, be less need for so many doctors. He found it difficult to see a specific and differentiated role for the psychiatrist working in the field of learning disabilities. He urged that those special skills that mental handicap specialists had acquired because of their medical training should be used with careful precision.

His message was clear. Those who worked in the field of learning disabilities, having been trained in psychiatry, should use their psychiatric skills for the benefit of those people with learning disabilities who needed psychiatric treatment. Those people with learning disabilities who did not need such specialist care should be supported and cared for outside of a medical framework.

Not unexpectedly, Godber's views had a profound impact on psychiatrists working within services for people with learning disabilities. There were those who believed that the psychiatrist was uniquely qualified to assume total control of those who lived in hospital. Others believed that the psychiatrist's main role had to be outside of the hospital and there was an urgent need to define and develop specialist psychiatric skills. The case for specialist psychiatry was presented in a collection of papers, *Psychiatric Illness and Mental Handicap* (James & Snaith, 1979). Clinical data were assembled which showed that significant numbers of people with learning disabilities had a major mental illness. The need for specialist psychiatry was given powerful support.

Developments in Scandinavia

Services in Scandinavia took a very different direction in the post-war period. In all of the Scandinavian countries policies for people with learning disabilities began to reflect what has been defined as 'normalisation'. In Sweden, under the leadership of Karl Grunewald (a psychiatrist), radical new policies for the development of community-based services based on the principle of normalisation were adopted with enthusiasm.

Bengt Nirje, the Swedish pioneer of normalisation, described it as:

> "making available to all mentally retarded people patterns of life and conditions of everyday living which are as close as possible to the regular circumstances and ways of life of society ... The application of the normalisation principle will not make retarded people more normal. But it will make their life condition as normal

as possible, respecting the degrees and complications of the handicap, the training received, and need and the social competence and maturity acquired and attainable." (Nirje, 1976)

Ironically, one of the policy initiatives which accompanied the introduction of the principle of normalisation in Sweden was a decision to stop recruiting specialist psychiatrists to work with people with learning disabilities!

Changing attitudes in the United States

In the US developments in the post-war period proceeded along a rather different path from those pursued in the UK and Scandinavia. Psychiatrists who had an interest in the needs of people with learning disabilities had always been thin on the ground. However, Kanner's work on autism had sparked interest in psychological issues regarding children with developmental disabilities, and during the 1950s there was growing interest in the emotional problems of people with learning disabilities. Relatively few psychiatrists were involved in clinical and diagnostic work, and it was generally educationalists and psychologists who planned and directed services.

In 1962 the report of a panel of experts appointed by President Kennedy sparked off a revolution in treatment, teaching, research and the development of new policy. There was a renaissance of professional interest in the needs of people with learning disabilities. Among those involved was Frank Menolascino, a psychiatrist from Omaha, Nebraska. In a retrospective review of these years he identified the roots of the changed attitudes as falling into four main areas.

Firstly, Menolascino identified the impact of the work of John Bowlby and Renee Spitz, which indicated that frequently it was not the underlying learning disability which led to behavioural problems and psychiatric disorders but rather the impersonal care which was provided in institutions. As newer principles of care were applied, it quickly became apparent that much of the abnormal behaviour, thought to be typical of an intellectually impaired person, was actually an expression of emotional detachment and therefore preventable if individuals were cared for in settings where there were better staffing levels and more stimulation and support.

Secondly, he attributed many of the changes in the lives of people with learning disabilities to improvements in primary health care. Improved management of epilepsy, better diagnosis and management of general medical disorders, and more effective diagnosis and understanding of motor and sensory impairments, all contributed to better emotional adjustment. In the institutions this permitted a drastic reduction in the use of mechanical restraint, of seclusion and the excessive use of medication. He saw these improvements in the treatment of mental illness in people with learning disabilities as flowing from a better understanding of the nature of psychiatric disorder. He asserted that any condition that renders a person less capable of handling reality-based demands makes that person more susceptible to mental illness.

Thirdly, he argued that the provision of more appropriate models of social care had a substantial impact on the mental health of people with learning disabilities. Providing more support to families and enhancing the quality of social care provided in community settings enabled family carers to be more involved and more effective. These changes had a significant impact on the mental health of the disabled person.

Fourthly, he argued that living through the 1960s and 1970s had brought mental health and learning disability professionals to a realisation that mental illness could frequently hinder the intellectual and adaptive growth of people with learning disabilities. Professionals discovered the benefits of working collaboratively to achieve better outcomes for their clients (Menolascino, 1983).

An ordinary life

In the UK the principles of normalisation were the sustaining force behind a set of reports published by the King's Fund (1980). The publication of *An Ordinary Life* focused attention on the need to harness the principles of normalisation to the everyday world of practice. These principles were already widely used in several parts of the US, notably in the Eastern Nebraska Office of Mental Retardation (ENCOR). It was the stimulus provided by a small group who had visited Nebraska and had seen what was being achieved that led to the King's Fund working party being set up. The objectives of the working party were remarkably simple:

> "Our goal is to see mentally handicapped people in the mainstream of life, living in ordinary houses in ordinary streets, with the same range of choices as any citizen, and mixing as equals with other, and mostly not handicapped members of their community." (King's Fund, 1980)

The report of that working party was enthusiastically received and provided the basis for many of the local services that we now see in the UK (see Towell, 1988, for a discussion of subsequent events).

Dual diagnosis

Interest in the concept of dual diagnosis arose in the US during the 1960s because of the need to make administrative distinctions. The administrators of Federal Government programmes needed to distinguish whether a person was primarily suffering from a learning disability complicated by an added emotional disturbance, or from a psychiatric disorder accompanied by a learning disability (Reiss, 1994). In other words was the person's primary handicap a mental illness or a learning disability? The distinction was important because the services were funded from separate sources. Those who had a learning disability as their primary problem would be entitled to services provided by developmental centres. Where the diagnosis was primarily of mental illness then the staff of a community mental health centre would be the appropriate providers.

The concept of dual diagnosis provided an alternative to the concept of primary and secondary handicaps. Instead of trying to guess which would be the appropriate service, both disorders would be diagnosed and appropriate services identified for each. Dual diagnosis has become the accepted term used in the US to describe the presence of psychiatric disorder in people with learning disabilities. It took some time for the concept to become established. It was considered that people with learning disabilities could not suffer from psychiatric problems because they had insufficient understanding of their feelings, and because few mental health professionals in the United States had experience in the field of learning disabilities they failed to recognise the needs of this population. In addition, there was the issue of diagnostic overshadowing, which means that clinicians tended to attribute abnormal behaviour to the underlying biological impairment instead of recognising coexisting psychopathology (Crews *et al*, 1994).

Challenging behaviour

In parallel with the growth of interest in dual diagnosis, there was rising concern in both the UK and the US about the management of people with learning disabilities who posed challenges to services because of their severely disturbed behaviour. The development of small group homes in the community and the closure of large institutions alerted service providers to the necessity for more effective ways of meeting the needs of these severely disturbed individuals.

In the US there had, for many years, been a strong interest among psychologists in behavioural approaches to the treatment of behavioural disorders. In the early 1980s there was a rapid expansion of interest among researchers in finding ways to meet the needs of those who engaged in severe forms of self-injurious behaviour. Service providers and carers became very concerned about the extreme measures which were increasingly being deployed to maintain a safe environment. Excessive amounts of medication, the use of seclusion and physical restraint all indicated the need for more effective therapies.

Durand and his colleagues played a leading role in the development of procedures that could reduce severe problem behaviour (Durand,

1990). These techniques, collectively known as functional communication training, have had a major impact, not only on the development of more effective intervention methods, but also on the ways in which we conceptualise severe behavioural problems. Some of the individuals with whom they worked engaged in such severe forms of self-injurious behaviour as to put their lives in danger. Other individuals behaved so aggressively that parents and care-givers became fearful for their own safety. Durand developed functional communication training as a way to manage these challenging behaviours more effectively. Guiding their approach was the assumption that:

> "such behaviour problems are not abnormalities. Instead, these responses are reasonable behavioural adaptations necessitated by the abilities of our students and the limitations of their environments. Therefore we have to look to the environment and its effect on the behaviours of our consumers." (Durand, 1990, p. 6)

By switching the emphasis away from locating possible sources of psychopathology within the individual to finding environmental triggers, Durand and his colleagues accepted that their approach diminished the role of physiological variables in the maintenance of these behaviours. They nevertheless recognised that physiological influences must play a part in the origins of these behaviours.

During these years a reaction against strict behavioural approaches had begun to gain in strength. Lovett wrote about the need to adapt behavioural approaches to the social context and emphasised the need to pay much more attention to the messages being communicated through challenging behaviour (Lovett, 1985). LaVigna & Donellan (1986) pursued similar themes in their book *Alternatives to Punishment*, where they drew attention to the need to pursue non-aversive methods. McGee *et al* (1987) in Nebraska took matters a stage further with their espousal of "Gentle Teaching" as a non-aversive approach to helping people with learning disabilities and challenging behaviour.

The term challenging behaviour has now crossed the Atlantic. When the term first came into use it represented an ideological shift in the way problem behaviour could be viewed. The nature of the challenge was to understand why the person behaved in culturally bizarre ways and to help them to develop socially acceptable ways to exercise control. The most widely used definition of challenging behaviour is:

> "Severely challenging behaviour refers to behaviour of such intensity, frequency or duration that the physical safety of the person or others is likely to be placed in serious jeopardy, or behaviour which is likely to seriously limit or delay access to and use of ordinary community facilities." (Emerson *et al*, 1987)

Challenging behaviour often serves as a means of communicating and controlling the environment around an individual with learning disabilities. This has focused our attention on the relationship between the individual and their social and material environment rather than just their problem behaviour. We need to recognise that in addition to any inherent psychopathological processes which may impinge on the person from within, the environment in which the person lives may provide an equally potent trigger for their challenging behaviour.

In a recent survey of referrals made to separate services for people with a dual diagnosis or challenging behaviour, few significant differences were evident between the populations using the two services, and those which were found related more to the severity of the problems than the clinical diagnosis (Allen & Kerr, 1994). This finding suggests that in meeting mental health needs we need to avoid a fragmented response. Challenging behaviour is not a clinical diagnosis, but we need to incorporate what the person with learning disabilities is communicating through their actions. The publication of the Mansell Report (Department of Health, 1993) has encouraged the development of a wide range of new approaches to the provision of more appropriate services for people with severely challenging behaviour.

Conclusion

Many of the shifts in understanding described in this overview have come about because we have come to think about the issues in new and different ways. New service philosophies, such as normalisation, have placed greater emphasis on the rights of people with learning disabilities to make choices and to speak for themselves. New ways of construing behavioural problems are forcing us to revise some of our traditional diagnostic approaches. Mercer (1992) has commented that within the field of learning disabilities there is no longer a single paradigm. There is little agreement on the nature of the phenomena being studied and consequently little agreement on treatments.

Many ambiguities persist, and in medical practice there continues to be a need to incorporate evidence from many different quarters. In the chapters that follow we shall explore a variety of themes which throw light on how to provide more effective diagnosis and treatment of psychiatric disorder in people with learning disabilities.

References

Allen, D. & Kerr, M. (1994) A survey of referrals to specialist services for people with learning disabilities who have a dual diagnosis or challenging behaviour. *British Journal of Learning Disabilities*, 22, 144–147.

Berrios, G. E. (1994) Mental illness and mental retardation: history and concepts. In *Mental Health in Mental Retardation* (ed. N. Bouras). Cambridge: Cambridge University Press.

Bickel, H., Gerrard, J. & Hickmans, E. M. (1953) The influence of phenylalanine intake on phenylketonuria. *Lancet, ii*, 812–813.

Clarke, A. D. B. & Clarke, A. M. (1984) *Mental Deficiency – the Changing Outlook*. London: Methuen.

Crews, W. D., Bonaventura, S. & Rowe, F. (1994) Dual diagnosis: prevalence of psychiatric disorders in a large state residential facility for individuals with mental retardation. *American Journal on Mental Retardation*, **98**, 688–731.

Department of Health (1993) *Services for People with Learning Disabilities and Challenging Behaviour or Mental Health Needs*. London: HMSO.

Durand, V. M. (1990) *Severe Behaviour Problems: a Functional Communication Training Approach*. London: The Gulford Press

Dykens, E. M. (1995) Measuring behavioral phenotypes: provocations from the "New Genetics". *American Journal on Mental Retardation*, **99**, 522–532.

Emerson, E., Toogood, A., Mansell, J., *et al* (1987) Challenging behaviour and community services: I. Introduction and overview. *Mental Handicap*, **15**, 166–169.

Godber, G. (1973) The responsibilities and role of the doctor concerned with the care of the mentally handicapped. *British Journal of Psychiatry*, **123**, 617–620.

Gould, S. J. (1981) *The Mismeasure of Man*. New York: W.W. Norton.

James, F. E. & Snaith, R. P. (eds) (1979) *Psychiatric Illness and Mental Handicap*. London: Royal College of Psychiatrists.

Kanner, L. (1943) Autistic disturbances of affective contact. *The Nervous Child*, **2**, 217–250.

—— (1960) Itard, Seguin, Howe: three pioneers in the education of retarded children. *American Journal of Mental Deficiency*, **65**, 2–10.

King's Fund (1980) *An Ordinary Life: Comprehensive Locally Based Residential Services for Mentally Handicapped People*. London: King's Fund.

Lane, H. (1976) *The Wild Boy of Aveyron*. Cambridge, MA: Harvard University Press.

LaVigna, G. W. & Donellan, A. M. (1986) *Alternatives to Punishment: Solving Behavior Problems with Non-Aversive Strategies*. New York: Irvington.

Lovett, H. (1985) *Cognitive Counselling and Persons with Special Needs: Adapting Behavioural Approaches to the Social Context*. New York: Praeger.

McGee, J. J., Menolascino, F., Hobbs, D., *et al* (1987) *Gentle Teaching: A Non-Aversive Approach to Helping Persons with Mental Retardation*. New York: Human Sciences Press.

Menolascino, F. J. & McCann, B. M. (eds) (1983) *Mental Health and Mental Retardation: Bridging the Gap*. Baltimore: University Park Press.

Mercer, J. R. (1992) The impact of changing paradigms of disability on mental retardation in the year 2000. In *Mental Retardation in the Year 2000* (ed. L. Rowitz). New York: Springer Verlag.

Nirje, B. (1976) The normalisation principle and its human management implications. In *Normalisation, Social Integration and Community Services* (eds R. J. Flynn & K. E. Nitsch). Baltimore: University Park Press.

Reid, A. (1982) *The Psychiatry of Mental Handicap*. Oxford: Blackwell Scientific.

Reiss, S. (1994) Psychopathology in mental retardation In *Mental Health in Mental Retardation* (ed. N. Bouras). Cambridge: Cambridge University Press

Rutter, M., Tizard, J. & Whitmore, K. (1970) *Education, Health and Behaviour.* London: Longman.

——, Cox, A., Tupling, C., *et al* (1975) Attainment and adjustment in two geographical areas. I. The prevalence of psychiatric disorder. *British Journal of Psychiatry,* **126**, 493–509.

——, Tizard, J., Yule, W., *et al* (1976) Isle of Wight Studies, 1964–1974. *Psychological Medicine,* **6**, 313–332.

Scheerenberger, R. C. (1983) *A History of Mental Retardation.* Baltimore: Paul Brookes Publishing.

Tizard, J. (1964) *Community Services for the Mentally Handicapped.* Oxford: Oxford University Press.

Towell, D. (ed.) (1988) *An Ordinary Life in Practice.* London: King Edward's Hospital Fund for London.

Von Gontard, A. (1988) The development of child psychiatry in 19th century Britain. *Journal of Child Psychology and Psychiatry,* **29**, 569–588.

Additional reading

Bouras, N. (ed.) (1994) *Mental Health in Mental Retardation.* Cambridge: Cambridge University Press.

Rowitz, L. (ed.) (1992) *Mental Retardation in the Year 2000.* New York: Springer Verlag.

2 Impairment, disability and handicap: categories and classifications

Tom Fryers

---

*Global categories • Partial categories • Frequencies in populations •
Intellectual impairment in developing countries*

The professional and scientific literature reveals a remarkable variety of incompatible terms, inconsistent categories and ambiguous concepts arising from diverse professional and scientific perspectives. Several equally important elements are difficult to reconcile in one taxonomy; genetic potential, aetiological diagnosis, brain damage and disorder, low measured intelligence, and social maladaptation. Each alone poses serious problems of classification, standardisation and measurement; together the difficulties are insuperable. Most cultures use social labels which are either stigmatising or promoted specifically because they are considered non-stigmatising, and these may change quite frequently. This should not affect professional and scientific terminology, although care professionals and researchers need to be aware of the differences between lay and professional language.

However, there has been little professional consensus on terminology, which has led to transient, culture-specific lay terms being used without discrimination or clear definition. The different needs of public acceptability, professional practice and scientific research cannot be accommodated in any one set of terms and categories. We require different taxonomies, categories and terms to serve different purposes, but always specified and defined.

The basic concepts of the World Health Organization (WHO) *International Classification of Impairments, Disabilities and Handicaps* (1980) provide a coherent structure for this. Impairment is a fault in an organ or body system; disability is a loss of function normal for any human being; handicap is social disadvantage accruing from the impairment and disability. These can be applied to define mental retardation as a whole (global categories), or to define groups which have an important but not exclusive relationship with mental retardation (partial categories). This is explored in detail in different ways in Fryers (1984), and especially in Fryers (1993). Discriminating multiple taxonomies within a common framework allows each to be researched or applied, both alone and in relation to others. Of course, no categories as such should determine the care individuals receive; that needs full individual assessment.

Current classification systems draw on three sources: firstly, the manual of definitions, *Mental Retardation: Definition, Classification, and Systems of Supports* (American Association on Mental Retardation, 1992); secondly, DSM–IV, International Version (American Psychiatric Association, 1995); thirdly, the latest WHO set of diagnostic categories found in the ICD–10 clinical descriptions and diagnostic guidelines (World Health Organization, 1992).

Box 2.1 summarises the taxonomy described below (after Fryers, 1993, 1996).

Global categories

Retaining the internationally recognised term 'mental retardation' for the field of study and activity in general, three types of global category are useful: intellectual impairment, generalised learning disability, and generalised dependency handicap.

Intellectual impairment

The fundamental global impairment is of the 'intellect', conceived as analogous to an organic body system in which lies the capacity to learn and reason. Intellectual impairment is measured, however inadequately, by intelligence tests, and summarised and simplified by the Intelligence Quotient (IQ). There is no reason to assume that this capacity is immutable and we know that its measurement is often prejudiced by other factors. Intelligence tests have long been discounted, but Berger & Yule (1985) have argued for their continued use in the absence of anything better.

Epidemiologically, IQs have provided the sole basis for comparison between studies, and only for a category defined by IQ < 50 representing 'severe intellectual impairment' (SII) (Fryers, 1984). Intelligence in human populations approximates to a normal distribution except for an excess at the lowest end representing brain damage and disorder, which mostly affects the prevalence of the severe group. 'Mild intellectual impairment' (MII; IQ 50–69 by convention) is largely a product of the population distribution.

Generalised learning disability

The primary function affected by intellectual impairment is learning, so learning disability is the appropriate term (qualified by 'generalised' to avoid confusion with American usage in educational contexts). It should be measured by standard tests of the learning function, but these are not well developed *per se*, and tests generally measure performance of specific skills such as memorisation and recall, reading, writing and numeracy,

---

Box 2.1 Taxonomies in mental retardation

Global (overall) categories

Intellectual impairment
  Criteria: intellectual
  Measures: intelligence or developmental tests
  Main categories: severe, IQ < 50; mild, IQ 50–69

Generalised learning disability
  Criteria: educational
  Measures: mostly proxies of learning achievement (rather than learning process) such as memory recall, reading, number, problem-solving
  Main categories: severe, moderate, and mild are used but in non-standard ways; often ill-defined

General dependence handicap (related to intellectual impairment) (also termed mental handicap or handicap due to mental retardation)
  Criteria: social – highly variable in different societies
  Measures: scales of dependency or maladaptation
  Main categories: severe (or severe and profound combined), commonly limited to IQ < 50, and therefore co-extensive with severe intellectual impairment (SII); mild, used with very variable criteria of social selection

Partial categories

Physical impairments, pathological and aetiological groups
  Criteria: commonly pathological or aetiological diagnosis
  Measures: usually clinical and laboratory
  Main categories: mostly neurological impairments providing 'medical' diagnostic groups

Syndromes of impairments and/or disabilities
  Criteria: agreed (consensus) grouping of signs and symptoms with epidemiological validation
  Measures: clinical, radiological, biochemical, etc.
  Main categories: epilepsies; cerebral palsies; pervasive disorders (mostly autism); psychiatric disorders

Specific disabilities
  Criteria: defined deficits in normal functions
  Measures: standardised assessments where available
  Main categories: specific motor, sensory, intellectual, emotional, and behavioural dysfunctions

Individual handicaps
  Criteria: social disadvantage
  Measures: very few standard measures available
  Main categories: income, housing, employment, education, access, stigma, abuse

Carers' concerns: handicaps of family members
  Social disadvantages as for disabled person

which are outcomes of the learning process. It is not clear how these should be combined to describe generalised learning disability.

In recent years in the UK, 'learning disabled' has become the favoured lay term for all groups of mentally retarded persons, but, as such, has no scientific validity. School-based categories of learning disability will have more validity for professional practice and administration of school systems, but will be of little value for epidemiological research unless the criteria for selection are accurately described, and measures are standardised and validated. If so, they can be studied in relation to various degrees of intellectual impairment. Of course, if a school category uses IQ < 50 as the sole necessary criterion (given that all people in this category will undoubtedly have severe generalised learning disability and severe dependency handicap), then we really have severe intellectual impairment in another guise.

In practice, categories of learning disability are likely to be determined by many more factors than IQ alone (e.g. in the UK by the 1981 Education Act), so they will not approximate to SII or any other categories defined by IQ. This is important, as many children (and adults, such as those in prison) have learning disabilities not related to especially low intelligence. Nor do all persons with the same level of IQ share the same degree of generalised learning disability, or types of specific learning disability. Current terms such as 'special needs' and 'learning difficulties', when used in an educational context, should probably be conceived as representing types of the learning disability category. Outside educational contexts, they are likely to represent types of the dependency handicap category.

Generalised dependency handicap

The principal global handicap, that is, the social disadvantage experienced by people with intellectual impairment, is dependency. As with all types of handicap, it is extremely variable in the experience of individuals but is a useful concept in populations. In this context, it is conceived as generalised dependency related to intellectual impairment and/or learning disability. Whatever fashionable term is applied to this group of people in a particular society – mentally retarded, mentally handicapped, learning disabled, developmentally disabled, and so forth – without precise and standardised measures of intelligence or learning function, the group is in reality being conceived as having generalised dependency handicap.

Many factors affect which people are called mentally retarded (or whatever label is in fashion) in any community. But if the definition of a *severe* group specifies IQ < 50 (whether adequately measured is another issue) as a sufficient and only essential criterion, this is again really severe intellectual impairment. *Mild* mental retardation, mental handicap or learning disability is never defined by IQ alone; many other clinical, personal, social, cultural, legal and organisational criteria, some recognised and some not, determine who is selected for this handicap group. These factors operate differently in different communities and at different times, so that the number thus selected is immensely variable. There is no basis for comparing studies because the key data – the criteria by which people are selected in each community – are not presented and may not be known. However, they could be, and this would form the basis of very interesting and valuable comparative studies.

Discriminating in this way between global impairment, disability and handicap in mental retardation encourages clarity of thinking, not least about causation. Causes of intellectual impairment are likely to be largely organic brain syndromes. Causes of learning disability may include these underlying processes, but also many other clinical conditions (e.g. cerebral palsy), especially those affecting communication. Social factors will also play a part. Causes of dependency handicap (even when related to intellectual impairment and/or learning disability) may include all these, but family and wider social and environmental factors will be equally prominent, and may be the most important in some cases. (For example, society's demand for universal literacy may handicap some who otherwise would fare well and live independently.)

Partial categories

Persons with intellectual impairment may, of course, experience any disease or disability, but here it is useful only to identify those 'partial categories' whose defining features are commonly related to mental retardation, although not exclusively so. Serious investigation of causes in these groups requires studies of total human populations, not only of groups exhibiting intellectual impairment or those selected as mentally retarded. Five types are usefully described:

Physical impairments: aetiological and pathological groups

These mostly relate to neurological impairments. They are rarely limited to specific degrees of intellectual impairment or learning disability, and many include people who would never be considered mentally retarded. Examples are phenylketonuria (including treated cases), Down's syndrome (including mosaics), and fragile X syndrome (including female carriers).

Syndromes of impairments and/or disabilities

These include the epilepsies, cerebral palsies, psychiatric disorders, autistic disorders, and 'challenging' behaviour. They are neither aetiological nor pathological entities, but are all important in the context of mental retardation, showing higher frequencies than in the general population. They can pose serious problems for clinical and psychological assessment.

Specific disabilities: losses of function

Motor and sensory disabilities are relatively common in people with intellectual impairment and may represent additional factors in selection as mentally retarded. Disability categories do not correlate with IQ categories, organic impairments or aetiological entities. Studies of specific disabilities such as 'mobility' or 'inability to feed oneself' can guide habilitative practice. The 'learning disorder' of DSM–IV (formerly 'academic skills disorders' in DSM–III) may be seen as a specific learning disability related partially to intellectual impairment.

Specific handicaps: social consequences

Specific handicaps are even less well defined, and there has been little research, but there is great potential in such studies for improving the lives of mentally retarded people. It is worth remembering that, for many individuals, it is the specific handicaps they experience in housing, employment, income, social networks, leisure opportunities, and so on, which gives them their greatest frustrations and their greatest sense of alienation.

Carers' concerns: parent and family handicaps

Only recently have these concerns been widely acknowledged, although there is a small body of research. In practice, a high proportion of care is provided by families, and professionals need to recognise the partnership involved. But 'informal' carers also have their own needs and handicaps which must be accommodated by professional services.

Frequencies in populations

Factors affecting frequencies

The two basic measures of disease or disorder in populations are incidence and prevalence. Incidence is a measure of events in a period of time, commonly new cases in a year, but similarly admissions to hospital, births and deaths. Incidence rates relate the frequency of these events to a population (as $n/1000$). Point prevalence is the number of people with a particular condition at a point in time; prevalence ratios (or rates) relate these numbers to the population ($n/1000$, often age- and sex-specific). The point in time can be a point in life-time rather than calendar time;

we use prevalence at birth (the number of babies with a particular condition in 1000 consecutive births) rather than incidence, to accommodate variations in birth rate. (This is sometimes called birth frequency, or wrongly called incidence at birth.) Variation in prevalence between successive birth cohorts will be masked, and comparative studies made difficult unless data are restricted to small age groups (e.g. five years).

Incidence and prevalence of a heterogeneous group such as 'people with mental retardation' are highly dynamic. However categories are defined, their frequencies are determined by the frequencies of very many disorders of widely varying genesis. Some disorders arise at conception and their causes must be looked for before conception; others arise in early foetal life, around birth, and in early postnatal life. New cases become progressively less frequent with age, with very few after 4 or 5 years of age. But mortality of abnormal foetuses follows a similar dynamic, being concentrated in early foetal life, around birth and in early infancy, then almost levelling off. Prevalence at any age is determined by both earlier inception rates and mortality rates; *known* prevalence also depends upon the identification rate. Prevalence ratios are also susceptible to differential migration.

These processes give rise to substantial variations in prevalence in different communities and at different times. The assertion common in the literature that prevalence ratios for severe mental retardation (or whatever term is used) are 'stable' or consistent is not true, even for clearly defined severe intellectual impairment. It would, indeed, be very strange if this were true, given the social determinants of population frequency of the causes of neurological impairment, which vary so much between cultures and communities. These social factors (e.g. diet in neural tube defects; patterns of fertility in Down's syndrome; alcohol price and supply in foetal alcohol syndrome; consanguinity in recessive genetic disorders) are most likely to offer scope for prevention.

Descriptive epidemiology of severe intellectual impairment (IQ < 50)

Severe intellectual impairment is co-extensive with the terms severe mental retardation, severe mental handicap, and severe learning disabilities, if these are defined by IQ < 50. The main points are shown in Box 2.2 and described in more detail below.

Point prevalence

Point prevalence varies between similar birth cohorts (concurrent age groups) in different communities. Reliable studies (see Fryers, 1984) found 1.62/1000 children born in 1951–55 in Salford, UK, and 7.34/1000 children born in 1957 in Amsterdam. Greater variation is expected in developing

---

Box 2.2 Basic epidemiology of severe intellectual impairment: prevalence in developed communities

There is geographical variation within similar birth cohorts: range at least 1.62–7.34/1000.

There is temporal variation in successive birth cohorts in the same community, e.g. 1.98–5.54/1000 in Salford children aged 5–9, 1961–1971.

There has been a similar pattern of temporal change in many developed countries, i.e. low prevalence for children born in the early to mid-1950s, high prevalence for children born in the early to mid-1960s.

There is variation by age due to variations between birth cohorts in incidence and mortality. Currently the highest prevalence ratios are in the age group 25–30 years. By 1997/1998, it will be 30–34 years.

There is increased survival at all ages and into old age. There are more people with SII aged > 45 than aged < 15.

There is probably a social class gradient in both incidence and mortality; there are excesses in lower socio-economic groups.

There are usually more males than females, but there are no consistent patterns in the sex ratio.

These features are typical of developed countries. They will also be true to varying extents for communities in developing countries depending upon development and economic status, demographic characteristics, vital statistics, and many other social indicators (see text).

---

countries. Prevalence varies with genetic, cultural, economic, environmental and service factors, largely by influencing the spectrum of biomedical causes and early mortality.

Sometimes there is one dominant cause, especially iodine deficiency disease, where more than 10% of village populations may be affected by congenital hypothyroidism. In other populations Down's syndrome often shows the greatest frequency of any one aetiological group, and in communities with traditions of late marriage, large families and taboos against contraception and/or abortion, may dominate the scene unless early mortality is very high. Congenital anomalies may be relatively high in small, isolated communities with traditions of consanguineous marriage, but few are associated with intellectual impairment. Mortality and survival are extremely variable and can generally be related to the 'development status' of the community.

Age-specific prevalence

Age-specific prevalence also varies over time in the same community, because the spectrum of causes and the extent of early mortality change. In Salford, prevalence for children aged 5–9 was 1.98/1000 in 1961, 5.54/1000 in 1971, and 3.86/1000 in 1980. The same factors affecting incidence and mortality which explain differences between communities, may explain changes over time in the same community.

Temporal change

A similar pattern of temporal change is seen throughout the developed world, with a low range of values for age-specific prevalence (1.8–4.0/1000) for children born in the early 1950s, a high range (3.3–5.5/1000) for those born in the early to mid-1960s, and falling prevalence ratios since then, at least well into the 1980s. The increase was almost certainly due to a rapid decrease in early mortality associated with developments in neonatal care; this has no doubt continued since. Such increased survival is well documented for Down's syndrome by life-table studies from birth. Other aetiological groups are too rare or too inconsistent in case definition or diagnosis to be studied in a similar way, but we can assume similar processes have operated, and continue to operate to increase survival. The progressive decrease in prevalence in young children since the late 1960s reflects many very different processes reducing inceptions; large-scale oral contraception led to both reduced mean maternal age and dramatic reductions in conceptions to women in the highest child-bearing age groups. This greatly reduced the incidence of Down's syndrome. Later, mostly in the 1980s, widespread amniocentesis and abortion programmes reduced Down's syndrome even more, although the impact was diminished by the lack of conceptions in older women. In recent years, the age of conception has tended to increase again, which will increase the number of Down's syndrome conceptions and the potential impact of abortion programmes.

All other contributions must each be very small because the number in each aetiological group is very small, but the cumulative effect may be significant. Postnatal screening programmes for inherited metabolic disorders and sporadic congenital hypothyroidism have been very successful. Perinatal factors, which were likely to have increased the number of babies with neurological defects surviving in the 1970s, probably produced far less neurological impairment in the 1980s, although proof is extremely difficult to generate.

In the UK, the reduction of encephalitis, encephalopathy and rubella syndrome by effective immunisation (and other measures for tuberculosis and bacterial meningitis) may have had a small effect in the 1970s and 1980s, but the major impact will be revealed in the 1990s since achieving

Table 2.1 Estimates of age-specific prevalence ratios (per 1000) for severe intellectual impairment (UK)

Age	Date		
	1.1.90	1.1.95	1.1.98
0–4	2.5?	2.00?	1.75?
5–9	3.0	2.25	2.00
10–14	4.0	2.75	2.25
15–19	4.5	3.50	3.00
20–24	5.0	4.00	3.75
25–29	4.5	4.50	4.25
30–34	4.0	4.00	4.50
35–39	3.5	3.75	4.00
40–44	3.0	3.25	3.50
45–54	2.5	2.75	3.00
55–64	2.0	2.25	2.50
65–74	1.0	1.25	2.00
75+	very few	1.00?	1.25?

immunisation rates of over 95%, which produces herd immunity, for pertussis, measles, mumps, haemophilus influenzae type B, and rubella.

The widespread adoption of early stimulation and training programmes for severely intellectually impaired infants, especially those with Down's syndrome, might have removed a few individuals from the severe group at later ages by improving their test performance, but the impact on prevalence rates must be extremely small and would be expected to be a one-off effect in any one community. Overall, although there are many small contributions possible, recent low prevalence figures do not seem to be fully explained.

Prevalence varies by age because of cohort differences from birth and early infancy. In many developed countries the highest age-specific prevalence is exhibited by those born in the early to mid-1960s, although this will not be 'in phase' everywhere. This means that, in the UK, for example, by 1998 the largest age group will be in their early 30s. Younger age groups (that is, later birth cohorts) have had progressively lower prevalence ratios. In most UK communities, this has enhanced the effect of smaller child cohorts on the numbers of children in school-age groups. The larger cohorts will move progressively through the age groups in future decades.

Prevalence also varies by age and time because reduced mortality has increased survival at all ages. In developed countries there are currently more adults over 45 than children under 15 in most communities, and there are now substantial numbers of elderly severely intellectually impaired people. The orientation of professionals and service planners needs to accommodate this.

From the prevalence and mortality data available, estimates can be made of age-specific prevalence ratios for severe intellectual impairment (Table 2.1). They can only be rough guides; they assume a stable population over the last half century and no unusual factors affecting particular important aetiological groups. The original estimates for a typical UK district at 1.1.90 were probably fairly reliable, but few new data have become available to confirm them or otherwise and estimates for later dates are increasingly speculative. Projected figures for the youngest age group and to a large extent those for the oldest age group are necessarily little more than informed guesses. However, what data have been published are generally consistent with the figures in Table 2.1, and they should be useful as guides for developing purchasing or commissioning strategies and planning service resourcing in a district.

However speculative these projections are, they illustrate the dynamics of the population which will inevitably move the statistics in the direction indicated. By 1998, the largest cohort will be aged 30–34.

There are usually more males than females at all ages, the ratio varying between 1/1 and 2/1, but with no clear pattern. It probably depends upon the particular spectrum of causes of central neurological damage and disorder in any population, but differential mortality may also affect it. Some biomedical causes favour males (e.g. fragile X syndrome), but males are generally also thought to be more vulnerable. Reduced mortality in recent years may have increased male excess.

Many early studies found severe intellectual impairment to be evenly distributed across socio-economic groups, a surprising finding given the social class differential of most measures of morbidity and mortality, and the social factors involved in the causes of severe intellectual impairment. More recent studies have tended to show the expected social class gradient. It seems likely that a differential in inceptions, masked by a similar differential in early mortality, has been revealed by much lower mortality.

Epidemiology of mild intellectual impairment

Prevalence of a group defined by IQ 50–69 reflects almost entirely the statistical distribution of IQs in populations, which is normal, that is, symmetrically distributed around the arithmetic mean. Standard intelligence tests must be validated for specific populations. Ideally, test means and standard deviations should be known from recent studies, because test means in particular populations change over time with developments in education and other cultural changes. That is, although tests were originally designed with a mean of 100, the test mean for a particular population may now be substantially greater. This requires adjustment of IQ scores, which only relate to the mean; unfortunately, current data are not available for most populations.

For a test of mean 100 (s.d. 15), 2.27% of the population will fall below IQ 70 (2 s.d. below the mean), plus a small effect mostly below IQ 50 from specific pathologies. The few populations providing data confirm this, with figures of 25–30/1000. Because measured intelligence in populations is a dynamic feature, studies of the effects on intelligence of early exposure to hazards such as those associated with birth, trauma, or ingestion of lead, must assess outcome in relation to population norms in a related cohort of births. A good example is a recent follow-up of children with treated phenylketonuria (Smith *et al*, 1991).

Mild learning disability; mild mental retardation

However defined in practice, these are never the same groups as mild intellectual impairment described in the previous section. Many individuals with mild intellectual impairment are identified as learning disabled at school, but most are not regarded as mentally retarded as adults. It is important to recognise that, as usually used for adults (and to a lesser extent for children) mild learning disability, mild mental handicap or mild mental retardation is always socially determined, though IQ (if known) and biomedical factors may be prominent among overt criteria. The vast variation in prevalence from studies of adults in the past 30 years (e.g. 2.97/1000 in Wessex, UK, and 77.91/1000 in Rose County, US, both published in 1968) illustrates the situation. These and all other studies use (or observe service systems using) different criteria for selection; there is no standardisation. There are no standard or representative data for prevalence of mild learning disability or mild mental retardation.

To be fruitful, research must recognise that who is called 'learning disabled' or 'mentally retarded' in a particular community or culture is a phenomenon to be explored and explained. Local registers are valid measures because they record precisely those for whom the label is perceived as appropriate in each community. We can only speak of 'underestimated' or 'hidden' mild learning disability in respect of those who fulfil local criteria but who have not been identified. In practice this is seldom known because many criteria are not overt, are ambiguous or are variable in application. Studies identifying and explaining the criteria for selection which operate in different communities, and which determine prevalence, would help us to understand the social context of service provision, the variants and determinants of stigma and discrimination, the concomitants of labelling, and the advantages and disadvantages to vulnerable people of being excluded from the group, and might guide much community care planning.

We know many factors that commonly affect selection as mentally retarded apart from perceived low intelligence (measured or not) and certain medical diagnoses (such as Down's syndrome) assumed to dictate selection. Legislation relating to mental health, education and criminal offences may all determine selection, as may regulations, institutional traditions, conventions of practice, and professional attitudes in health, education and social services. For example, 'mild mental handicap' dramatically reduced in the UK as social services took over the lead from health, because social workers did not label people in that way as often as doctors. People with mild intellectual impairment are more likely to be selected if they also have communication problems, multiple physical disabilities, mental illness or, especially, challenging behaviour, and if they suffer unemployment, low socio-economic status, a poor home environment or inadequate parental care. There are also some people in long-stay institutions who would not now be labelled learning disabled, but who have been inherited by current services. These many factors in selection are summarised in Box 2.3.

It is these selection criteria, recognised or unrecognised, which lead to the commonly observed characteristics of the groups called mildly learning disabled or mildly mentally retarded. There may be few precise aetiological diagnoses, but many neurological impairments and motor and sensory disabilities. Epilepsy, cerebral palsy, mental illness and challenging behaviour are more common than in the general population; so are social deprivation, educational failure and poor employment records. Since selection criteria change in all societies, prevalence of the

---

Box 2.3   Factors affecting selection as 'mentally retarded'

Legislation: criminal, health, education, social welfare, and employment law all relevant.

Service structures and traditions: in education, health, social welfare, etc.

Professional cultures: concepts, perceptions, expectations, labelling, etc.

Patterns of employment and unemployment: work and training opportunities.

Social class and social attitudes: cultural expectations, deprivation, discrimination.

Family support: structures and security of families.

Historical service patterns: older people inherited from earlier situations, e.g. in institutional care.

Perceived low intelligence: with or without additional factors, e.g. antisocial behaviour, mental illness, motor, sensory or communication disabilities, multiple disabilities.

Certain medical diagnoses, especially Down's syndrome.

group and the balance of characteristics will change over time. However, most individuals have the basic capacity to be independent and to enjoy an essentially normal lifestyle, and successful rehabilitation, or simply maturing, may move people out of the category as they get older.

Intellectual impairment in developing countries

There are few reliable sources for estimating prevalence in most countries, but the data suggest wide variations related to the varying spectrum of organic causes, mortality, and social situations (see Fryers, 1996). Conceptual and methodological problems are also harder for researchers in developing countries to solve. Precise comparative statistics are not crucial in this context. However, descriptive epidemiological work identifying groups of people with particular needs, establishing the aetiological processes and factors which are locally preventable, and estimating the order of size of the group for resourcing service developments are all extremely important (Tao, 1988; Belmont, 1984).

Severe intellectual impairment (IQ < 50), whatever it is called, will be recognised in all societies, but mild intellectual impairment may not be. A non-technological, non-literate society may impose no handicap on many of those with limited learning and reasoning powers; they may have acceptable roles and adequate support in the family and community. But increasing technological demands, and universal education requiring reading, identifies those who function well below average as having problems and may handicap them in their prospects for employment and marriage. The rapid and universal urbanisation of society may also increase handicap for the less able, as extended family networks are disrupted.

References

American Association on Mental Retardation (1992) *Mental Retardation: Definition, Classification, and Systems of Supports.* Washington, DC: AAMR.

American Psychiatric Association (1995) *Diagnostic and Statistical Manual of Mental Disorders* (4th edn) (DSM–IV International Version). Washington, DC: APA.

Belmont, L. (1984) *International Epidemiological Studies of Childhood Disability: Final Report.* Utrecht: Bishopp Becker Institute.

Berger, M. & Yule, W. (1985) IQ tests and assessments. In *Mental Deficiency: the Changing Outlook* (4th edn) (eds A. M. Clarke, A. D B. Clarke & J. M. Berg), pp. 53–96. London: Methuen.

Fryers, T. (1984) *The Epidemiology of Severe Intellectual Impairment: The Dynamics of Prevalence.* London: Academic Press.

—— (1993) Epidemiological thinking in mental retardation: issues in taxonomy and population frequency. *International Review of Research in Mental Retardation*, **19**, 97–133.

—— (1996) Mental retardation in developing countries. In *Psychiatry for the Developing World* (eds D. Tantam, L. Appleby & A. Duncan). London: Gaskell.

Smith, I., Cook, B. & Beasley, M. G. (1991) Review of neonatal screening programme for phenylketonuria. *British Medical Journal*, **303**, 333–335.

Tao, Kuo-Tai (1988) Mentally retarded persons in the People's Republic of China: a review of epidemiological studies and services. *American Journal on Mental Retardation*, **93**, 193–199.

World Health Organization (1980) *International Classification of Impairments, Disabilities and Handicaps*. Geneva: WHO.

—— (1992) *The ICD–10 Classification of Mental and Behavioural Disorders: Clinical Descriptions and Diagnostic Guidelines*. Geneva: WHO.

Additional reading

Fryers, T. (1984) *The Epidemiology of Severe Intellectual Impairment: The Dynamics of Prevalence*. London: Academic Press.

—— (1990) Pre- and perinatal factors in the aetiology of mental retardation. In *Reproductive and Perinatal Epidemiology* (ed. M. Kiely). Florida: CRC Press.

—— (1993) Epidemiological thinking in mental retardation: issues in taxonomy and population frequency. *International Review of Research in Mental Retardation*, **19**, 97–133.

—— (1996) Public health approaches to mental retardation: handicap related to intellectual impairment. In *Oxford Textbook of Public Health* (3rd edn) (eds W. W. Holland, R. Detels, E. G. Knox, *et al*). Oxford: Oxford University Press.

3 Applied epidemiology

Tom Fryers and Oliver Russell

Aetiology and prevention of neurological impairments ● Major
aetiological groups ● Programmes to prevent impairments ● Disabilities
and handicaps related to intellectual impairment

Epidemiology is the study of health, disease and disorder, and factors affecting them, in human populations. Its methods are primarily statistical, but interpretations require knowledge of demographic, social, organisational and environmental sciences concerned with the collective experience and behaviour of human beings, and of clinical and pathological sciences. Epidemiology provides the foundation of public health practice, informing preventive programmes and the planning, organisation, development and evaluation of services.

Using epidemiological methods, we can validate taxonomies, discriminate categories, measure and compare the community dimensions and characteristics of health problems, search for causes, and evaluate treatments and services. These need population data from well-designed studies or accurate and comprehensive information systems, both dependent upon high quality clinical and personal data. For much of this work we use the four classical designs of analytic study – cross-sectional, case control, cohort and intervention studies. However, descriptive studies are important to generate hypotheses and are essential for planning, development and monitoring services. Definitions must be precise and consistent, measurements accurate and standardised, analysis creative as well as statistically valid. Clarity has not characterised work in this field, but the World Health Organization *International Classification* (World Health Organization, 1980) offers a useful structure for taxonomies suited to a variety of purposes.

Aetiology and prevention of neurological impairments

Cause and outcome in individuals and populations

Whatever definitions are used for mental retardation, causes of neurological impairment are of fundamental importance. Cause is a complex idea which should be conceived in terms of causal processes, causal factors, and a variety of precise outcomes. For example, the rubella virus can be said to cause rubella syndrome, but what determines maternal infection, foetal infection and foetal response to infection? In Down's syndrome we know a great deal about the processes of causation, but nothing of the ultimate causal agents. Aetiological studies must try to relate specific causal factors to specific pathological outcomes; multiple exposure variables and multiple outcome variables almost always preclude clear conclusions, as illustrated by the many studies of perinatal factors.

In epidemiology, cause encompasses a different concept: the epidemiologist seeks out factors and processes, mostly social and environmental, which increase frequencies in populations. It is often these that offer most potential for prevention (Fryers, 1990).

Types and frequencies of organic syndromes

The main organic syndromes related to intellectual impairment are summarised systematically in Box 3.1. Many of the hundreds of syndromes are so rare as to pose extreme difficulty in establishing frequency data; nevertheless a few are major contributors.

Pure primary disorders are present from conception, an autosome or sex chromosome aberration in one gamete producing an abnormal chromosome constitution. Trisomy 21 is the archetype, but trisomies 13 (Patau's syndrome), 18 (Edward's syndrome) and others also occur. Sex chromosome disorders are seldom associated with significant intellectual impairment. X linked disorders have recently gained prominence with the elucidation of fragile X syndrome.

Primary disorders with secondary neurological damage do not affect the general constitution, but a genetically determined specific defect affects development, with or without environmental provocation. Phenylketonuria is the commonest of many disorders in which enzyme defects prejudice normal metabolism. Sporadic congenital hypothyroidism leads to cretinism if not identified and treated from early infancy.

Pure secondary disorders arise from environmental insults to a normal zygote after conception. Prenatal causes include neural tube defects, iodine deficiency disease, rhesus incompatibility, and the effects of communicable diseases and other agents such as alcohol, drugs and radiation. Perinatal processes are complex, the main factors being hypoxia, hypoglycaemia, cerebral thrombosis and haemorrhage, and gross trauma. Factors increasing vulnerability in the baby include a very large baby, a very small baby, immaturity and pre-existing abnormality. Other factors are to be found in the mother and in the quality of midwifery and neonatal care. Postnatal causes include encephalitis and encephalopathy from communicable disease, trauma, and metabolic disasters in infants.

Major aetiological groups

Down's syndrome (trisomy 21) constitutes a significant proportion of severe intellectual impairment in all communities. About 94% are due to nondisjunction of chromosome 21, about 3–5% are familial, due to translocation, and should be identified after birth for genetic counselling. Of the nondisjunctions, 1–3% show mosaicism, which may explain the rare Down's syndrome person of normal intelligence and achievements.

Seventy-five to eighty-five per cent of nondisjunctions are of maternal origin, mostly from the first meiotic division, and therefore occurring in the mother's foetal life. Prevalence at birth increases with maternal age (0.7/1000 at 20–24 years to 4.5/1000 at 35–39, 16/1000 at 40–44 and over 55/1000 at 45–49). Between 5–20% of nondisjunctions are of paternal origin, also mostly at the first division. These may arise just prior to fertilisation; occupational exposures may be relevant.

Overall prevalence at birth is lower where maternal age has lowered (McGrother & Marshall, 1990, estimate a 45% reduction in the UK since 1941) and where amniocentesis and abortion programmes have had an impact. There is a very high mortality of Down's syndrome foetuses early in gestation; it is likely, but not certain, that prevalence at conception is also related to maternal age. In developed countries, postnatal survival has increased from about 50% at one year 40 years ago, to 80–90% at five years now, most deaths being among the 25–40% with serious heart defects.

Generally the Down's population has an IQ range of 20–55. There is increased survival into middle and old age, where Alzheimer's dementia is common and has an early onset. Demographic changes in the UK have affected family structures: 'typical' mothers of Down's babies used to be elderly with several children; they are now often having their first child in their 30s (Gath, 1990).

Fragile X syndrome

Fragile X syndrome is an important contributor to severe intellectual impairment, but not all those with the condition exhibit low intelligence. Fragile X may be as common as Down's syndrome but prevalence figures vary quite considerably between studies. However, it is generally agreed that the birth prevalence is between 0.5/1000 and 1.0/1000 male births.

Fragile X syndrome is usually associated with an expansion in a gene called FMR1 which is located on the X chromosome at the Xq27.3 'fragile' locus and consists of multiple CGG trinucleotide triplet repeats. In normal individuals the number of repeats is less than 54, but phenotypically and cytogenetically normal carriers have between 50 and 150 (so-called 'premutations'). Through transgenerational progression these CGG repeats may expand and proceed to a full mutation to the fragile X syndrome with more than 200 triplet repeats (Turk, 1995).

Intelligence may be impaired and about 80% of affected boys will have an IQ < 70, including some with IQ < 50. About 30% of girls with the mutation will have IQs of 50–69, rarely lower, while 70% are unaffected carriers, half of whose male children and a sixth of whose female children

Box 3.1 Aetiology of organic syndromes related to intellectual impairment (frequencies are approximate)

Primary disorders: chromosome aberrations which are present at conception.

Trisomy 21 (Down's syndrome)
Nondisjunction trisomy (94% of all Down's). Birth prevalence varies with maternal age. Age 20, 0.5/1000; age 30, 1.0/1000; age 35, 2.5/1000; age 40, 10/1000; age 45, 40/1000; age 50, 150/1000.
Trisomy mosaics (1–3%). Birth prevalence 0.03/1000.
Translocation (3–5%). Birth prevalence 0.03/1000.
All except a few mosaics are intellectually impaired, mostly severely. IQ range generally 30–55.

Trisomy 18 (Edward's syndrome)
Birth prevalence 0.3/1000; 10% survive to age one year; all have severe intellectual impairment.

Trisomy 13 (Patau's syndrome)
Birth prevalence 0.2/1000; 18% survive to age one year; all have severe intellectual impairment and seizures.

5p syndrome (Cri du Chat syndrome)
Rare. Partial deletion of short arm of chromosome 5; 50% not severely impaired.

Sex chromosome disorders
Birth prevalence 2–3/1000; only occasionally severely or mildly intellectually impaired.

Non-specific disorders associated with intellectual impairment
Recessive. Birth prevalence ?0.5/1000.
X-linked. Birth prevalence 1/1000; most boys but few girls are intellectually impaired.

Doubtful aetiology
Cornelia de Lange syndrome (Amsterdam dwarfism). Always intellectually impaired, often show self-injurious behaviour.
Williams syndrome. Often hypercalcaemic; usually intellectually impaired by later childhood.
Rubinstein–Taybi syndrome.
Prader-Willi syndrome.

Primary disorders with secondary neurological damage

Defects of protein metabolism
Phenylketonuria (PKU). Birth prevalence 0.05–0.2/1000.
At least five others; aggregated birth prevalence 0.1/000 (all severely intellectually impaired if untreated).

Defects of carbohydrate metabolism
Galactosaemia. Birth prevalence 0.02/1000 (all severely intellectually impaired and die early if untreated).

Box 3.1 continued

Defects of lipid metabolism
Tay–Sach's disease. Birth prevalence 0.04/1000 in Ashkenazi Jewish communities; rare elsewhere.
Batten's disease. Frequency uncertain (all severely intellectually impaired and die early).

Defects of mucopolysaccharide metabolism
Birth prevalence for all types combined 0.1/1000. MPS 1: Hurler's/Schie's; MPS 2: Hunter's; MPS 3: Sanfilippo; MPS 4: Morquio's. All severely intellectually impaired.

Defects of hormone system
Sporadic congenital hypothyroidism. Birth prevalence 0.1–2.0/1000 (intelligence variably but seriously affected unless treated from very early infancy).

Mechanism not clear
Tuberous sclerosis. Birth prevalence 0.01/1000
Neurofibromatosis. Birth prevalence 0.33/1000; some cases of microcephaly (effect on intelligence very variable).

Secondary disorders (damaged after conception)

Antenatal factors
Iodine deficiency disorders (cretinism). Frequency of severe intellectual impairment very variable; can be more than 10% of whole populations.
Neural tube defects. Birth prevalence 1–8/1000; possibly 10% are intellectually impaired.
Rhesus incompatibility. Intellectual impairment varies.
Communicable diseases. Very varied frequency of infection and of brain damage after infection.
Alcohol: foetal alcohol syndrome. Many cases show severe intellectual impairment.
Drugs; irradiation; heavy metals: no satisfactory data.

Perinatal factors
Gross trauma, hypoxia, hypoglycaemia, and cerebral thrombosis. Often associated with cerebral palsy and epilepsy. Definitions are problematic and the frequency of damage is virtually unmeasurable.

Postnatal factors (all very variable in frequency)
Physical trauma; accidents.
Communicable diseases; meningitis and encephalitis or encephalopathies.
Chemical agents: lead may reduce intelligence a little.
Nutritional/metabolic: high solute baby feeds combined with fever.

(After Fryers, 1984)

will be affected (Simon *et al*, 1990). Twenty per cent of males with fragile X syndrome have epileptic seizures. The epilepsy usually presents in childhood. Nuclear magnetic resonance studies have found anatomical abnormalities in the cerebellar vermis.

Because the behaviour of many fragile X children fulfils diagnostic criteria for autism, it was thought that there was a link between the conditions. However, recent evidence confirms that only 2–3% of autism can be shown to be associated with the fragile X syndrome. According to some studies fragile X children appear to be more hyperactive, more restless and to have poor concentration. The most subtle effect of the fragile X gene may involve personality changes including shyness and a predisposition to anxiety or depression (Einfeld & Hall, 1994).

Autosomal recessive genetic disorders

These disorders are especially frequent (up to 5% of births) where there are high rates of consanguinity, usually communities isolated by geography or social status, or those with cultural traditions of consanguinity. There are 138 autosomal recessive conditions which have to date been reported to be associated with intellectual impairment, but they are mostly very rare conditions and the total number of affected individuals is quite small. Prevention requires education and wider opportunities for marriage.

Rett syndrome is a neurologically progressive syndrome which only affects girls and has only come to attention in the past 20 years. The disorder may present as early as five months. The affected child shows regression in intellectual function, curious stereotypical hand-wringing movements and then shows progressive motor disabilities.

Prevalence rates of 1/15 000 girls have been reported both in Scotland and in Sweden (Hagberg, 1993). Rett syndrome appears to be more prevalent in certain geographical areas than in others. A highly significant increased rate of consanguinity among both paternal and maternal ancestors of girls with Rett syndrome has been reported from Sweden. A clustering of cases has been reported in islands in Western Norway and in Northern Tuscany. Although such concentrations of cases support a genetic origin, no conclusive proof has been reached.

Inherited metabolic disorders

Congenital hypothyroidism occurs sporadically in all communities (0.1–2.0/1000 births) unrelated to iodine deficiency. Unless identified very early (preferably before the age of three weeks) by screening, and treated with L-thyroxine, cretinism will result. Since the late 1970s neonatal screening programmes for congenital hypothyroidism have been set up in countries with advanced healthcare systems. Before these screening programmes were introduced any affected child would not be diagnosed and treated until after the neonatal period, by which time the lack of thyroid hormone would have seriously affected neurological development. The major complications of late-treated congenital hypothyroidism were impaired intelligence and a range of abnormalities of neurological function, especially poor motor coordination. However, it now seems that even early treatment does not necessarily eliminate all problems, perhaps because low levels of thyroid hormone in the prenatal environment impede brain maturation and development.

A recent British study (Simons *et al*, 1994) showed that although the mean IQ scores in children with early-treated congenital hypothyroidism generally fell within 2 s.d. for the control population, those children who at birth had more severe forms of hypothyroidism had persisting deficits in their IQ scores at the age of ten years. While early treatment of congenital hypothyroidism does not completely eliminate difficulties with coordination, they appear to be diminished. Children may have minor difficulties with balance or rapid fine manipulation (Grant, 1995).

In contrast, a major American study, the New England Congenital Hypothyroidism Collaborative Study, found no intellectual impairment at any age among those screened and treated. No relation between severity of hypothyroidism and outcome was apparent in the American study. Reasons for these different findings have been debated.

From a public health perspective the congenital hypothyroidism screening programme provides a model for a population-based approach to a disorder which occurs sporadically. Screening programmes are usually shared with those for phenylketonuria and several other even rarer metabolic disorders in which absence of an enzyme prejudices metabolism of particular proteins, carbohydrates or lipids in the normal diet. In these disorders brain damage and severe intellectual impairment arise if the hazardous dietary component is not excluded from infancy.

Phenylketonuria is perhaps the most intensively studied inborn error of metabolism. It is an autosomal recessive condition and is the most frequent of the inherited metabolic disorders, with a prevalence of 0.05–0.2/1000 births. It was once thought to be a simple disorder easily recognised by the simplest of chemical tests, but it is now known to be a much more complex metabolic condition, and over 40 different mutations of the phenylalanine hydroxylase gene have been discovered. Untreated phenylketonuria is, above all, a disorder of the nervous system in which various degrees of serious brain disorder, such as epilepsy, become apparent in early infancy. The introduction of the Guthrie test, which provided an economic and effective method for the universal screening of all newborn infants, enabled all those who were at risk to be recognised and offered an appropriate phenylalanine-free diet. Treatment needs to begin within 20 days.

The remarkable story of phenylketonuria and its recognition and treatment encouraged physicians to search for other metabolic disorders which might also respond to dietary restriction. A few such disorders have been found but none as remarkable as phenylketonuria. The intellectual status of early-treated subjects is not as good as was thought a few years ago. The subtle but global intellectual impairments that have been documented are to a very substantial degree determined in the preschool years, long before there is any question of stopping or relaxing treatment (Medical Research Council Working Party on Phenylketonuria, 1993).

For the new generation of women with treated phenylketonuria a new set of problems arise. There is a high risk of foetal damage in the offspring of women with phenylketonuria. Fortunately dietary intervention from before conception seems to have a favourable influence on outcome.

Tay-Sachs disease is important from an epidemiological point of view because it has a high prevalence but only among a restricted population, namely Ashkenazi Jews. About 1 in 30 Jews is heterozygous for the gene, compared with 1 in 300 heterozygotes in the non-Jewish population. The condition is brought about by a disorder in lipid metabolism and results in early death.

The *mucopolysaccharidoses* is the name given to a group of rare disorders which are characterised by deficiency of specific lysosomal enzymes. The different types are most commonly known by their eponymous titles (e.g. Hurler's, Hunter's, San Filippo). It has been estimated that the prevalence of all types of the mucopolysaccharidoses combined is about 0.1/1000 births. The most common type is MPS III or San Filippo syndrome. This disorder is of particular interest because children who suffer from this disorder begin life as normal children and then develop a severe neurodegenerative disorder accompanied by intellectual deterioration and major behaviour disturbance. The prevalence of MPIIIA, the commonest subtype, is probably about 0.05/1000 live births. In the UK the Society for Mucopolysaccharide Diseases has been formed by the parents of affected children, playing a very important role in providing mutual support and encouraging further research.

Autosomal dominant genetic disorders

Forty-one autosomal disorders have been reported to be associated with intellectual impairment.

Tuberous sclerosis

Tuberous sclerosis is the commonest dominantly inherited condition causing epilepsy and intellectual impairment. The clinical expression is so variable that the true prevalence of the disorder is still unknown. The prevalence at birth has been estimated at 1/6000 (Webb & Osborne, 1995) and a Swedish study found a prevalence of 1/6800 among children aged

11–15 years. The majority of children present with an epileptic seizure and a substantial number of children with infantile spasms will be found to have tuberous sclerosis. However, a significant number of children with the condition will not come to attention until a more severely affected member of the family is identified. Until DNA techniques allow population screening to be carried out prevalence rates will have to be estimated.

Neural tube defects

Neural tube defects vary in frequency, and recent research has identified dietary deficiency of folic acid as a major cause (DoH Expert Advisory Group, 1992). Education to change the diet or the provision of folate supplements can prevent defects, but folate sufficiency must be established before conception because the defects arise extremely early in development, usually before a woman knows that she is pregnant. Supplementation should always be provided for women after one neural tube defect birth. General community programmes of supplements and health education for all fertile women are not yet established in all districts in the UK.

Foetal alcohol syndrome

Foetal alcohol syndrome is extremely variable in frequency. There is no known 'safe' dose during pregnancy, and there is evidence of lesser degrees of foetal damage even when the full syndrome does not arise. The best advice remains to avoid alcohol completely during pregnancy.

Iodine deficiency disease

Iodine deficiency disease has been largely forgotten in the UK, and few remember why table salt is iodised. Throughout the world cretinism brought on by iodine deficiency is by far the most frequent cause of severe intellectual impairment, and this is especially important because it is preventable. It affects large parts of Asia, Africa and South America, but especially Himalayan communities and various mountain areas of China, where over 10% of the population of some villages may show frank cretinism, and goitre is even more rife (Hetzel. 1989). The commonest medium for iodine supplementation is salt, where supplies are well controlled. Iodised oil injections to fertile or pregnant women can be successful, the effects lasting about three years, and there are currently hopes of an effective oral iodised oil.

Perinatal factors

Causal processes around birth are a complex of factors affecting vulnerability, the hazards of birth, and survival. Epidemiologically there are very serious difficulties in relating specific factors to specific outcomes (Fryers, 1990; Escobar *et al*, 1991). Precise definition and accurate measurement of exposure and outcome variables are extremely difficult or impossible. Comparing outcomes with relevant norms is prejudiced by inadequate population data. It is difficult to know the status of babies before they enter the perinatal period; many syndromes, for example those associated with cerebral palsy, long considered perinatal in origin, may arise earlier. Evaluation of the perinatal period is affected by increases in amniocentesis and abortion, and changes in fertility and mean maternal age.

The dynamic relationships between healthy survival, damaged survival and death make even basic numbers hard to estimate. Communities in which major perinatal problems abound are likely also to have high mortality. Other communities have fewer hazards and lower mortality. This has virtually precluded evaluation of changes in perinatal care; decreased mortality is certain, but effects on the frequency and degree of impairments and disabilities are far less sure. There probably were more damaged survivors in the late 1960s and early 1970s, but they have probably diminished since. No statistics can be recommended with confidence (Aylward *et al*, 1989). Few doubt, however, that perinatal causes contribute importantly to intellectual impairment in most communities.

Programmes to prevent impairments

Universal screening of newborn infants

Universal screening of neonates is now common for phenylketonuria, several similar disorders treatable by diet, and sporadic hypothyroidism. It has been extremely effective in the UK in preventing intellectual impairment.

Screening healthy adult populations

Screening healthy populations was successful for Tay Sach's disease in Ashkenazi communities in the US where the implications of premarital genetic counselling were accepted, but not elsewhere. Tay-Sach's disease is now almost eliminated from American Jewish populations. Genetic registers can also be helpful and may in time play a larger role.

Antenatal screening for Down's syndrome

Screening for foetal abnormalities, especially Down's syndrome, has become an increasingly important part of antenatal care. When amniocentesis was first introduced it was confined to women in 'high risk' groups, specifically those over 35 years of age. Those who were found to be carrying a foetus with Down's syndrome or another serious abnormality were offered an abortion. In population terms the programme was judged to be a failure. It has been estimated that in England and Wales between 1980 and 1985, the number of infants with Down's syndrome was only reduced by 10% (see Vyas, 1994). Data from the Office of Population Censuses and Surveys also suggests that there has been little change in prevalence at birth in recent years.

The introduction in 1992 of new serum testing techniques opened up the possibility that all women could be offered antenatal serum screening for Down's syndrome. The test is offered at 16–18 weeks of pregnancy and is based on the triple assay of maternal serum alpha foetoprotein, unconjugated oestriol and human chorionic gonadotrophin. Each of these measurements, separately or in combination, enable a risk calculation to be made. Those whose test results suggest they are at high risk are offered an amniocentesis or chorionic villus sampling which, if positive, would normally be followed by termination. These techniques make it possible for all women to be aware of their individual risk.

Women are required to make decisions at three points: before the prescreening tests, before amniocentesis and before termination. Adequate counselling before the prescreening test is necessary to enable women to make an informed choice about whether to undergo the testing. Serum screening for Down's syndrome is now offered on some basis by nearly all obstetricians in England and Wales. There is a major degree of concern about the adequacy of the counselling available.

There are clearly many ethical issues involved in the abortion of the foetus with Down's syndrome. Williams (1995) has drawn attention to the 1993 report of the Nuffield Council on Bioethics which states: "Genetic screening should only be instituted for serious diseases; screening for characteristics with a genetic component, but which cannot be classified as diseases should not be included in such programmes" (quoted in Williams, 1995). Although the Nuffield Council did consider Down's syndrome to be a disease this view has been challenged. Many people with Down's syndrome have expressed their views on the subject and talk proudly of the Down's syndrome as being part of their identity – they do not see themselves as having a disease.

Antenatal screening for other conditions

Amniocentesis and abortion are not truly preventive but have been accepted in many communities, not only in respect of Down's syndrome, but also for the termination of pregnancies with a foetus affected by rubella or a neural tube defect. The availability of serum screening for alpha-foetoprotein enabled the antenatal detection of neural tube defects, and the introduction of the ultrasound scan has enabled other foetal abnormalities to be identified.

Postnatal testing of mothers

To avoid further affected children with a familial disorder, postnatal testing of the mothers of affected babies can detect familial translocation in Down's syndrome and carrier status in fragile X syndrome. The opportunity should be taken to facilitate counselling and choice about subsequent pregnancies.

Rhesus immunisation

Immunisation of Rhesus negative mothers against sensitisation by Rhesus positive cells after the first child is important in rhesus incompatibility.

DNA screening of selected populations at high risk

Over the last 10 years fragile X syndrome has been recognised as a significant cause of mental retardation. Recent technical advances in diagnostic methods have made it possible to consider screening populations at risk using DNA testing. This should enable all potentially affected families to be forewarned by DNA-based screening for the mutation (Sabaratnam *et al*, 1994). The inheritance has an unusual X-linked pattern. Although the majority of males inheriting the mutation are affected it has been found that in 20% the gene is non-penetrant: their intellect and appearance are normal but they are nevertheless carriers of the disorder. Thirty per cent of females who inherit the mutation have some degree of intellectual impairment, but there are no specific dysmorphic features. For the 70% of female carriers who are intellectually normal there may be no outward sign at all of their risk of having intellectually impaired children, and it is frequently only after the birth of a second child with learning disabilities that a genetic cause is suspected. Screening for carriers is clearly important. DNA-based screening for fragile X syndrome is now technically feasible and is being carried out with selected populations in special schools (Slaney *et al*, 1995). A check-list is used to identify a subset of children at particularly high risk of fragile X syndrome. Female relatives can be counselled and further conceptions avoided. Accurate prenatal diagnosis and selective termination of affected foetuses can be offered.

Communicable diseases

Although no one organism is numerically important in mental retardation, collectively they are important, not least because of the potential for prevention. Rubella syndrome arises during early foetal life and can be prevented by immunisation. Cytomegalovirus is common but so is natural immunity and vaccine development is incomplete.

In the case of toxoplasmosis there is a paucity of information about the frequency of the infection, the disease rate after intra-uterine infection and the frequency of specific impairments. Only rough estimates of risk are possible (but they are probably very small), and with the limitations of current tests and risks of treatment a general antenatal screening programme is not justified (Hall, 1992). There is no consensus on intervention other than advocating good hygiene.

Tuberculosis and syphilis have been important in all countries. Early diagnosis and effective treatment has almost eliminated these conditions in developed countries, but not elsewhere. The congenital syndromes which are associated with these conditions bring about neurological damage and intellectual impairment.

Malaria should not be ignored in countries where the disease is prevalent. The various causes of meningitis and encephalitis, or encephalopathy, include measles, mumps, pertussis and haemophilus influenzae, all of which are preventable by immunisation which reduces individual risk. However, it is more important to minimise communicability by achieving herd immunity, generally requiring about 95% coverage in the population. Rubella, measles, mumps and pertussis are particularly relevant to intellectual impairment. Effective immunisation programmes for measles will also prevent late-onset subacute sclerosing pan-encephalitis.

Dietary advice and education

Dietary advice and education are important for improving nutrition in general, especially during pregnancy. Specific advice on folates probably requires supplementation programmes to be widely effective in preventing neural tube defects. Where there is endemic iodine deficiency disease, community programmes of salt iodisation or alternatives require high levels of political will and effective community organisation. Health promotion to avoid alcohol consumption in pregnancy is also variable in effect but very important where alcohol consumption is high.

Accident prevention

Accident prevention is complex and difficult, involving behavioural, environmental, economic and political factors; there have been some successes and some failures. Prevention of non-accidental injury to children is even less certain. Avoidance of specific environmental toxins may be important in some communities, particularly heavy metals. Only lead has been much investigated; it does not create recognised intellectual impairment, but evidence of a general reduction in intelligence of a few points is still disputed. General health of women and children are still major issues in the developing world and affect vulnerability to disease and damage.

Disabilities and handicaps related to intellectual impairment

Certain disorders are always prominent in groups of people with intellectual impairment. Epilepsy and cerebral palsy, syndromes of neurological impairments and specific disabilities, may arise as part of the same aetiological process as intellectual impairment, before, during or after birth. Proportions necessarily vary, but a range gives rough guidelines. Epilepsy, often fully controllable by drugs, is reported in 20–50% of people with severe intellectual impairment; cerebral palsy in 15–40%; serious visual problems in 10–30%; hearing problems in up to 5%; serious problems with speaking in 60–85%. These illustrate the multiple disabilities and multidisciplinary needs which characterise the group. Groups with lesser degrees of intellectual impairment have much lower frequencies of these disorders, but they are still important contributors to overall handicap.

The pervasive developmental (autistic) disorders are disability syndromes overlapping severe or mild intellectual impairment. Prevalence of autistic disorder as defined by Wing's triad of impairments is currently estimated to be 2 per 1000. Recognition as a clinical entity does not imply a single aetiology. Many psychiatric disorders may be conceived as syndromes of disability in the absence of known organic impairments. Studies usually show more psychiatric problems in people with intellectual impairment than the general population, but if behaviour disorders are excluded, a true excess of clearly defined psychiatric illness is less certain, given the difficulties of assessment and comparison in people with learning disabilities.

Measuring disabilities

The taxonomy and measurement of disabilities in populations has received little attention, and it is difficult to discriminate discrete syndromes and standardise instruments. Clinical and behavioural observation scales can provide useful individual profiles for professional practice but are difficult to handle for research; they include the AAMD Adaptive Behaviour Scales (Nihira *et al*, 1974), the Vineland Social Maturity Scale and the Development Record (Doll, 1953), among others. Wing's Medical Research Council Handicaps, Behaviour and Skills Schedule, developed for research, has been used successfully in community studies in several countries (Wing, 1980). Derived from this, a short Disability Assessment Schedule (DAS) has been used for both service and research applications. There are computer analysis programmes for both. There is a need for more epidemiological studies of disability related to normal populations, and evaluation research on procedures and programmes intended specifically to minimise disability.

Individual handicaps

This is a little explored field for the epidemiologist. Most handicaps, or social disadvantages, are not specific to people called learning disabled or mentally retarded, although they may experience a unique combination of them. There is no accepted taxonomy, few measures, and little interest in research. A long-term project following up all those identified as mentally retarded in Aberdeen in the 1950s is one of the few sources of information on the adult problems of those identified in childhood. Recent papers by Richardson *et al* (1988) have examined marriage, peer relationships, and work experience.There have also been a few studies of economic and other burdens on families with severely mentally handicapped children. We need data on handicap because the ultimate aim of services is to diminish handicap, and we need the tools with which to evaluate those services.

References

Aylward, G. P., Pfeiffer, S. I., Wright, A., *et al* (1989) Outcome studies of low birth weight infants published in the last decade: a meta-analysis. *Journal of Paediatrics*, **115** 515–520.

Department of Health Expert Advisory Group (1992) *Folic Acid and the Prevention of Neural Tube Defects*. London: DoH.

Doll, E. A. (1953) *Vineland Social Maturity Scale*. Minneapolis: American Guidance Service.

Einfeld, S. L. & Hall, W. (1994) Recent developments in the study of behaviour phenotypes. *Australia and New Zealand Journal of Developmental Disabilities*, **19**, 275–279.

Escobar, G. J., Littenberg, B. & Petitti, D. B. (1991) Outcome among surviving very low birthweight infants: a meta-analysis. *Archives of Disease in Childhood*, **66**, 204–211.

Fryers, T. (1984) *The Epidemiology of Severe Intellectual Impairment: The Dynamics of Prevalence*. London: Academic Press.

—— (1990) Pre and perinatal factors in the aetiology of mental retardation. In *Reproductive and Perinatal Epidemiology* (ed. M. Kiely). Florida: CRC Press.

Gath, A. (1990) Down's syndrome children and their families. *American Journal of Medical Genetics Supplement*, **7**, 314–316.

Grant, D. B. (1995) Congenital hypothyroidism: optimal management in the light of 15 year's experience of screening. *Archives of Disease in Childhood*, **72**, 85–89.

Green, J. M. (1994) Serum screening for Down's syndrome: experiences of obstetricians in England and Wales. *British Medical Journal*, **309**, 769–772.

Hagberg, B. (ed.) (1993) Rett syndrome: clinical and biological aspects. *Clinics in Developmental Medicine*, No. 127. Cambridge: Cambridge University Press.

Hall, S. M. (1992) Congenital toxoplasmosis. *British Medical Journal*, **305**, 291–297.

Hetzel, B. S. (1989) *The Story of Iodine Deficiency; An International Challenge in Nutrition*. Oxford: Oxford University Press.

McGrother, C. W. & Marshall, B. (1990) Recent trends, incidence, morbidity and survival in Down's syndrome. *Journal of Mental Deficiency Research*, **34**, 49–57.

Medical Research Council Working Party on Phenylketonuria (1993) Phenylketonuria due to phenylalanine hydroxylase deficiency: an unfolding story. *British Medical Journal*, **306**, 115–119.

Nihira, K., Foster, R., Shellhaas, M., *et al* (1974) *Adaptive Behaviour Scales*. Washington, DC: American Association on Mental Deficiency.

Richardson, S. A., Koller, H. & Katz, M. (1988) Job histories in open employment of a population of young adults with mental retardation. *American Journal on Mental Retardation*, **92**, 483–491.

Sabaratnam, M., Laver, S., Butler, L., *et al* (1994) Fragile X syndrome in North East Essex: towards systematic screening: clinical selection. *Journal of Intellectual Disability Research*, **38**, 27–35.

Simon, V. A., Abrams, M. T., Freund, L. S., *et al* (1990) The fragile X phenotype: cognitive, behavioural and neurobiological profiles. *Current Opinion in Psychiatry*, **3**, 581–586.

Simons, W. F., Fuggle, P. W., Grant, D. B., *et al* (1994) Intellectual development at 10 years in early treated congenital hypothyroidism. *Archives of Disease in Childhood*, **71**, 232–234.

Slaney, S. F., Wilkie, A. O. M., Hirst, M. C., *et al* (1995) DNA testing for fragile X syndrome in schools for learning difficulties. *Archives of Disease in Childhood*, **72**, 33–37.

Turk, J. (1995) Fragile X syndrome. *Archives of Disease in Childhood*, **72**, 4–5.

Vyas, S. (1994) Screening for Down's syndrome *British Medical Journal*, **309**, 753–754.

Webb, D. W. & Osborne, J. P. (1995) Tuberous sclerosis. *Archives of Disease in Childhood*, **72**, 471–475.

Williams, P. (1995) Should we prevent Down's syndrome? *British Journal of Learning Disabilities*, **23**, 46–50.

Wing, L. (1980) MRC Handicaps, Behaviour and Skills (HBS) Schedule. *Acta Psychiatrica Scandinavica*, **suppl. 62**, 275–284.

World Health Organization (1980) *International Classification of Impairments, Disabilities and Handicaps*. Geneva: WHO.

Additional reading

Fryers, T. (1984) *The Epidemiology of Severe Intellectual Impairment: The Dynamics of Prevalence*. London: Academic Press.

—— (1987) Epidemiological issues in mental retardation. *Journal of Mental Deficiency Research*, **31**, 365–384.

—— (1993) Epidemiological thinking in mental retardation: issues in taxonomy and population frequency. *International Review of Research in Mental Retardation*, **19**, 97–133.

—— (1996) Public health approaches to mental retardation: handicap related to intellectual impairment. In *Oxford Textbook of Public Health* (3rd edn) (eds W. W. W. Holland, R. Detels, E. G. Knox, *et al*) Oxford: Oxford University Press.

—— (1996) Mental retardation in developing countries. In *Psychiatry for the Developing World* (eds D. Tantam, L. Appleby & A. Duncan). London: Gaskell.

Weatherall, D. J. (1991) *The New Genetics and Clinical Practice* (3rd edn). Oxford: Oxford University Press.

4 The diagnosis of psychiatric disorder

Oliver Russell

Conceptual issues ● *Epidemiological studies* ● *Clinical studies*
Diagnostic rating scales used in research ● *Conclusion*

"Mental illness in the mentally handicapped child or adult is usually
a question of nuances, of degree, of an opinion or an attitude of
those concerned." (Kirman, 1979)

In the years since Kirman made this comment there have been major
changes in the ways we approach the diagnosis of mental health problems
in people with learning disabilities. Although serious forms of psychiatric
disorder affect relatively few individuals with learning disabilities,
substantial numbers are vulnerable to problems such as hypersensitivity
to criticism, excessive dependency and social inadequacy. For people
who may be living in relatively isolated circumstances, such problems
may give rise to much misery and distress. Identifying those who may be
at risk and providing them with psychological support is an increasingly
important task for the psychiatrist.

Several studies have suggested that behavioural and psychiatric
disorders occur more frequently among people with learning disabilities
than in the general population, possibly 40% of adults with severe learning
disabilities being affected by such disorders (Corbett, 1979; Reiss, 1990).
We now recognise the need for more precise and rigorous diagnostic
procedures. While clinical interviews, behavioural check-lists and the study
of case notes all have a part to play in the process of arriving at a diagnosis,
the confirmation of the nature of the disorder depends on a careful
examination of the person by a trained clinician using agreed diagnostic
criteria.

But where can we find these criteria? Should we base our clinical
diagnosis of mental health problems in people with learning disabilities
within the same framework as that used for those in the general
population? Should we classify all of the apparently inappropriate
behaviours seen in people with learning disabilities as psychiatric disorder
– or are some of these behaviours a natural, and perhaps not unexpected,
response to living in a chaotic or deprived social environment? Is the way
in which a behaviour disorder manifests itself related in some way to the
severity of the learning disability? Do those people with learning disabilities
who have brain damage suffer a similar range of emotional problems as
those who do not?

Conceptual issues

Although a substantial amount of research has been carried out on the mental health needs of people with learning disabilities, there is still considerable confusion and uncertainty about the exact nature of the disorders which psychiatrists and psychologists are called upon to diagnose and treat. Behavioural or emotional disturbances can be the consequence of physical illness, for example a confusional state may be precipitated by a severe respiratory infection. An emotional disturbance may also be the result of psychological stress. Depression may be triggered by a personal loss, for example as a consequence of prolonged grief after being bereaved, or the depressed mood may reflect a biochemical or endocrine imbalance. An unexpected, or unprepared for, change in a living situation may set off a profound behaviour disturbance – as when an aggressive outburst occurs after a person has been moved from a familiar ward in a hospital to a new and unfamiliar group home in the community. There is clearly a wide spectrum of potential triggers, any one of which may precipitate an emotional or psychological reaction.

People with learning disabilities appear to be much more sensitive to stress than other members of the community. In particular they are likely to be more vulnerable to the consequences of physical ill health, social isolation, physical abuse and environmental pressure. For some people there may be additional social and emotional problems consequent upon their failure to develop adequate language skills or the complications associated with repeated epileptic seizures. In addition to their social vulnerability they may also be less physically robust on account of physical disability, metabolic disorder or brain damage.

Although the immediate trigger for the change in behaviour may be visible, the roots of the problem will often be concealed because the person may not be able to express their thoughts and feelings. Consider these examples:

> Is the severely disabled boy who silently rocks himself back and forward in a chair simply bored, or is he depressed?
> Is the young woman who repeatedly strikes her face till it bleeds responding to physical pain, or is she hallucinating as a consequence of a psychotic illness?
> Is the elderly man who seems lost in his thoughts suffering from dementia or was he never able to communicate with others?

The interpretation of such behaviours is fraught with difficulty. Observation of a person's behaviour will enable us to extend the picture, but because a person with learning disabilities may not be able to give a coherent account of their thoughts and feelings there is a high chance that they will be misunderstood and that their problems will be poorly diagnosed.

While the occurrence of abnormal behaviour patterns may suggest the presence of a psychiatric disorder this will not always be the case. Aggressive or self-injurious behaviour may reflect frustration or anger in response to perceived threats in a hostile environment. Emotional withdrawal may represent unexpressed fear.

'Problem behaviour' or psychiatric illness?

Before considering the diagnosis of psychiatric disorder in more detail we need to examine some of the ways in which abnormal behaviour in people with severe learning disabilities is labelled. Descriptions such as 'problem behaviour', 'challenging behaviour' and 'behaviour disorder' are all currently in use but are applied in different ways.

Problem behaviour

People with learning disabilities in institutions have to adapt to living in noisy environments where they have to cope with the conflicting demands of others. For many people the process of adaptation is not easy and some may respond in inappropriate ways. Their behaviour may then be described as problem behaviour if it satisfies at least some of the following criteria (Zarkowska & Clements, 1994). The behaviour:

(a) is inappropriate given a person's age and level of development;
(b) is dangerous either to the person or to others;
(c) constitutes a significant additional handicap for the person by interfering with the learning of new skills or by excluding the person from important learning opportunities;
(d) causes significant stress to the lives of those who live and work with the person and impairs the quality of their lives to an unreasonable degree;
(e) is contrary to accepted social norms.

Clinical psychologists have developed sophisticated strategies to assess problematic behaviours and devise appropriate interventions (for details see chapter 11).

Challenging behaviour

In the mid-1980s many mental health professionals felt that the term problem behaviour was unhelpful. It was recognised that the 'problem' was often to be found in the environment rather than within the person. Challenging behaviour is, however, not a clinical diagnosis. It is a term which was introduced to signify that for some people the available services were not meeting their needs and that their aggressive or self-injurious behaviour reflected their frustration and anger. Those who first used the term emphasised that it was the professionals and the service providers who were being challenged.

> "The term challenging behaviour is used to emphasise the fact that the issue is a challenge to those who provide services, and to the rest of society, not just a problem carried around by the individual. The challenge is ours to find effective ways of helping people to behave and express themselves in ways which are acceptable to society." (Blunden & Allen, 1987)

Psychiatrists, psychologists and other professionals were asked to face that challenge by looking more closely at the social and environmental factors that might have initiated such behaviour. Sadly, the phrase challenging behaviour has lost its original meaning and is now often used as a synonym for problem behaviour.

Behaviour disorder or psychiatric disorder?

Behaviour disorder is a term which is used to describe emotional disturbance in children and adolescents, but may also be used with reference to people with learning disabilities. The term 'behaviour disorder' is much more specific than 'problem behaviour' or 'challenging behaviour'. Although the terms are often used as though interchangeable, behaviour disorders are specific disorders for which diagnostic criteria are available. DSM–IV (International Version; American Psychiatric Association, 1995) and ICD–10 (World Health Organization, 1992) both provide a resource for reference and a diagnostic listing of all recognised behaviour disorders and behavioural syndromes. It is now possible using a multi-axial classification to include a diagnosis of behaviour disorder alongside other psychiatric diagnoses. Behaviour disorders do not relate clearly or simply to any known disease process. In the UK until recently, relatively little attention has been given to the diagnosis of behaviour disorder, but the situation seems to be changing (Sturmey, 1993, 1995).

Behaviour disorders may arise in all sorts of ways. The behaviour may be a learned response acquired in a socially deprived environment, where there is a lack of social interaction. The disturbance may be triggered by physical illness, for example by pain from a peptic ulcer or by discomfort from an untreated dental abscess, or it may be triggered by environmental stress (living in noisy or overheated rooms) or by social pressure (being pressurised or abused by other people). Behaviour disorders are especially likely to manifest themselves in people with learning disabilities who have sensory deficits or communication problems. Such behaviours will often take the form of self-injury or aggression. The clinician needs to be able to distinguish between those behaviours which are the manifestation of a treatable psychiatric condition and those which are psychological reactions to environmental or interpersonal stress. Clearly there will often be degrees of overlap, especially among emotional disorders such as anxiety states and obsessional behaviours. The distinction may not be useful where the approach to treatment is likely to be similar. However, the distinction is important where there is a need for specific pharmacological intervention, as in schizophrenia or bipolar depressive disorders.

The need for a psychiatric diagnosis

A diagnosis may be required for several reasons:

To diagnose the nature of a clinical condition. When a person presents with abnormal behaviour there is a need to establish whether a clinically recognised condition is present. Once a person with a learning disability is suspected of having a mental health problem, a differential diagnosis will be considered and further diagnostic tests will be carried out to identify the precise nature of the psychiatric disorder. Diagnostic guidelines may be used as a framework for the classification of the disorder, but until the precise nature of the condition has been diagnosed it may be difficult to embark on appropriate treatment.

To evaluate the outcomes of treatment. A second reason for having a diagnosis is to have the means to assess the severity of a disorder and thus be able to monitor the outcome of treatment. This is particularly important when evaluating the effect of drug treatments (Sturmey, 1995).

To establish causal connections between pathology and psychiatric disorder. Diagnostic precision is necessary if we are to understand the connections between biological, psychological and social processes and psychiatric symptomatology. For example, if we are to understand how disruption of metabolic pathways causes personality change, or how social or environmental deprivation relates to mood disorder, we need to have clear diagnostic categories. Clinical research has to be based on clinical information which is valid and reliable.

To identify those who may need treatment through the screening of populations at risk. Lastly, we need to have diagnostic rating scales in order to screen populations of people with learning disabilities for the presence of psychiatric disorder. The benefits of early intervention are now recognised and we need to identify those children and adults with a learning disability living in the community who have a psychiatric disorder so that they may receive appropriate treatment. Various diagnostic instruments have been used to screen populations at risk.

Psychiatric symptoms

Distinguishing a psychiatric disorder from other abnormal behaviours may be very difficult. Some believe that the distinction is not justified and that there is no need to separate psychiatric disorder from behaviour disorder (Szymanski, 1994), and that all abnormal behaviours should be included within a single classificatory system. Others believe that it is important to make distinctions.

When making a diagnosis of a psychiatric disorder in an individual who does not have learning disabilities, we rely extensively on what the person tells us about their thoughts, perceptions and feelings, and we augment that information with our observations in the clinical interview. As clinicians we are seriously disadvantaged if the person is unable to give an account of their inner feelings.

It has been suggested that before an individual can accurately report on their own emotional state they need to be able to show not only that they can recognise different emotions, but also what it means to be happy, sad or frightened (Reed & Clements, 1989). In practice people with severe learning disabilities may be able to say virtually nothing about their thoughts and feelings and we may have to rely almost entirely on our observations of the person's behaviour. As Kirman reflected in the sentence quoted at the beginning of this chapter, we may be guided, not by clinical signs and symptoms, but by rather vague impressions. Such a situation is clearly very unsatisfactory.

When a person who does not have learning disabilities presents to a psychiatrist they will usually: complain of a problem, perhaps in terms of their emotional feelings such as despair, depression, fear or panic; report some loss of adaptive functioning (perhaps they cannot sleep or can no longer face other people); present themselves for treatment. In a person with learning disabilities the process may be different (Sturmey *et al*, 1991; Sturmey, 1995):

> It is usually someone other than the patient who complains about the problem.
>
> Although there may be a loss of adaptive functioning it is often the family or carers who complain.
>
> Changes in a carer's tolerance may result in the referral of someone whose behaviour has not objectively changed.
>
> Changes in the carers themselves may result in an old problem, which had perhaps long been tolerated, being referred for treatment.
>
> Changes in the social environment may result in what had once been seen as a minor irritant escalate into an intolerable problem behaviour.

Dual diagnosis

There is also another fundamental issue. When we identify a psychiatric symptom, can we be sure that it is not simply a part of that person's normal repertoire of behaviour? There has been concern among clinicians that the mental health needs of people with a learning disability might be overlooked because any psychiatric symptoms which were present were often assumed to be an intrinsic part of whatever pathology caused the learning disability. In the US the concept of dual diagnosis has been adopted to try to overcome this problem and recognise that psychiatric disorder and learning disability frequently coexist. The concept of a dual diagnosis enables the mental health needs of such a person to be properly recognised.

In attributing a dual diagnosis we make a number of assumptions. We assume that psychiatric disorders in people with learning disabilities are likely to follow the same pattern as in people without learning disabilities. In the absence of a spoken account of an individual's feelings we may consider that our assessment of their non-verbal behaviour is sufficient to make a diagnosis. Also, we expect that the process and potential outcome of a psychiatric disorder will be the same (or similar) in people with and without learning disabilities.

Epidemiological studies

The pioneering work of Michael Rutter and colleagues marked the beginning of the modern epidemiological approach to the diagnosis of psychiatric disorder. In 1965 they conducted a study of all 10–12-year-olds in the Isle of Wight to identify those who had a psychiatric disorder (Rutter *et al*, 1970). Their studies involved the use of rating scales which were completed by carers, teachers or others who knew the child well. They defined psychiatric disorder as "abnormalities of emotions, behaviour, relationships or thinking which are inconsistent with the patient's intellectual level and of sufficient duration or severity to cause persistent suffering or handicap to the person and/or distress and disturbance to those in daily contact with him or her".

Rutter *et al* found that emotional and behavioural disorders were very much commoner in intellectually retarded children and in children with specific reading retardation. They explored the relationship between psychiatric disorder and chronic disability. They found that where the disorder involved the central nervous system (as in cerebral palsy or epilepsy) the rate of psychiatric disorder increased fivefold. In subsequent studies in London and elsewhere, Rutter and others in his team also explored the outcomes for children with head injuries. Here they again found a strong association between brain injury and psychiatric disorder.

Rutter concluded that psychiatric disorder is most likely to occur when there is abnormal neurophysiological activity. The type of activity may also be important, as indicated by the greater psychiatric risk associated with psychomotor seizures. The consistent association between autism and certain biological syndromes, but not others, and the characteristic form of self-mutilation associated with Lesch-Nyhan syndrome highlights the importance of looking for an underlying medical condition whenever psychiatric disorder is diagnosed (Rutter, 1981).

The research of Rutter *et al* also illuminated the importance of social factors. Quite apart from the neurological considerations, the psychiatric consequences of brain injury are also very substantially influenced by the child's behaviour prior to the injury, and psychosocial and environmental influences play a significant role in the emergence of a psychiatric disorder.

The epidemiological studies which were undertaken by Corbett (1979) in Camberwell in the 1970s provided a baseline for our current knowledge of the prevalence of psychiatric disorders in adults with learning disabilities. Corbett limited his survey to children and adults with severe and profound disabilities. Using ICD–9 criteria he found that in a community sample of 140 children, 47% met the criteria for a diagnosis of psychiatric disorder. Among adults he found that 37% of those who were living at home had a psychiatric disorder. Corbett concluded his paper by remarking that the psychiatrist is presented with a wealth of behavioural pathology but with only tenuous and fragmentary clues with which to establish a coherent system of classification.

Clinical studies

During the 1970s most of the diagnostic studies which were undertaken of psychiatric disorder in adults were based upon the diagnostic framework used in general adult psychiatry. Most psychiatrists relied on traditional categories of psychiatric disorder, even though it was sometimes difficult to formulate diagnoses in respect of people who had no language skills. Psychiatrists believed that there were no fundamental differences in the ways that psychiatric disorders affect people with learning disabilities as compared with the non-disabled population. In other words the classical signs of mental illness are found in people with learning disabilities, no matter whether or not they have an inherent biological problem. Any psychiatric disorder was seen as being superimposed on the learning disability.

Reid (1972) carried out a study of schizophrenia in people with learning disabilities and found that he could make a diagnosis of schizophrenic psychosis in 12 patients and of paranoid psychosis in a further seven. This gave a prevalence rate for schizophrenic psychosis (including paranoid disorders) of 32 per 1000 hospital residents. He used ordinary clinical methods to diagnose psychiatric disorder in those who had verbal skills, but found that he could not make a reliable diagnosis in those without verbal skills. Very similar rates were found by Heaton-Ward (1977) in Bristol.

Cluster analysis

There has been a tendency to overdiagnose schizophrenic symptoms in long-stay hospital populations of people with learning disabilities, by including within this category all those socially withdrawn and profoundly handicapped adults who show prominent mannerisms and stereotyped movement disorder. Reid *et al* (1978) developed an alternative diagnostic framework. They submitted observational data systematically collected on 100 hospitalised patients to cluster analysis. Each patient was independently assessed by nursing staff, by scrutiny of hospital notes and by an interview with a psychiatrist. Eight behavioural syndromes were identified in this analysis (Box 4.1). Reid was very tentative in putting these results forward, but they marked an important advance in classifying behavioural syndromes, although cluster analysis did not provide a device for assessing psychopathology.

In a 16–18 year follow-up study, Reid & Ballinger (1995) found that their overall ratings were significantly persistent, both in presence and in degree. Some individuals had moved in or out of the pathological range and there was some tendency for the most severe degree of psychiatric disorder to abate, but this did not reach statistical significance.

The use of a multi-axial classification

The presence of a psychiatric disorder can only be established when the signs and symptoms of a particular condition are present. Diagnostic criteria for psychiatric disorders are to be found in DSM–IV and ICD–10. The World Health Organization has also published a set of diagnostic criteria for research (DCR; World Health Organization, 1993); these have been carefully evaluated (Clarke *et al*, 1994).

The diagnostic criteria for research offer a multi-axial system for recording information. Multi-axial systems have been developed to allow information about different disorders or aspects of behavioural function to be communicated quickly in a standard format. Clarke *et al* (1994) used the following axes:

Axis I   Basic data (age, sex, living arrangements)
Axis II   Cognitive level (degree of learning disability)
Axis III   Physical disorders (Down's syndrome, etc.)
Axis IV   Psychiatric disorder
Axis V   Functional assessment (self-help skills, vision, hearing, etc.).

Clinicians involved in the trial found the DCR to be a useful and comprehensive system. There were problems when behavioural disorders occurred in the absence of a psychiatric disorder.

Problems in diagnosing psychiatric disorder in people with learning disabilities are most acute in the case of schizophrenic and paranoid

---

Box 4.1 Behavioural syndromes identified by cluster analysis (Reid *et al*, 1978)

Clusters 1 & 2	Patients with relatively little serious psychiatric pathology (47%)
Cluster 3	A hyperkinetic syndrome, persistent in some cases and progressing in some to a hypokinetic syndrome in adult life (6%)
Cluster 4	A stereotypy/emotional withdrawal syndrome presenting in some cases with features of grown up early childhood autism (16%)
Cluster 5	A high arousal syndrome with severe and multiple behavioural disturbance (8%)
Cluster 6	A small group with affective disorders (9%)
Cluster 7	A syndrome of pathological social withdrawal having an almost paranoid quality (7%)
Cluster 8	A group of predominantly older patients who were abnormally socially and emotionally withdrawn. Their behaviour could be construed as a response to institutionalisation (9%)

---

disorders. Because the person may not be able to talk about their delusional ideas or hallucinatory experiences, the clinician is forced into making a diagnosis solely on the evidence of observed behaviour. The differentiation of schizophrenia from depression and other psychiatric disorders in people who are non-verbal is extremely difficult because there is no defined nucleus of non-verbal symptoms for schizophrenia in people with intellectual impairments (Wright, 1982; Meadows *et al*, 1991). Clarke *et al* (1994) confirmed this view.

Diagnostic rating scales used in research

For research purposes three methods of diagnosis are currently in use: diagnostic interviews, retrospective analysis of case notes, and observational check-lists completed by third parties. Because of the wide range of intellectual competence found among people with learning disabilities, each instrument has had to be adapted or modified for different populations.

Brief diagnostic rating scales for people with severe or profound learning disabilities

Aberrant Behaviour Check-list

The Aberrant Behaviour Check-list (Aman *et al*, 1985) was devised to assess treatment effects and to provide an instrument for the assessment of general behaviour in people with learning disabilities. The items on the scale are divided into five subscales: irritability, agitation and crying; lethargy, social withdrawal; stereotypical behaviour; hyperactivity, non-compliance; and inappropriate speech.

A version adapted for use in community settings (the ABC-C) has now been validated and found to be a useful assessment tool (Aman *et al*, 1995).

Diagnostic Assessment Scale for the Severely Handicapped (DASH)

The Diagnostic Assessment Scale for the Severely Handicapped (DASH) was developed by Matson *et al* (1991) to provide an instrument specifically for people with severe and profound handicaps. The scale covers 13 major psychiatric disorders and is based on 83 items derived from DSM–III–R. It is a multidimensional instrument which can be used to assess the severity of symptoms as well as their frequency and duration.

In studies of institutional populations, Matson *et al* (1991) found that direct care staff could provide psychiatric ratings of profoundly and severely learning disabled individuals with generally acceptable interrater reliability and internal consistency.

Brief diagnostic rating scales for people with mild or moderate learning disabilities

Reiss Screen for maladaptive behaviour

The Reiss Screen was also developed in the US. This is a 38-item assessment instrument with eight scales evaluating the probability that the person has an aggressive disorder, psychosis, autism, depression, avoidant disorder, dependent personality disorder and paranoia. The Reiss Screen is completed by a carer, teacher or other person who knows the subject well enough to report validly on maladaptive behaviour. The scoring system produces 14 numbers for the type of disorder and a total score for severity. If the results exceed a cut-off point then the person is referred for a full diagnostic assessment (Reiss, 1988).

The Psychopathology Inventory for Mentally Retarded Adults (PIMRA)

The inventory is available in a self-report format as well as a version for use by a third party. The PIMRA (Matson *et al*, 1984) is designed for use with people with mild learning disabilities. It comprises 56 items based on DSM–III. It is subdivided into eight scales: schizophrenia, affective disorders, psychosexual disorder, adjustment disorder, anxiety disorder, somatoform disorder, personality disorder and poor mental adjustment. Each item is rated on a 'yes' or 'no' basis. One interview is between the clinician and an informant, such as a carer or teacher; the other interview is between the clinician and the person with learning disabilities. The results of the interview are interpreted clinically. The PIMRA has proved to be useful but it is essentially a questionnaire rather than a detailed diagnostic instrument.

In the UK, Bouras & Drummond (1992) developed an assessment tool, the Clinical Psychopathology Mental Handicap Scale (CPMHS), which is based on the PIMRA. The CPMHS consists of a list of signs and symptoms explicitly related to psychiatric disorders. The CPMHS was used on all 381 new referrals over a period of 8 years. A psychiatric diagnosis was recorded for 41% of those with expressive language skills who could be interviewed.

Diagnostic interview schedules

The Psychiatric Assessment Scale for Adults with Developmental Disability (PAS–ADD)

In the UK a substantial advance was made when Moss and colleagues developed a diagnostic instrument to use with older people with moderate and severe learning disability (Moss *et al*, 1993; Patel *et al*, 1993). The need for a new instrument was dictated by the wish to have a detailed instrument that could be used directly and without dependence on third-party reports. The PAS–ADD is a semistructured instrument which allows for a considerable degree of flexibility in its use. The main body of the interview concentrates on the more common neurotic conditions found in people living in the community, with additional modules available to cope with less frequently encountered psychiatric conditions.

The PAS–ADD is derived from the Present State Examination (PSE), which was developed for use in general psychiatry. PAS–ADD has a number of special features which make it especially suited for diagnosis in people with learning disabilities: the patient and the informant are interviewed in parallel (Moss *et al*, 1996), the two sets of data being subsequently combined to increase sensitivity; there is a three-tier structure which is designed to make the interview sufficiently flexible for use with people of a wide range of linguistic abilities; the device of choosing a 'memorable event' helps to focus the content of the discussion on events in the four weeks prior to the interview; the items have been organised so that the interviewer can 'skip' items and maintain the patient's attention.

The research team reported that the instrument was successful in detecting cases of major depression, generalised anxiety, panic disorder and agoraphobia. It is currently being expanded to cover a wider range of disorders, including pervasive disorders of development.

Conclusion

The diagnosis of psychiatric disorder is now firmly grounded in methods which are tried and tested, but there is still little agreement as to how many people with learning disabilities have a psychiatric disorder. In 1982 Jacobson reported a study of over 30 000 children and adults with learning disabilities living in New York State. Among the adult population he found 12.4% had been classified as having a psychiatric disability. Iverson & Fox (1989), using a cut-off point based on PIMRA, found that 35.9% of a random sample of 165 adults were rated as having a psychiatric disorder. Using the Reiss Screen, Reiss (1990) found a prevalence rate of psychiatric disorder of 39% in a study of those attending a community-based day programme in Chicago. He found that only a small minority suffered from severe psychiatric disorders. Very similar findings have been reported in the UK.

Although depressive disorders are not that common (Reiss, 1990, found that between 3% and 6% of those in his sample were depressed, and Bouras, 1988, found 8% in his referrals), these disorders are important because they are frequently associated with aggressive behaviour. People who become aggressive are frequently frustrated or misunderstood.

The diagnosis of mental health problems is especially important now that effective psychological and pharmacological treatments are available for most categories of psychiatric disorder. Appropriate treatment ultimately depends on sensitive assessment using reliable diagnostic measures. The psychatrist needs to be equipped with an appropriate combination of clinical tools to undertake these tasks.

References

Aman, M. G., Singh, N. N., Stewart, A. W., *et al* (1985) The Aberrant Behavior Checklist: a behavior rating scale for the assessment of treatment effects. *American Journal of Mental Deficiency*, **89**, 485–491.
——, Burrow, W. H. & Wolford, P. L. (1995) The Aberrant Behavior Checklist – Community: factor validity and effect of subject variables for adult group homes. *American Journal on Mental Retardation*, **100**, 283–292.
American Psychiatric Association (1995) *Diagnostic and Statistical Manual of Mental Disorders* (4th edn) (DSM–IV, International Version). Washington, DC: APA.
Blunden, R. & Allen, D. (eds) (1987) *Facing the Challenge: an Ordinary Life for People with Learning Difficulties and Challenging Behaviour*. London: King's Fund.
Bouras, N., Drummond, K., Brooks, D., *et al* (1988) *Mental Handicap and Mental Health: a Community Service*. London: National Unit for Psychiatric Research and Development.

—— & Drummond, C. (1992) Behaviour and psychiatric disorders of people with mental handicaps living in the community. *Journal of Intellectual Disability Research*, **36**, 349–357.

Clarke, D. J., Cumella, S., Corbett, J., *et al* (1994) Use of ICD–10 research diagnostic criteria to categorise psychiatric and behavioural abnormalities among people with learning disabilities. *Mental Handicap Research*, **7**, 273–285.

Corbett, J. (1979) Psychiatric morbidity and mental retardation. In *Psychiatric Illness and Mental Handicap* (eds F. E. James & R. P. Snaith), pp. 11–25. London: Gaskell.

Heaton-Ward, W. A. (1977) Psychosis in mental handicap. *British Journal of Psychiatry*, **130**, 525–533.

Iverson, J. C. & Fox, R. A. (1989) Prevalence of psychopathology among mentally retarded adults. *Research in Developmental Disability*, **10**, 77–83.

Jacobson, J. W. (1982) Problem behaviour and psychiatric impairment within a developmentally disabled population. 1: Behaviour frequency. *Applied Research in Mental Retardation*, **3**, 121–139.

Kirman, B. (1979) Mental illness and mental handicap: reflections on diagnostic problems and prevalence. In *Psychiatric Illness and Mental Handicap* (eds F. E. James & R. P. Snaith), pp. 3–9. London: Gaskell.

Matson, J. L., Kazdin, A. E. & Senatore, V. (1984) Psychometric properties of the Psychopathology Instrument for Mentally Retarded Adults. *Applied Research in Mental Retardation*, **5**, 881–889.

——, Gardner, W. I., Coe, D. A., *et al* (1991) A scale for evaluating emotional disorders in severely and profoundly mentally retarded persons: development of the Diagnostic Assessment for the Severely Handicapped (DASH) scale. *British Journal of Psychiatry*, **159**, 404–409.

Meadows, G., Turner, T., Campbell, L., *et al* (1991) Assessing schizophrenia in adults with mental retardation: a comparative study. *British Journal of Psychiatry*, **158**, 103–105.

Moss, S., Patel, P., Prosser, H., *et al* (1993) Psychiatric morbidity in older people with moderate and severe learning disability. I: Development and reliability of the Patient Interview (PAS–ADD). *British Journal of Psychiatry*, **163**, 471–480.

——, Prosser, H., Ibbotson, B., *et al* (1996) Respondent and informer accounts of psychiatric symptoms in a sample of patients with learning disability. *Journal of Intellectual Disability Research*, **40**, 457–465.

Patel, P., Goldberg, D. & Moss, S. (1993) Psychiatric morbidity in older people with moderate and severe learning disability. II: The prevalence study. *British Journal of Psychiatry*, **163**, 481–491.

Reed, J. & Clements, J. (1989) Assessing the understanding of emotional states in a population of adolescents and young adults with mental handicaps. *Journal of Mental Deficiency Research*, **33**, 229–233.

Reid, A. H. (1972) Psychoses in mental defectives. *British Journal of Psychiatry*, **120**, 213–218.

——, Ballinger, B. R & Heather, B. B. (1978) Behavioural syndromes identified by cluster analysis in a sample of 100 severely and profoundly retarded adults. *Psychological Medicine*, **8**, 399–412.

—— & —— (1995) Behaviour symptoms among severely and profoundly mentally retarded patients: a 16–18 year follow-up study. *British Journal of Psychiatry*, **167**, 452–455.

Reiss, S. (1990) Prevalence of dual diagnosis in community based day programs in the Chicago Metropolitan Area. *American Journal on Mental Retardation*, **94**, 578–585.

Rutter, M. (1981) Psychological sequelae of brain damage in children. *American Journal of Psychiatry*, **138**, 1533–1544.

—, Tizard, J. & Whitmore, K. (1970) *Education, Health and Behaviour*. London: Longman.

Sturmey, P. (1993) The use of DSM and ICD diagnostic criteria with people with mental retardation: a review of empirical studies. *Journal of Nervous and Mental Diseases*, **181**, 38–41.

— (1995) Diagnostic based pharmacological treatment of behavior disorders in persons with developmental disabilities: a review and a decision making typology. *Research in Developmental Disabilities*, **16**, 235–252.

—, Reed, J. & Corbett, J. (1991) Psychometric assessment of psychiatric disorder in people with learning disabilities (mental handicap): a review of measures. *Psychological Medicine*, **21**, 143–155.

Szymanski, L. (1994) Mental retardation and mental health: concepts, aetiology and incidence. In *Mental Health in Mental Retardation* (ed. N. Bouras). Cambridge: Cambridge University Press.

World Health Organization (1992) *The ICD–10 Classification of Mental and Behavioural Disorders: Clinical Descriptions and Diagnostic Guidelines*. Geneva: WHO.

— (1993) *The ICD–10 Classification of Mental and Behavioural Disorders: Diagnostic Criteria for Research*. Geneva: WHO.

Wright, E. C. (1982) The presentation of mental illness in mentally retarded adults. *British Journal of Psychiatry*, **141**, 496–502.

Zarkowska, E. & Clements, C. (1994) *Problem Behaviour and People with Severe Learning Disabilities: the STAR Approach* (2nd edn). London: Chapman & Hall.

Additional reading

Berry, P. & Gaedt, C. (1995) Psychiatry of mental retardation. *Current Opinion in Psychiatry*, **8**, 293–300.

Bouras, N. (ed.) (1994) *Mental Health in Mental Retardation*. Cambridge: Cambridge University Press.

Russell, O. (1985) *Mental Handicap*. Edinburgh: Churchill Livingstone.

5 Behavioural phenotypes

Tom Berney

Assessment • *Prevalent syndromes* • *Psychiatric issues* • *Conclusions*

Improved genetic techniques mean that ever more people with learning difficulties can expect an aetiological diagnosis (Table 5.1). This progress in laboratory precision encourages a matching clarity in our clinical definition of phenotype, both somatic and psychological. Although this chapter focuses on the latter, the two are so closely intertwined that some somatic features must be mentioned. Most syndromes are so pervasive, leaving few systems untouched, that any catalogue of stigmata is lengthy and better summarised by photograph (Baraitser & Winter, 1983).

Assessment

Assessment has tended to concentrate on ability and skills – the cognitive phenotype. Personality assessment, contentious enough in the rest of the population, is hampered by limited communication which blocks access to subjective perceptions and attitudes. This shifts the emphasis to the more observable aspects of personality – behavioural style or temperament. This, the characteristic manner in which the person approaches and responds to the world about, can be dissected into a number of variables. Ideally these variables should be independent of each other; they can be grouped to give recognisable profiles (Table 5.2) (Ganiban *et al*, 1990). An alternative model identifies the independent dimensions of emotionality, activity, sociability and adaptability (Buss & Plomin, 1984).

The behavioural phenotype includes temperament as well as all the other facets of behaviour, such as stereotypy, self-injury and eating habits. This outward sign of an inward congenital predisposition unfolds with development as it is shaped by other, innate factors (such as the mix and degree of mental, physical and sensory disabilities) and by its interaction with the environment.

Thus, after some elements have been amplified and others muted, a single aetiology can eventually produce such a wide range and variety of behaviours (the phenomenon of pleiotropy) that it is hard to see any common thread until a large number of people have been examined. Thereafter further assessment is hindered because of the popular expectation that every person with that syndrome will have that phenotype. In practice, only a small minority

Table 5.1 The inheritance of genetic syndromes

Syndrome	Prevalence	Inheritance	Degree of learning disability
Cornelia de Lange	1/40 000–100 000 live births	Sporadic –?autosomal dominance (?3q 26.3)	Throughout ability range but majority severe–profound
Down's	1/600 live births dependent on maternal age: ranges from 1/2500 (< 30 years): 1/80 (> 40 years): 1/32 (at 45 years)	21-trisomy. 95% non-disjunction 1–3% translocation 1–2% mosaic	Throughout ability range (10% are low normal)
Duchenne muscular dystrophy	1/3500 male births	X-linked recessive at Xp21	Mostly borderline but 10% severe
Fragile X	1/1000–3000 live births	Multiple CGG repeat (>50) at Xq27.3	Mild–moderate with performance deficit relative to verbal
Lesch-Nyhan	1/100 000–1 200 000 population	Sporadic mutation at Xq(26–27)	Mild–moderate but disputed as masked by physical disabilities
Neurofibromatosis Type 1	1/2500–4000 live births	Autosomal dominant at 17q11.2 50% due to sporadic mutation usually of the paternal allele	Low average ability with only 10% significant learning disability
Phenylketonuria	1/4500–15 000 population	Autosomal recessive at 12q(22-24.1)	Variable expression across whole ability range
Prader-Willi	1/15 000 live births 12–15/100 000 population	Lack of paternal 15q(11-13) by deletion or maternal disomy	Borderline–moderate
Rett	1/10 000–15 000 females	Probable sporadic mutation on X chromosome	Severe–profound
Tuberous sclerosis	1/7000 population	Autosomal dominant with genetic heterogeneity – linkages shown to 9q34 and 16p3	Majority of normal intelligence, however where there is learning difficulty, it is usually profound
Williams	1/25 000 live births	Sporadic – possibly 7q11.23 (a gene for elastin synthesis)	Moderate–severe with selective deficits in visuospatial and motor skills, and good verbal skills

will have the 'full hand' of features in their full intensity; most cases will have a paler reflection or fragments of the phenotype, if indeed it surfaces at all. Behavioural phenotypes are age-specific and must be seen in the context of both chronological and developmental ages. There is also their environmental context. For example, if the group has grown up in an institution, any innate predisposition may be hidden by a spurious, acquired uniformity. A number of methodological problems, outlined below, complicate the study of behavioural phenotypes.

There are a large number of assessment schedules, many poorly validated, designed for use by observation, interview or questionnaire. No single schedule will encompass the full range of abilities, skills and behaviour, and thought must be given to the appropriate instrument (O'Brien, 1992).

Behavioural assessment requires a balance to be struck between the use of direct observation, necessarily for brief periods, and the reports of carers which will draw on a greater period of time and a wider variety of circumstances. Unfortunately carers' reports are coloured by their own view of the behaviour; one man's restless overactivity might be another's healthy inquisitiveness. Allowance must be made for this, for example by an assessment of the informant's own characteristics as well as by obtaining a consensus account from several carers.

Although a phenotype has to be defined against some standard, no single comparison group can be entirely satisfactory; a frequent choice is whether to match for age or for ability. If the comparison group does not have a comparable degree of disability then, although an attribute might be specific to the syndrome studied, equally it might simply be a characteristic of learning difficulty. Selecting a group with an equivalent degree of disability can be complicated further by disparities between verbal and non-verbal ability or between receptive and expressive language.

Comparison with another syndrome of specific aetiology, frequently Down's syndrome, allows both age and ability to be matched. However, any differences are relative, being attributable either to their presence in the syndrome under study or, equally, to their absence in Down's syndrome. A variant of this trap is the use of autism as a comparison group, treating it indiscriminately both as a behavioural syndrome and as a homogeneous aetiological diagnosis.

The rarity of many syndromes has encouraged the use of small samples of widely varied age and ability.

Selection pressures have led to unrepresentative samples biased by the severity of disturbance or learning difficulty.

Prevalent syndromes

The problems outlined above have led to the growth of a phenotypic mythology based on tentative conclusions awaiting confirmation (Dykens

Table 5.2 Temperamental traits (Thomas *et al*, 1968)

Temperamental quality	Description	Temperamental category			
		Easy	Difficult	Slow to warm up	
Quality of mood	Relative amount of friendly, pleasant, joyful behaviour	Positive	Negative	Slightly negative	
Intensity of reaction	Energy of response regardless of its quality or direction	Low/mild	Intense	Mild	
Approach/withdrawal	Response to a new situation or person	Approach	Withdrawal	Initial withdrawal	
Adaptability	Flexibility/rigidity of adaptation to changes in environment	Very	Very	Slowly	
Activity level	The proportion of active periods to inactive ones	Varies	Varies	Low/moderate	
Rhythmicity	Regularity of hunger, excretion, sleep and wakefulness	Very regular	Irregular	Varies	
Attention span and persistence	The amount of time devoted to an activity and the effect of distraction on the activity	High/low	High/low	High/low	
Distractability	Degree to which extraneous stimuli will alter behaviour	Varies	Varies	Varies	
Threshold of responsiveness	Intensity of stimulation required to evoke a discernible response	High/low	High/low	High/low	

et al, 1994; Dykens, 1995). The hunt is on with phenotypes being identified for any discernible syndrome; the following examples have been selected for their prevalence or their interest. Further detail may be obtained from a specialist text (Flint & Yule, 1994; Flint, 1996; O'Brien & Yule, 1996).

Down's syndrome

This disorder is unusual in that the obvious somatotype allows diagnosis at birth, laboratory confirmation is readily available, and there is a widespread awareness of the disorder and its characteristics. Although long recognised and with a high prevalence, much of the large body of research is spoiled by methodological shortcomings. No system is unaffected but there is no single abnormality, other than the trisomic genotype, which is either invariable or characteristic of Down's: indeed, there is a substantial overlap between all the autosomal trisomies.

The pattern of development comprises a mixture of elements such as intelligence, self-help, social and language skills. There is a downward shift of the IQ by about 50 points and subsequent slowing in the developmental trajectory results in a widening gap between the Down's child and his unimpaired peers. There is no loss of skills but their acquisition progressively diminishes until a static state is reached in late childhood: a picture which may give the superficial impression of a dementia as the child progressively falls behind (Hartley, 1986). Some of this reflects an unwillingness and/or an inability to exploit the environment unaided. There is an impassioned debate as to how far this can be offset by intensive tuition or enrichment, as in the Headstart and Doman–Delacato programmes (Cummins, 1988). Unfortunately, later on there is the early onset of true dementia, apparent in about 45% of those over 45 years.

Behaviour and intelligence cannot be divorced from the somatic phenotype: for example, cognitive and language development are limited by deafness and predicted by the degree of hypotonia. Childhood behaviour disorder, sleep disturbance and eventual maternal stress, are linked with disability and poor health, notably recurrent respiratory problems. Hypothyroidism occurs frequently, usually borderline in degree and probably autoimmune in type, as often the levels of antithyroid and antimicrosomal antibodies are raised.

In a society which places a high value on physical attractiveness, an individual may live down to a characteristic appearance. Anything which enhances a person's appearance is likely to have a widespread effect on their self-esteem, social development and integration. In theory it should be worthwhile to use cosmetic surgery to modify the facial appearance which brands a person with Down's syndrome. In addition, it is argued, reduction of the overlarge tongue will help the articulation and tone of speech, drooling, breathing and the ability to eat as well as reducing the proneness to infections. Parents and doctors have found cosmetic surgery to be extremely successful overall. However, their accounts indicate that specific improvements were less obvious and more rigorous studies, using controls, photographs, videotapes and external raters, not only failed to find any significant improvement but even hinted at adverse effects. Speech difficulties are cognitive rather than anatomical in origin and mask the person's overall ability. Educational methods, including behavioural training in speech, social and assertive skills, might be a more cost-effective approach to tongue protrusion, eating difficulties and social behaviour and integration. Surgery might be considered an adjuvant to these techniques rather than as a replacement (Katz & Kravetz, 1989). Finally, although less emotive than sterilisation, it is an elective and permanent procedure which requires equal scrutiny where there is any doubt about the ability to give valid consent.

Is there then a characteristic behavioural phenotype? Langdon Down, demarcating this group from that of congenital hypothyroidism, gave a vivid description of children who were humorous and good-natured mimics, albeit stubborn. The stereotype has been confirmed by subsequent case reports, encapsulated as the 'happy puppy', and established by Tredgold as "a group of cheerful and happy disposition who are affectionate and easily amused". Only lately has this been tested by more systematic studies. One such found schoolchildren to be clownish, sociable, affectionate and self-confident. The comparison group, of similar age and ability, were more often confused, nervous, tense, unstable and uncooperative. Clearly the contrast merely might indicate a high level of unease in other forms of learning difficulty. Other studies, although identifying temperamental characteristics such as "impassivity" and a "readiness to approach novel circumstances", emphasise the wide scatter and the overall similarity to non-handicapped children. This applies particularly where comparison with the siblings allows compensation for the family climate (Ganiban *et al*, 1990).

Pervasive developmental disorder occurs in about 5% of people with Down's syndrome, about half of the prevalence to be expected in those of an equivalent degree of learning disability.

Fragile X syndrome

It was well known that nearly a quarter of the cases of learning disability were inherited in a sex-linked pattern. The identification of the chromosomal fragile site at Xq27.3 gave a marker for the abnormal gene. The chromosomal constriction was the result of a repeating sequence of a DNA triplet (CGG) which led to the methylation of the adjacent CpG island which then turned off the FMR-1 gene. The multiple CGG replication grows across generations, particularly with passage through females, and is reflected in the severity of the clinical syndrome which accounts for about 8% of the males with learning disability. The syndrome includes testicular enlargement, a large head with a long face, prominent ears, a high arched palate and a widespread connective tissue disorder with lax joints, flat feet, cave chest and mitral valve prolapse.

The degree of learning disability is very variable but usually in the mild to moderate range. As in Down's syndrome, slowing of cognitive development, especially in early adolescence, gives a falling IQ which may represent merely the inability to cope with sequential information as well as abstract reasoning. The cognitive profile is uneven, visuospatial and short-term memory deficits being combined with relative strengths in verbal and adaptive behaviour. The selective impairment of a range of abilities, particularly numerical, as well as poor executive function suggests that the fault might be a deficit in the fronto-parietal axis.

The association with autistic disorder has furnished a vigorous debate about research methodology. Various studies have found 5–46% of people with fragile X to be autistic and 0–16% of autists to have fragile X. As the studies were often of small groups selected by their disturbed (autistic) behaviour and lacking control comparison, any link may merely represent the chance overlap to be expected from the study of two conditions that are overrepresented in learning disabilities – in short, from ascertainment bias. On the other hand Cohen *et al* (1991) argued that the overlap exceeds any expectation derived from their separate occurrence. Fragile X will be only one of a number of causes of autism and, as most of the cases of fragile X will not be autistic, it might be expected that any causal link would be swamped by the other, unlinked cases.

There is another explanation. Fragile X is associated with social avoidance and gaze aversion, particularly marked in greeting, although these are rooted in shyness rather than autistic indifference. The speech is abnormal, being 'cluttered' with a fast, garbled, repetitive quality and articulation difficulties. However, it is characterised by perseveration rather than echolalia, a litanic pitch rather than monotony, and an interest in communication which hurries the person into unintelligibility. There are other unusual phenomena such as hyperactivity, impulsiveness and distractibility with wrist-biting and an explosiveness under stress, often from stimulus overload. The frequency of depression and other psychiatric disturbance may be increased. Here are the makings of a behavioural phenotype, perhaps a subtype of autism, but more likely to be that of a sociable but shy person in whom the superficial features mimic autism closely enough to cause confusion (Turk, 1992). In the end much depends on the clinical definition of autism and the way in which the diagnosis is arrived at (Rutter *et al*, 1994).

Throughout it is important to remember that any features will vary in extent and degree and, furthermore, that about a fifth of males and half of females show no penetrance (see Dykens *et al*, 1994, for an overview).

Sex aneuploidy

Klinefelter's syndrome (XXY) and its variants occur in 1/2000 male neonates. Additional X-somes result in a degree of impairment which is variable, debatable and perhaps limited to a specific language deficit and infertility. The testes are small and the development of the pubertal secondary sexual characteristics reduced. Also reported are increased passivity, apprehensiveness, shyness, impulsiveness and, unsurprisingly, poor relationships with others (Theilgaard, 1984). Levels of gonadotropins are increased and those of testosterone reduced; many symptoms are said to respond to supplementary testosterone.

Additional Y-somes occur in 1/1000 male neonates. People with *XYY syndrome*, although more assertive and restlessly impulsive, probably have more in common with, than differing from, those with XXY. Both syndromes make for a tall individual, possibly with a degree of cognitive deficit and some immaturity of personality, so it is not unexpected that the prevalence should be greater where the screening is limited to tall men and/or the inhabitants of institutions including prisons.

The female equivalent, *Turner's syndrome* (XO) occurs in about 1/2500 female neonates after a high rate of spontaneous abortion. There are widespread somatic stigmata and growth retardation. Overall intelligence is unimpaired but there is a specific cognitive phenotype of a strong verbal ability with visuomotor and visuospatial difficulties (El Abd *et al*, 1995). Psychiatric disturbance is frequent, particularly anxiety and depression, with problems in social relationships.

Prader-Labhart-Willi syndrome

The somatic phenotype includes obesity, mild mental handicap, hypogonadism, short stature, small extremities and poor muscle tone (Clarke *et al*, 1995). It was described in 1956 (popular usage omits Labhart's name; only first authorship is safe). Subsequent additions fleshed out a picture of a pervasive and puzzling dystrophy with a characteristic facies and frequent spinal deformity. The risks of corrective thoracotomy are raised by a combination of friable connective tissue, increased bleeding and softer bone. There is also sleep apnoea with daytime drowsiness, a variable degree of mental impairment, and an expressive language disorder compounded by poor articulation. Visual perceptual skills may be a particular strength and extend to hyperlexia (Cassidy & Ledbetter, 1989).

The aetiology is clearly genetic in its lack of paternal 15(q11–13), usually achieved by deletion but also by maternal disomy. There is also a remarkably high frequency of pre- and perinatal abnormality which begs the question as to how often, in other forms of learning disability, there is a genetic basis to the perinatal adversity usually blamed for the impairment.

Initially the hypotonia leads to feeding difficulties and poor weight gain, but an insatiable hunger drive develops from about three years old. This, coupled with a defective sense of satiety, soon leads to the obesity and its complications which eventually dominate the picture. A lower metabolic rate suggests a contributory reduction in caloric requirement. However, in comparison with other forms of obesity, the proportion of fat (30–40%) is unusually high and is not reflected in skin-fold measurements. Thus the lower metabolic rate may be appropriate to the fat-free mass which is small relative to height, weight, surface area and age.

Outbursts of violent temper result from thwarting the appetite but non-food-related belligerence also occurs. In fact, there is a high incidence of psychiatric disturbance with incessant skin-picking, compulsive or anxiety neuroses and occasional reports of self-limiting psychotic episodes.

Therapies abound but only fenfluramine has been reported as having some partial success, improving both appetite and mood – the reluctance to use it contrasts oddly with the enthusiasm it found as a treatment of autism. Trials of potential satiety factors, whether pancreatic polypeptide, cholecystokinin or sucrose, have come to naught as has treating the opioid system with naltrexone.

Angelman's syndrome stands in genetic and phenotypic contrast. Here the child, lacking a maternal contribution to chromosome 15(q11-13), has an equally characteristic facies, has a severe learning disability, ataxic and jerky movements and an affectionate and cheerful disposition. These led to the epithet of 'Happy Puppet' although there is some doubt as to whether the laughter really signals happiness or is simply a paroxysmal tic. Associated problems include epilepsy, gastrointestinal problems (reflux, rumination and pica), attention deficit syndrome and sleep disturbance.

Tuberous sclerosis or epiloia

This well-recognised syndrome, which peppers the body with hamartomata, is associated with hyperkinetic and autistic features. It is associated with infantile spasms, their presence identifying those children who will be left with the more severe learning disabilities and the most intractable epilepsy. Difficult behaviour is frequent, with sleep problems, hyperactivity, aggression or self-injury and a non-compliant obsessiveness. All this, as well as an association with autism, may be specific to tuberous sclerosis (Hunt & Shepherd, 1993) but, alternatively, might often represent their common link with the combination of severe learning disability and severe epilepsy. The site of the intracranial hamartomata also might be relevant, but any conclusion must wait on further studies which will control for these interlaced variables.

Inherited by a dominant gene, about half of the cases arise from spontaneous mutation. Because it is often expressed partially it means that case identification must be followed by the close examination and counselling of the immediate relatives.

Neurofibromatosis Type I (Von Recklinghausen disease)

The combination of neurofibromata (increasing from puberty) and café-au-lait spots (from early childhood) was considered largely a cosmetic and anatomical problem, albeit overshadowed in a third of cases by malignant change, skeletal deformity and hypertension. It is now evident that this goes with an overall low average level of ability; that about 10% have a significant learning disability; and that about half of the remainder have specific learning disabilities, particularly visuospatial, memory and motor, as well as literacy and numeracy problems. Add distractibility and impulsivity, and it is unsurprising that this group should show a downward socio-economic drift in relation to their parents. There is also a surfeit of psychiatric disturbance and problems with social relationships. These may stem partially from the disfigurement as well as relating to communication problems – speech delay and articulation difficulties.

Duchenne muscular dystrophy

Abnormalities at Xp21 result in a failure to produce dystrophin and an insidiously progressive muscular deterioration over the course of 20 years. This starts with a delay in motor development and the use of a wheelchair becomes necessary towards the end of childhood with a general increase in weakness. Eventually respiratory or cardiac failure brings death in late adolescence or early adulthood.

There is a range of non-progressive cognitive deficits with impaired ability, particularly verbal with delayed language development. Although most individuals are of low–normal/borderline ability, about 20% have significant learning disabilities, of which about half are severe. There is also a high rate of psychiatric disturbance with depression seeming more frequent than expected in other forms of chronic disability.

Cornelia de Lange syndrome

This sporadic syndrome probably has a genetic basis, whose expression is variable and age-dependent. It comprises a moderate/severe learning disability, growth retardation, limb abnormalities, and a distinctive facies with a small, turned-up nose, a down-turned mouth and eyebrows which meet in the middle (synophrys). The personality is likely to be coloured by the many physical problems, but particularly by the discomfort and danger of gastro-oesophageal reflux, as gastrointestinal malformation and malfunction are frequent.

This was one of the earliest conditions to be ascribed a behavioural phenotype, which included self-injurious and autistic behaviour as well as characteristics associated with severe learning disability so that it is difficult to sort out the significance of their co-occurrence. It has yet to be seen how far this picture will hold with larger studies and more effective and earlier treatment.

Lesch-Nyhan syndrome

This holds a particular interest as compulsive self-mutilation, the scourge of the more severely handicapped, here afflicts people of normal ability and has a specific biochemical deficit.

This X-linked syndrome is almost exclusive to males. The classical picture is one of normal development in early infancy except perhaps for orange, uricosuric sand in the nappy. Hypotonia then heralds a progressive motor deterioration to spastic choreo-athetosis, dysphagia and dysarthria, with seizures in about 50%. The compulsive self-mutilation that follows seems to be as distressing to the child as to the observer and there is a preference for imposed restraint, making it qualitatively different to other forms of self-injury. Over time this waxes and wanes, perhaps with a temporary improvement in early adolescence. There is also a more generalised aggression with tantrums directed against objects and people. Specific or moderate learning disabilities may become apparent as well as marked growth retardation and a failure of secondary sexual development. Respiratory or renal failure usually brings death in early adulthood.

The disorder is spectral being closely related to the degree of deficiency of hypoxanthine-guanine phosphoribosyl transferase (HPRT), an enzyme essential to the process of salvage in purine synthesis. The inability to recycle puts a greater reliance on *de novo* synthesis, and the basal ganglia, which appear particularly vulnerable to this distortion, develop deviant dopamine terminals. Uric acid is released in excess but the use of allopurinol to reduce its levels yields no psychological benefit. Animal models suggest the self-injury to be mediated by supersensitive D1 receptors and therefore potentially responsive to their selective blockade by compounds such as clozapine and fluphenazine. Clinically the issue is less clear-cut and reports are few. Dramatic success has been reported with fluphenazine, but other accounts indicate a more mixed and idiosyncratic response to a variety of compounds including anti-epileptics, tetrabenazine, carbidopa-levodopa, bromocryptine, hypoxanthine and xanthine oxidase (Jankovic, 1988). Other measures include splinting, extraction of the primary teeth, and behavioural measures, the last being even less successful than in other forms of self-injury.

Williams syndrome

The main features, including supravalvular aortic stenosis, a characteristic 'elfin' facies, and mild to moderate learning disabilities, are only the iceberg tip of a progressive, multisystem syndrome. Cardiovascular complications are common, including hypertension, arterial stenosis and mitral valve prolapse. Contractures occur with progressive joint limitation, kyphosis and scoliosis. A variety of urinary and gastrointestinal problems, particularly constipation, contribute to chronic ill-health and discomfort. Calcium levels may be raised, especially in infancy, and this syndrome overlaps with the idiopathic infantile hypercalcaemia caused by hypervitaminosis D.

There is a peculiar cognitive and personality profile with an extraordinary verbal facility which contrasts with that in other forms of learning disability. It has been compared to the 'cocktail-party speech' of hydrocephalic children (which is fluent, well-articulated and accompanied by an over-familiar manner but is littered with stereotyped phrases and clichés, repetitive responses and irrelevant personal experiences, which makes it superficial and meaningless). In Williams syndrome there is indeed a hyperverbal subgroup, but their speech is meaningful rather than empty chatter, with a tendency to remember and use adult phrases and vocabulary. This gives an impression of ability which misleadingly masks their severe visuospatial and motor deficits. There is also a hypersensitivity to sound, expressed in an exaggerated startle reflex, with a resultant anticipatory anxiety, distractibility and hyperactivity. Earlier reports stressed a polite and gentle charm, but recent work suggests a more difficult temperament. This has passed unnoticed in the brief, formal interview where their sociable tendency to approach people contrasts with the avoidance so frequently associated with learning difficulty. Many of the traits may be the natural consequence of coping with the combination of a peculiar profile of cognitive handicaps, underlying physical discomfort in general and hyperacusis in particular. Einfeld & Hall (1994) have challenged this view; they consider that the behaviour is a unique pattern of psychopathology and that Williams syndrome ought to be listed as a specific condition in psychiatric classification systems.

Rett syndrome

Only recently recognised, this occurs in females and, although distinguished by its clinical course as well as its appearance, previously it was probably misdiagnosed as autism.

After 6–18 months of nearly normal development, the child starts to dement and head growth slows. Typically there is an autistic withdrawal accompanied by seizures, stereotypic movements (notably hand-wringing), agitation, hyperventilation and breath-holding. Then follows a truncal ataxia, spasticity and dystonia to leave an adult who is severely mentally and physically handicapped. Depression and anxiety are frequent, with self-injury and panic when threatened.

An underlying enzyme deficiency or mitochondrial abnormality have been proposed. However, the lack of a consistent pathophysiological basis hints that, here too, there may be a varied aetiology, perhaps including an X-linked dominant inheritance, emerging by a final common pathway to produce a disorder lethal in boys (Percy *et al*, 1990; Hagberg *et al*, 1993).

Phenylketonuria (PKU)

An autosomal recessive disorder underlies a variable deficit in hepatic phenylalanine hydroxylase. The resultant rise in phenylalanine levels gives a spectrum of disorder which ranges from benign hyperphenylalaninaemia (where the levels are sufficiently low for it to be doubtful whether treatment is merited), through mild PKU, to classical PKU. Quite distinct is atypical PKU which arises from a deficit in biopterin synthesis (a coenzyme of the hydroxylase) and which is unresponsive to diet. PKU can be detected by routine neonatal screening (between days 6 and 14) allowing the early restriction of dietary phenylalanine.

Untreated, the consequence can be severe with microcephalic mental impairment, autism and epilepsy. Phenylalanine affects myelination and the immature central nervous system is most vulnerable, although susceptibility continues into adulthood. This may be the effect of a combination of direct neurotoxicity, competitive blockade of the uptake of other amino acids (notably valine, leucine and isoleucine) and, lacking tyrosine and tryptophan, a reduction in the synthesis of serotonin and dopamine.

The focus of management, reducing phenylanine intake by a restricted and expensive diet, inevitably affects family functioning, particularly in adolescence when it is compounded by changing dietary requirements and the issue of independence. In family studies there is little that is distinct from the general population except for a suggestion that they are less cohesive and more routine and inflexible. However, there is a considerable variation within this population and one potentially useful categorisation might be into 'child-centred' and 'PKU/diet-centred' families.

Even with the effective control of phenylalanine levels there can be an overall irritability, anxiety and social isolation with a reduction in concentration and cognitive ability, particularly in visuomotor and spatial abilities. This may represent either pre-diet damage or the failure to hold to a very narrow therapeutic window, for too low a level of phenylalanine also carries a cognitive penalty. Frequently the diet is discontinued, usually in adolescence, to be followed by a delayed global deterioration – cognitive, emotional and motor – ranging from the subtle to the gross. This includes upper motor neurone abnormality, which is reflected in delayed visual evoked potentials, slowing of the EEG spectrum and abnormality on MRI scan. This, supported by reports of reversible change, suggests that only life-long control is safe. In addition, there are sufficient reports of a general improvement in previously untreated adults to warrant a trial of treatment even where severe learning disabilities and abnormal behaviours appear entrenched.

There is hope that an alternative approach might lie in the competitive blockade of phenylalanine uptake across the blood–brain barrier with an augmentation of those amino acids felt to be lacking. This might be achieved by a low-protein diet together with a supplement of the competing and deficient amino acids, the regimen being both more acceptable and palatable.

Maternal hyperphenylalaninaemia causes cardiac defects and microcephaly, often with learning disabilities, in the non-PKU foetus. This means that dietary control must be in place before conception; a painful confrontation for many who were unaware of, or thought they had grown out of, their disorder and its restrictions.

Foetal alcohol syndrome

In addition to the characteristic facies, growth deficiency and multiple systemic impairments that characterise this syndrome, there is a mild learning disability with speech and language problems, particularly expressive, although there may be a prolific verbal output. Starting with an infantile withdrawal syndrome which may range from hypertonic jitteriness to frank seizures, the later picture is one of irritability and hyperactivity. The diagnosis is often missed as the expression is neither consistent nor specific to prenatal alcohol and probably depends on a combination of the amount, duration and timing of alcohol intake relative to the pregnancy, binge drinking being especially suspect.

This has been proposed as one of the more common identifiable causes of learning disability in the Western world and, as such, to pose a huge challenge in public health (Waterson & Murray-Lyon, 1990). However, it is questionable as to whether the syndrome is as prevalent as proposed. Many of the effects ascribed to it might have as much to do with associated disease, social deprivation and cigarette smoking.

Congenital hypothyroidism (cretinism)

In the developed world this usually is the consequence of an innate deficit in the foetus which, on discovery by neonatal screening, is remedied by early and energetic treatment with thyroid hormone. Elsewhere, *foetal iodine deficiency disorder* reigns as a common but often unrecognised cause of intellectual impairment. The clinical picture ranges from visuo-motor deficits, through a more pronounced (albeit euthyroid) neurological disorder, to the widespread intellectual impairment of myxoedematous hypothyroidism. The choice of outcome depends on the timing and degree of maternal iodine deficit, genetic predisposition and, in the myxoedematous form, an underlying autoimmunity. Furthermore, geographical differences indicate rather more than a simple nutritional deficiency as the iodine uptake is affected by other goitrogens specific to the geological site (Hetzel, 1989).

Psychiatric issues

Many clinical problems do not coincide with the aetiological diagnosis but run as themes through these phenotypes. Notable are sleep and feeding problems, as well as recurrent idiosyncrasies such as an aversion to the scalp being touched.

Autism

This protean diagnosis often leads to confusion. The primary (genetic) disorder of autism is often confused with the behavioural syndrome of autism, secondary to a variety of disorders which may include fragile X syndrome, de Lange syndrome, untreated PKU and tuberous sclerosis (Rutter *et al*, 1994; Bailey *et al*, 1996).

A further example of this confusion is provided by Sotos syndrome of cerebral gigantism. Although associated with a wide range of varied cognitive impairment, the deficits in socialisation and frequent aggressive outbursts form a common thread (Rutter & Cole, 1991) which may extend to autism on occasion. However, the entity of Sotos syndrome itself is under attack as further cases reveal that it too might have a varied aetiology including fragile X.

Self-injurious behaviour

This may be more frequent (or simply more pronounced) in syndromes such as Prader-Willi and de Lange. It remains to be determined how frequent or specific self-mutilation is and whether there is an association with other characteristics such as an altered awareness of pain or autism. There are indications of clinical subtypes which may distinguish those that are predominantly innate from those that are environmentally driven; for example, that seen in Lesch-Nyhan syndrome driven by its inner compulsion, compared with that in de Lange which appears more habitual and often a response to physical discomfort.

Other psychiatric disorder

We are beginning to perceive genetic links with psychiatric disorder both within the individual and in the family. Examples are the associations between fragile X syndrome and depression, autism and manic–depressive disorder, and Down's syndrome and dementia. That depression should be a recurrent familial theme may indicate an innate vulnerability in the neurotransmitters.

Cognitive deficits

Although a learning disability provides a common denominator to many syndromes, there is variation in both the degree and the profile of deficits. Both Down's and fragile X syndromes have trajectories of cognitive development which slow at the end of childhood. Similarly, although visuomotor and spatial deficits seem ubiquitous, they are disproportionate to the other disabilities in some syndromes, such as Williams, Turner's and fragile X.

Physical illness

Most syndromes are associated with chronic and distressing physical disorders, notably gastrointestinal disturbance. Although often unnoticed by the literature, these may well contribute to disturbance and even be the major factor in syndromes such as de Lange and Williams. Active epilepsy probably contributes to many phenotypes and, in particular, to those with autism.

Appearance

How far does a syndromal appearance, which reduces expectations, lead to secondary handicap? The accounts of cosmetic surgery so far are limited to Down's and de Lange syndromes but merit wider discussion. As success often appears to lie in the eye of the beholder, this must be approached cautiously and on an individual basis.

Conclusions

Diagnosis of a syndrome carries the risk that those afflicted will be expected to conform to their stereotype, living down to their label. Against this must be balanced the help that it can bring: genetic counselling, prognosis and acceptance of the disability are put on a firmer footing.

Recognition carries with it eligibility for a parent support or contact group which brings a number of advantages:

- It alleviates some of the sense of isolation.
- Many aspects of the handicap are put into a more concrete context; you can see how others have turned out and the range of possible variation.
- Recognition of such behavioural traits as are specific to the syndrome; particularly valuable where the parent has felt responsible for what is, in reality, a bruising mismatch of temperaments.
- The opportunity to discover which remedies have worked for others.

- The national networks and their documentation can be of great help to the psychiatrist, both when faced with an unusual syndrome, of which he might see only a few cases, and as a source of fresh ideas for the management of the more prevalent disorders such as Down's syndrome or autism.
- For both parents and professionals, they encourage a collaborative approach to problems, driving forward the development of better services and further research.

This is a burgeoning field reflected in the rapid growth of the Society for the Study of Behavioural Phenotypes, established in 1990. However, there is the risk of following Sheldon's path and, with the eye of enthusiasm, imposing a behavioural phenotype where only a somatotypic link exists. This is particularly problematic where a recurrent disability or discomfort gives a spurious uniformity to behaviour, for example, where social isolation follows deafness or irritability follows gastrointestinal pain. Would these secondary phenomena constitute a behavioural phenotype or should we accept only traits that have a direct genetic link?

References

Bailey, A., Phillips, W. & Rutter, M. (1996) Autism: towards an integration of clinical, genetic, neuropsychological and neurobiological perspectives. *Journal of Child Psychology and Psychiatry*, **37**, 89–126.

Baraitser, M. & Winter, R. (1983) *A Colour Atlas of Clinical Genetics*. London: Wolfe Medical.

Buss, A. H. & Plomin, R. (1984) Theory and measurement of EAS. In *Temperament: Early Developing Personality Traits*. New Jersey: Lawrence Erlbaum.

Cassidy, S. B. & Ledbetter, D. H. (1989) Prader-Willi Syndrome. *Neurologic Clinics*, **7**, 37–54.

Clarke, D. J., Boer, H. & Webb, T. (1995) Genetic and behavioural aspects of Prader-Willi syndrome. *Mental Handicap Research*, **8**, 38–53.

Cohen, I. L., Sudhalter, V., Pfadt, A., *et al* (1991) Why are autism and the Fragile-X syndrome associated? Conceptual and methodological issues. *American Journal of Human Genetics*, **48**, 195–202.

Cummins, R. A. (1988) *The Neurologically Impaired Child: Doman-Delacato Techniques Reappraised*. Kent: Croom Helm.

Dykens, E. M. (1995) Measuring behavioral phenotypes: provocations from the "New Genetics". *American Journal on Mental Retardation*, **99**, 522–532.

——, Hodapp, R. M. & Leckman, J. F. (1994) *Behavior and Development in Fragile X Syndrome*. London: Sage.

Einfeld, S. L. & Hall, W. (1994) Recent developments in the study of behaviour phenotypes. *Australia and New Zealand Journal of Developmental Disabilities*, **19**, 275–279.

El Abd, S., Turk, J. & Hill, P. (1995) Psychological characteristics of Turner syndrome. *Journal of Child Psychology and Psychiatry*, **36**, 1109–1126.

Flint, J. (1996) Behavioural phenotypes: a window onto the biology of behaviour. *Journal of Child Psychology and Psychiatry*, **37**, 355–368.

—— & Yule, W. (1994) Behavioural phenotypes. In *Child and Adolescent Psychiatry* (eds M. Rutter, E. Taylor & L. Hersov), pp. 666–687. Oxford: Blackwell Scientific.

Ganiban, J., Wagner, S. & Cicchetti, D. (1990) Temperament and Down syndrome. In *Children with Down Syndrome: A Developmental Perspective* (eds D. Cicchetti & M. Beeghly), pp. 63–100. Cambridge: Cambridge University Press.

Hagberg, B., Wahlstrom, J. & Anvret, M. (eds) (1993) *Rett Syndrome: Clinical and Biological Aspects*. Clinics in Developmental Medicine no. 127. Cambridge: Cambridge University Press.

Hartley, X. Y. (1986) A summary of recent research into the development of children with Down's syndrome. *Journal of Mental Deficiency Research*, **30**, 1–14.

Hetzel, B. S. (1989) *The Story of Iodine Deficiency: An International Challenge in Nutrition*. Oxford: Oxford University Press.

Hunt, A. & Shepherd, C. (1993) A prevalence study of autism in tuberous sclerosis. *Journal of Autism and Developmental Disorders*, **23**, 323–339.

Jankovic, J. (1988) Orofacial and other self-mutilations. In *Advances in Neurology, 49: Facial Dyskinesias* (eds J. Jankovic & E. Tolosa), pp. 365–381. New York: Raven Press.

Katz, S. & Kravetz, K. (1989) Facial plastic surgery for persons with Down syndrome: research findings and their professional and social implications. *American Journal on Mental Retardation*, **94**, 101–110.

O'Brien, G. (1992) Behavioural phenotypy in developmental psychiatry. *European Journal of Child Psychiatry*, **1** (suppl. 1), 1–61.

—— & Yule, W. (eds) (1996) *Behavioural Phenotypes*. Clinics in Developmental Medicine. Cambridge: McKeith Press.

Percy, A., Gillberg, C., Hagberg, B., *et al* (1990) Rett syndrome and autistic disorders. *Neurologic Clinics*, **8**, 659–676.

Rutter, M., Bailey, A., Bolton, P., *et al* (1994) Autism and known medical conditions: myth and substance. *Journal of Child Psychology and Psychiatry*, **35**, 311–322.

Rutter, S. C. & Cole, T. R. P. (1991) Psychological characteristics of Sotos syndrome. *Developmental Medicine and Child Neurology*, **33**, 898–902.

Theilgaard, A. (1984) A psychological study of the personalities of XYY- and XXY-men. *Acta Psychiatrica Scandinavica*, **69** (suppl. 315), 1–133.

Thomas, A., Chess, S. & Birch, H. (1968) *Temperament and Behaviour Disorders in Children*. New York: New York University Press.

Turk, J. (1992) The fragile X syndrome: on the way to a behavioural phenotype. *British Journal of Psychiatry*, **160**, 24–35.

Waterson, E. J. & Murray-Lyon, I. M. (1990) Preventing alcohol-related birth damage: A review. *Social Science in Medicine*, **30**, 349–364.

6 Emotional, behavioural and psychiatric disorders in children

Mary Lindsey

Epidemiology • *Causes of behavioural and psychiatric disorder* •
Syndromes and disorders • *Assessment* • *Prevention* • *Interventions*

The recognition of emotional needs has come much later for children with learning disabilities than for children of normal intelligence. Practices that are ordinarily regarded as unacceptable in the care of children, such as institutional care, are frequently prescribed to meet special needs or to relieve families of the burden of care. The attitudes of parents and professional people toward learning disabilities generally reflect the attitudes of a society that values intelligence and conformity. The psychiatrist working with this group of children should therefore be aware of their disadvantaged position and counter this by viewing them first as children with normal emotional needs, and then addressing any special needs or problems within that context.

The classification systems most applicable to children with learning disabilities are those that are multiaxial. Child psychiatrists in the UK are more likely to use the system based on ICD–10 (Rutter, 1989; World Health Organization, 1992), whereas psychiatrists in the US are more likely to use DSM–IV (American Psychiatric Association, 1994). Psychiatrists for people with learning disabilities may use either of these diagnostic codes or the American Association on Mental Retardation's system (1992).

For severely and profoundly disabled children it is often very difficult to make psychiatric diagnoses in relation to the presenting problems and it may be useful to introduce more objective and descriptive measures such as the Adaptive Behaviour Scale published by the American Association on Mental Deficiency (Nihira *et al*, 1974; Einfeld & Tonge, 1996*a,b*) or the Medical Research Council's schedule of handicaps, behaviours and skills (MRC–HBS) (Wing, 1981); or the Developmental Behaviour Checklist (Einfeld & Tonge, 1991). Training is needed in the reliable use of these assessments.

Epidemiology

It has been widely shown that the rate of disturbed behaviour and of handicapping psychiatric disturbances, such as autism, is greater in children with learning disabilities (Rutter *et al*, 1970) (see chapter 4).

Table 6.1 compares two studies: a study of children aged 0–15 years with severe learning disabilities living in southeast London (Corbett, 1985), and a study of 13–17-year-olds in an urban population in Sweden (Gillberg *et al*, 1986). The most commonly reported diagnoses in the group with severe learning disabilities were childhood psychosis, hyperkinesis and conduct disorder. In the Gillberg *et al* (1986) study, psychotic behaviour included infantile autism, language and social impairment, severe social impairment or, more rarely, schizophrenia and Asperger syndrome.

More mildly disabled children are generally reported to have a lower rate of disturbance than those in the severely disabled group but greater than in the general population. The types of disorder become more like those seen in the general child psychiatric population, with less severe self-injurious behaviour and more cases of depression, anxiety and fearfulness (Box 6.1).

Table 6.1 Reported rates of psychiatric disorders in children with learning disabilities (Corbett, 1985; Gillberg *et al*, 1986)

Diagnostic categories	Corbett (1985) 0–15-year-olds, IQ < 50 *n* = 140	Gillberg *et al* (1986) 13–17-year-olds, IQ < 70 *n* = 149	
		IQ < 50	IQ 50–70
No psychiatric disorder	53%	36%	43%
Childhood-type psychosis	17%	n/a	n/a
Psychotic behaviour	n/a	50%	14%
Hyperkinetic disorders	4%		11%
Conduct disorder	4%	4.5%	12%
Severe stereotypies and pica	10%	n/a	n/a
Depressive syndrome	n/a	1.5%	4%
Neurotic disorders	4%	n/a	n/a
Emotional disorder	n/a	4.5%	10%
Isolated habit disorders	2%	n/a	n/a
Psychosomatic disorder	n/a	3%	4%
Adjustment reaction	6%	n/a	n/a
Other	n/a		2%
Total with psychiatric disorders	47%	64%	57%

n/a, category not examined. These studies were done on children of different ages and using different diagnostic categories. In Gillberg *et al* (1986) some children had more than one diagnostic category and a hierarchy was used. Thus, for example, a child with hyperkinesis and social impairment would be placed in the psychotic behaviour category. Gillberg *et al* also used a much broader definition of psychotic behaviour, including infantile autism, language and social impairment, severe social impairment, and schizophrenia and Asperger's syndrome.

Box 6.1 Prevalence of psychiatric symptoms and disorders in children with IQs above and below 70

IQ < 70
More prevalent: autistic traits (social impairment); hyperkinesis; uncontrolled rage (tantrums); severe self-injurious behaviour; sleep disturbances; unsocialised conduct disorder; pica

IQ ≥ 70
More prevalent: anxiety and phobic states; depressive syndromes; school refusal; socialised conduct disorder; Asperger's syndrome; schizophrenia; anorexia nervosa and bulimia

---

The prevalence and type of disturbed behaviour also varies according to the cause and nature of the disability of the child. The reported rates in Down's syndrome vary considerably but there is general agreement that these are much less than in the learning disabled group as a whole, although probably greater than in the general population (Turner & Sloper, 1996). Gath & Gumley (1986) found that 38% of their sample of children with Down's syndrome had significant behaviour disorder as compared with 49% of the age-matched controls. The most common diagnostic group among the controls was psychosis (17.5%), but in the children with Down's syndrome 9% had severe psychiatric morbidity, although to label them as having 'psychosis' was not felt to be satisfactory. Gath & Gumley noted that just under 40% of the children with Down's syndrome in their sample had sufficiently severe and distressing problems as to require a broad range of psychiatric skill and understanding. In her longitudinal study of children with Down's syndrome, Carr (1995) found that around a third of the children showed specific behaviour problems, including aggressiveness, temper tantrums and difficult behaviour in public. Buckley & Sacks (1987) also found 30% of their under-14-year-olds with Down's syndrome having temper tantrums.

A number of behaviours and psychiatric problems have been described in association with other syndromes (Table 6.2) but, as many of the problems are common among children with severe learning disabilities, it requires careful research to be sure that it is more than a chance association (Taylor, 1991). Many behaviours are non-specific and do not occur in all the individuals with the condition (see chapter 5).

It is very easy to ascribe stereotypes to particular disorders and this can lead to possibly harmful and self-fulfilling expectations. There is always a great deal of individual variation and other personality attributes may be more significant. On the other hand, positive use of the information

Table 6.2 Syndromes associated with learning disabillities, behavioural and psychiatric disorders

Syndrome	Main physical features	Behavioural/psychiatric associations
Tuberous sclerosis/Bourneville disease	Infantile spasms; seizures (often hard to control); skin pigmentation/depigmentation; tubers and fibromata throughout body; rhabdomyoma in heart; malignancy in brain	Autism; hyperactivity; self-injury, screaming; aggression/destructiveness; pica, rumination, aerophagy; schizophrenia-like psychosis
Infantile hypercalcaemia/Williams syndrome	Growth deficiency; elfin-like facies; supravalvular aortic stenosis; renal complications	Hyperactivity; anxiety; loquaciousness/overfriendliness
Fragile X syndrome	Facial appearance; macro-orchidism	Autistic traits; hyperactivity, anxiety; self-injury
De Lange syndrome	Facial appearance; congenital heart disease	Self-injury; autistic traits
Untreated/poorly treated phenylketonuria	Blond hair, blue eyes (untreated); spasticity (untreated); epilepsy	Autism; hyperactivity; anxiety
Rett syndrome	Overbreathing/breathholding; increasing spasticity; epilepsy	Stereotypic hand-wringing; autistic traits; anxiety; air-swallowing; teeth-grinding; pica; self-injurious handbiting; sleep disturbances
Rubella syndrome	Major sensory impairments, congenital heart disease	Autistic traits; self-injury
Lesch–Nyhan syndrome	Spasticity and athetosis; epilepsy; renal complications	Self-injury; aggression; linguistic outbursts; vomiting/spitting
Prader–Willi syndrome	Obesity; hypotonia; cryptorchidism; small hands and feet; other congenital abnormalities	Hyperphagia; hyperactivity; anxiety; self-injury; autistic traits; compulsions
Sanfillipo syndrome	Steady deterioration; slight coarsening of features; diarrhoea; epilepsy; increasing spasticity	Hyperactivity in early stages; sleep disturbances
Down's syndrome	Characteristic facies and somatotype; other congenital anomalies; infantile spasms more common; prone to thyroid disorders	Hyperactivity; conduct disorder; autistic traits (rare but probably greater than chance and may follow infantile spasms)

can lead to more understanding, more realistic expectations and avoidance of blame.

Causes of behavioural and psychiatric disorder

It is unusual for any one cause to operate in isolation and there is often an interactive effect (Fig. 6.1). The skills of the psychiatrist lie in teasing out the important factors and dealing with as many as possible.

Organic factors

It is widely accepted that the organic factors causing the learning disability are also the cause of the psychiatric disorder in affected children. The epidemiological findings support this point of view, as does the association of particular psychiatric problems with certain disorders (Table 6.2). It is the mechanism through which the brain abnormality leads to psychological disorder that requires further elucidation, and the study of anatomically localised lesions and of the phenotypes of inherited disorders may help this process (Taylor, 1991; Flint, 1996). Other organic factors associated with psychiatric and behavioural disorder include epilepsy, sensory deficits and physical discomfort.

Degenerative disorders

In some of the degenerative disorders, such as the Sanfilippo syndrome (a mucopolysaccharidosis), some of the lipidoses, sub-acute sclerosing pan-encephalitis and congenital neurosyphilis, the regression may in the early stages present as a behavioural disturbance. The signs of a general decline in the level of functioning, neurological signs or epilepsy are, however, usually evident.

Self-esteem

There seems little doubt that in many children organic factors play a major part, especially when there are autistic symptoms. Nevertheless, it is also probable that being handicapped, stigmatised and/or disadvantaged will predispose children to emotional problems, either in addition to any organic causes or as a major cause alone.

Family factors

There is general agreement that most families with a child with learning disabilities face many stresses that will test their capacity to adapt and to cope. It was assumed that this was a major disadvantage to any family but more recently it has been found that many respond to these challenges

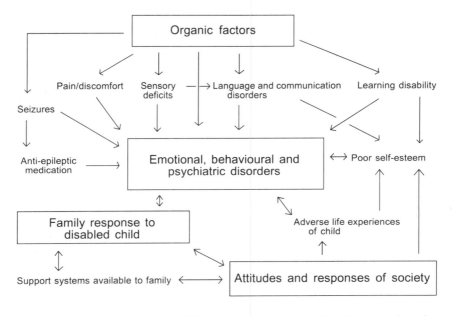

Fig. 6.1 Interaction of possible causes of emotional, behavioural and psychiatric disorders in learning disabled children.

in a resourceful and adaptive manner. Identified stresses include the process of grieving for the 'normal' child that has been lost, and coming to terms with the reality of the disability, especially when the child and family fail to complete the usual developmental tasks within the family life-cycle.

There are many practical stresses arising from excessive and prolonged dependence and the demands of caring for and educating the child. The separation and sexual issues of adolescence are particularly difficult for many families. Feelings of failure and stigmatisation exacerbate the problems for families, but since society has gradually become more tolerant and sympathetic to disabled people this has been less of an issue, although there are ethnic and cultural variations.

The family's capacity to organise effectively to deal with these potential stresses and to meet the needs of all the children is critical. Some families are able to define and interpret their child's disability in a positive way or as a fairly routine component of daily living and the level of stress in such families is likely to be relatively low. Case study 1 describes a family who have found effective coping strategies for dealing with a profoundly handicapped child with severe behaviour problems. The child appears to have a role in stabilising relationships and providing the family with a common sense of purpose.

Case example 1

AB is 9 years old and has tuberous sclerosis (TS). He has a profound learning difficulty with many autistic features to his behaviour. He is non-ambulant due to a moderate spastic diplegia and already weighs 8 stone (51 kg) following a precocious puberty. He has no self-care skills and is doubly incontinent. Despite many anti-convulsant regimes A has continued to have partial seizures, tonic seizures (drop fits) and tonic–clonic seizures. They particularly occur during sleep, and wake AB and his mother on many occasions during the night. Since entering puberty when 6 years of age he has had frequent episodes of high-pitched screaming which can last for hours at a time. A has three siblings, two older and one younger. Mrs B. can be described as child- and home-centred in her values and has no wish to have a job or career. Her social life revolves around her immediate and extended family and a few close friends. She also cares for her elderly father who lives nearby. Mr B. works long hours in a job he enjoys. Decision-making on nearly all issues of family finance and activity is undertaken by Mrs B. and there were major conflicts from time to time in the past when Mr B. challenged this situation. He left home on two occasions when A was a baby and Mrs B. coped well without him. Since then the marital relationship has improved. Both parents perceive A as very precious and know that children badly affected by TS have a reduced life expectancy. They are very afraid he will die during a seizure. Mrs B. will only let her sister and husband share A's care and rarely lets him out of her sight. He does not attend school because he sleeps most mornings and waking him causes a seizure. His mother feels that teachers cannot guarantee his safety if he has a severe seizure at school. Family life is controlled to some extent by A's needs but the positive and tolerant attitudes of his parents are shared by his siblings who also experience very positive parenting. A is taken out frequently and there are many visitors to the home. He receives good stimulation at home. Mr and Mrs B. believe that the bouts of screaming (reported also in other children with TS) have a medical or physiological basis and need to be investigated, tolerated and treated medically rather than behaviourally. Mrs B. has learnt to cope with only a few hours sleep a night and does not regard this as a major problem. Four years ago the professionals involved with the family regarded Mrs B. as overprotective especially because she would not allow A to attend school at 5 years of age. The family were persuaded to attend a family therapy session at that time but made it clear to the therapists that they did not believe they had any problems and had no wish to receive help. The other children in the family were happy and well adjusted and there were medical reasons for A's non-attendance at school. No further sessions were offered and home tuition was arranged and used when A's seizures were less frequent. The only other services the family use are occupational therapy for practical aids, district nursing for incontinence aids, and medical services for epilepsy and other health problems.

Parental belief systems have a major influence on their perception of stress, on family adjustment and on psychological distress (Fraser & Rao, 1991). The internal resources of the family, such as their capacity to adjust and to solve problems, are also most important. Parental psychological well-being has been reported to be associated with a problem-focused coping style, perceived control and with the absence of wishful thinking. A close, confiding marital relationship also appears to have a positive effect in reducing stress. The external resources available, especially the informal network of extended family and friends, are another key factor in terms of practical and emotional support and are reported to be more important than professional help.

It has been suggested that different family interactional patterns will affect the development of the child and that the child with learning disabilities is at greater risk of dysfunctional family responses, especially if there are family, marital, financial or other stresses. The family processes are no different to those occurring in families without a handicapped child, but the families of children with learning disabilities appear to be at greater risk.

Adverse life experiences

A child with learning disabilities is at risk of a number of adverse life experiences.

If the family solves its problems in a dysfunctional way or by excessive use of institutional care then the child may have to cope with extra stress. The parents of children with behavioural difficulties more often seek out-of-home placements and there is evidence that the behaviour problems cause stress that can impair family functioning (Carr, 1990). It is often very difficult to disentangle cause and effect with, in some families, a spiralling of stress and behaviour problems leading to rejection of the child (Fig. 6.2).

Children with learning disabilities are also at risk of segregation, stigmatisation, discrimination, rejection by peers and abnormal friendship patterns. As adolescents they often have poor self-esteem and self-image, which is hardly surprising when living in a society which values achievement, independence and conformity. They are frequently excluded or patronised by normal peers and the scope for sexually orientated relationships is usually severely limited. Segregation may not only stigmatise a child but also fail to provide good opportunities for modelling on and learning from a peer group.

The greater average parental age in some groups, such as children with Down's syndrome, increases the probability of the experience of bereavement through loss of parents or grandparents. Carers often have difficulty in offering appropriate help to the child or adolescent suffering from bereavement.

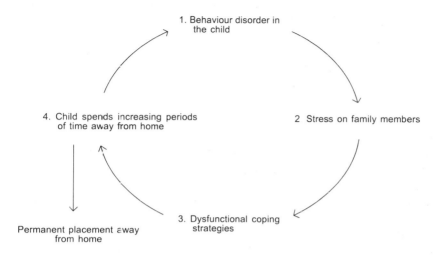

Fig. 6.2 The stress cycle often seen in families with a child with learning difficulties and behavioural disturbance. The usual method of breaking the cycle is to find a residential placement (boarding schools are often used in this way), but intervention at any of the first three points can, especially in the early stages, also break the cycle.

There is little research on abuse of children with learning disabilities but there is no doubt that it occurs and that such children are at greater risk (Tharinger *et al*, 1990). Behaviour problems can be indicators of sexual or emotional abuse.

Social expectations

The ability to learn and use social rules is important if behaviour is to be socially acceptable. It is also essential to have the opportunity to learn these rules and both skilled teaching and direct experience may be necessary for this to occur. Experience of repeated failure and lack of satisfaction from achievement can occur if educational or parental goals are too ambitious (case example 2).

> **Case example 2**
> FG was 17 years of age and had Down's syndrome. His parents had encouraged his placement in ordinary schooling with ancillary support until he was 16 years old and he then attended a College of Further Education on the Special Needs course. He was friendly, compliant and always eager to please. His tutors were very pleased with his progress and arranged work experience in a local supermarket. It was hoped that he would be able to enter open employment when he left college. He had an older sister who had

just left home and his mother had recently returned to employment. He attended the local Gateway Club for people with learning difficulties and had several friends there. His parents noticed, over a period of several weeks, that he had become very withdrawn, disinterested and uncommunicative. His appetite was reduced and his sleep pattern disturbed. He was late in getting to sleep and would wake them in the early hours of the morning by talking to himself or by rocking in his bed. He seemed tense and would frequently wring his hands. His performance at work and college also deteriorated. A diagnosis of depression was made and his sleep pattern improved after a few days on antidepressant medication. There was a gradual improvement in his mood until he was able to participate with his therapist both verbally and by drawing. It then became evident that he felt he could not cope with open employment and was very afraid of failure. Previous assessments by the educational psychologist showed that, although he was socially competent and had basic academic skills, his IQ was approximately 50 and his cognitive skills were quite limited. F was supported in expressing his feelings to college staff and to his parents. He explained to them that he would prefer to transfer to the Training Centre attended by some of his friends but still with the possibility of entering employment when he felt more confident. F also explored with his therapist his feelings that he had been abandoned by his sister and mother and felt very lonely and frightened when he arrived home from college to an empty house. There had been so much emphasis on his independence that his dependency needs and feelings of inadequacy had not been recognised. Family sessions were used to explore these issues and to help his parents accept and value him as he was, rather than constantly pushing him to achieve more. He was encouraged to be more assertive and less compliant and his parents saw that they needed to give him more opportunity to express himself and to make his own decisions. At two-year follow-up he had suffered no further episodes of depression. He was still attending the Training Centre but had, of his own accord, asked for a part-time sheltered work placement.

Disorders of language and communication

Linguistic deficits in expression and comprehension are very common in children with learning disabilities and have been reported to be associated with behaviour problems. This association is very easy to understand because of the enormous importance of effective and appropriate communication in human relationships (Fraser & Rao, 1991). It is often thought that aberrant behaviour has a communicative function.

Temperament

There is a paucity of research regarding temperament in learning disabled children except in relation to specific syndromes, but there is no reason to suppose that it has any less an influence than in children generally. It has been suggested that those temperamental characteristics associated with behavioural problems may be more common in children with learning disabilities.

Iatrogenic factors

These not only include the side-effects of medication such as anti-epileptic, psychotropic and hypnotic drugs, but also environmental factors due to inappropriate or poor quality services. Environmental deprivation and institutionalisation are well known factors in the predisposition of children to emotional and behavioural problems.

Syndromes and disorders

Pervasive developmental disorders (Pdds)

DSM–IV provides operational definitions of Pdds, which are similar to the diagnostic guidelines provided in ICD–10. Childhood disintegrative psychosis and Rett syndrome are included under the Pdds.

Pervasive developmental disorders have several characteristics in common. Their main features are impairments of reciprocal social interaction skills, communication skills, or the presence of stereotyped and restricted interests and activities. Pervasive developmental disorder is usually evident during the first few years of the child's life and is often associated with some degree of learning disability (Lord & Rutter, 1994).

The use of the term pervasive is not wholly appropriate as it suggests a concept of a global impairment more in keeping with traditional views of severe learning disability. The developmental disorders in the autistic spectrum may be quite specific or partial rather than pervasive, and hardly applicable to those young people with Asperger's syndrome studying for A levels.

Autism and Asperger's syndrome

Autism is characterised by difficulty in understanding and using language, poverty of imagination and impaired social relationship skills (Trevarthen *et al*, 1996; Wing, 1996). Many children with learning disabilities do not meet all the criteria for the syndrome but have autistic features or symptoms. If this group is included the prevalence is very high compared with non-disabled children (Gillberg, 1990).

Asperger's syndrome is also seen in children with mild learning disabilities, and in such children a qualitative impairment in social interaction is associated with obsessional preoccupation with specific and often bizarre topics (see chapter 7 and Wing, 1991).

Attention deficit hyperactivity disorders/hyperkinetic disorders

Attention deficit hyperactivity disorders are characterised by a developmentally inappropriate degree of inattention, impulsiveness and hyperactivity and are common in children with learning disabilities. This is usually evident at home, school and in social situations, but to varying degrees depending on the demands being made on the child and on the external controls and reinforcers (Taylor, 1991; Taylor *et al*, 1991; McArdle *et al*, 1995).

A high level of activity and short attention span may also be a secondary feature of autism, although the child may have an excellent concentration span when following obsessional pursuits. The diagnosis in such cases should be that of the primary disorder.

A number of children with atypical and intractable forms of epilepsy also have behaviour problems and are hyperactive. Improvement in seizure control or change of anti-epileptic medication does not necessarily produce an improvement in the behavioural problems.

Conduct disorders

Antisocial or disruptive behaviours are more likely to be impulsive, unplanned and carried out without a peer group. Only a few children with learning disabilities have the opportunity to truant or steal from outside the home and, if accused of delinquent acts, it often transpires that they have been encouraged or left to take the blame by more able peers. Persistent wandering from home without awareness of danger is a more common problem. Inappropriate sexual behaviours may be due to lack of sex education and poor knowledge of social rules. The possibility of sexual abuse should also be considered.

Fears and anxieties

Fears and anxieties may engender avoidance or clinging behaviours including separation anxiety and school refusal. Very often, however, non-attendance at school is more obviously due to parental anxieties or may relate to a parental inability to accept the education offered because it conflicts with the parental perception of the ability or needs of the child.

Affective disorders and schizophrenia

Psychiatric illnesses are more common among adults with learning disabilities than in the general population and it is likely that this is also the case in children. Depression has been reported to be identifiable and prevalent, but the criteria for diagnosis are generally poorly defined. Depression must be differentiated from normal unhappiness in reaction to the many frustrations, rejections, losses, failures and other stresses experienced by people with learning disabilities (case examples 2 and 3). It is often the cyclical nature of disturbed behaviour which draws attention to the presence of a manic–depressive disorder. Affective and schizophrenic disorders present the same diagnostic problems as in adults but must also be differentiated from the disinhibited fantasy life and wishful thinking sometimes seen in adolescents (case example 3). When studied these are qualitatively different from delusional or hallucinatory symptoms and are not accompanied by the other pathognomonic features of a psychotic disorder.

Case example 3

H was 15 years of age and had Down's syndrome. She was the youngest child in a family of four children; her siblings had all left home and were married with their own children. Her parents were in their 50s and her father had recently recovered from a heart attack. H attended a local special school where she presented as a happy and well-adjusted teenager. She could read and write at a simple level and had basic numeracy skills. She had good peer relationships with the other children at school but did not have any friendships or social life of her own outside the school. Her parents included her in their social life and she also spent a lot of time with her married sister and her family. They all treated her as a much younger child. When H got home from school she would routinely go to her bedroom to change her clothes. Her parents would then hear her talking loudly, apparently to the pop-star posters on her wall. She addressed them by name and told them about the events of the day. She would sometimes have similar conversations with her imaginary friends in the presence of her mother. She often told her mother that she had arranged to meet them. She avoided such conversations with her father who would get angry about it. At school and when with her sister she talked about the pop-stars she liked but did not fantasise about them. Following her father's illness and hospitalisation H's preoccupation with her pop-idols increased to the point that her mother sought psychiatric referral. H was having prolonged conversations with imaginary people, was insistent that they were her friends and became angry if her mother challenged her on this. She generally became more argumentative and assertive. During a session with H followed by three family sessions, it was possible to explore her loneliness and sense of being different to her siblings, her anxiety about her father's illness which had never been discussed with her, and her strong desire to have a boyfriend and social life of her own. Her parents were able to see that she had credible opinions and feelings and stopped treating her as a child. Her worries about her father were explored and her parents were honest with her about his illness. They gave H more responsibility and helped her to develop her own social life. This led to a friendship with a boy in her class who she regarded as her boyfriend. Her parents were able to regard this, and H's new-found assertiveness, as a normal and healthy sign of adolescence and were helped in this by including H's sister in one of the family sessions. H's symptoms diminished and gradually disappeared.

Obsessive–compulsive disorders, stereotypies and self-injury

While children may behave in a way that suggests an obsessive–compulsive disorder this is always difficult to diagnose because of the subjective features of the definition. Obsessional thoughts and conversation occur in Asperger's syndrome. Obsessional behaviours are also a feature of children with autistic symptoms, but the term repetitive activity may be a more accurate description that also includes their stereotypies. Stereotyped behaviours such as rocking, mannerisms, finger posturing, twirling and hand-shaking are common especially in children with more severe learning disabilities and with autistic traits. Self-injurious behaviour has a compulsive quality and is often regarded as a stereotypy. It can be particularly difficult to manage. There are a number of theories regarding the reasons for these behaviours. The onset may be associated with minor illnesses, but maintenance is most usually attributed to boredom, self-stimulation or to blocking out external stimuli which are disturbing to the child. Self-injurious behaviours are thought to cause the release of endorphins in the body which have an effect similar to opiates.

There is a danger of stereotypic behaviour being confused with neuroleptic-related dyskinesias and with the mannerisms of Gilles de la Tourette syndrome.

Aggressive and other challenging behaviours

Aggression may be caused by disinhibited rage as in a temper tantrum, but may also have a more instrumental function. The aetiology and management of challenging behaviours is multifaceted and requires detailed assessment. It is most important to deal with them effectively in childhood to prevent their persistence into adult life by which time they are often intractable.

Physical symptoms

Eating disorders

These occur, but anorexia nervosa and bulimia are very rare, and hyperphagia is more common. Some children, often those with autism, will only eat a very restricted range of foods although this generally improves with age. Pica is fairly common especially among younger children; vomiting and rumination also occur and may be associated with gastro-oesophageal reflux which will need treatment.

Sleep disturbance

This is common especially in children with autism, hyperactivity and severe epilepsy. It tends to reduce with age but can be so disruptive to family life that intervention is essential. Tolerance to hypnotics usually develops quickly and their use needs to be combined with other approaches.

Incontinence

Secondary incontinence may be a sign of stress, but enuresis and encopresis are similar to any children in presentation and management. It is important to exclude constipation as a cause.

Hysterical symptoms

These are rare and may take the form of pseudoseizures. Hypochondriacal behaviours are more common. With all such disturbances care must be taken to exclude physical causes.

Psychosomatic conditions

These occur in the same manner as in other children although the sources of stress may be more difficult to identify.

Assessment

Developmental level

When there is a discrepancy between mental and chronological age a judgement has to be made regarding reasonable expectations. A child with a developmental level below three years is very likely to be active, to have a short attention span and to have tantrums when thwarted. Size, stamina and strength make practical management more difficult. A diagnosis of attention deficit hyperactivity disorder is inappropriate in such children. This does not exclude the possibility of successful intervention, but may mean that a developmental approach is more likely to be successful than the use of medication or exclusion diet.

Assessment must include an understanding of the cognitive, motor, language, practical and emotional development of the child and of the present level of attainments. A psychological assessment is very helpful in this respect. The principles of assessment are well described by Graham (1991). Figure 6.3 delineates stages of the assessment process.

History-taking

Most children with learning disabilities have limited or no language skills. Description of internal emotional states is difficult even for older mildly disabled children because it requires a capacity to abstract and generalise from the emotional states of other people. Self-reports of distress and discomfort are therefore less usual and emotional disturbance is more likely to be inferred from behaviour. This may be identified by direct observation or through information provided by carers.

Taking a history must involve identification of the possible causes of the disabilities and of their effect on the child and the carers. It is usually helpful to meet the entire family, and parents generally expect and deserve a partnership with professionals in which they are treated with respect and as equals.

There is often a social worker involved who will have useful insights into the situation. The special educational requirements of learning disabled children usually mean small classes and a close relationship with their teacher, who is also a valuable source of information. If a child is already receiving respite care, the carers in that situation will have useful information about the child. It is therefore helpful to meet with everyone involved either initially or later in the assessment. If a meeting is impractical or contraindicated, the various agencies are usually willing to supply reports.

Physical examination

A physical examination is indicated to confirm or assist in the diagnosis of the cause of the learning disability and of other associated problems. It is usually much more difficult for parents to come to terms with a disability in a child if no cause can be identified. It is nearly always worth exploring the parent's understanding of the reasons for their child's problems, the extent to which they feel able to accept them, and the nature of any residual blame or guilt.

It is important to establish the presence and nature of any sensory deficits and motor problems. The paediatric services should be involved if necessary or, if already involved, it is important to liaise with them. Further investigations may be indicated such as an electroencephalogram or serum anticonvulsant levels in a child with epilepsy.

Psychiatric and psychosocial assessment

The psychiatric assessment should include a detailed history of the behaviours, direct observation of the child, and must also consider the environmental and family systems. When considering the significance of behaviours that cause concern it is important to identify the reason the behaviour is regarded as a problem. There may have been a change in the normal behaviour pattern of the child, or there may be an expectation of different behaviour based on other children with similar disabilities or on non-disabled children of the same age or developmental level. Sometimes there is a practical or emotional change in the environment

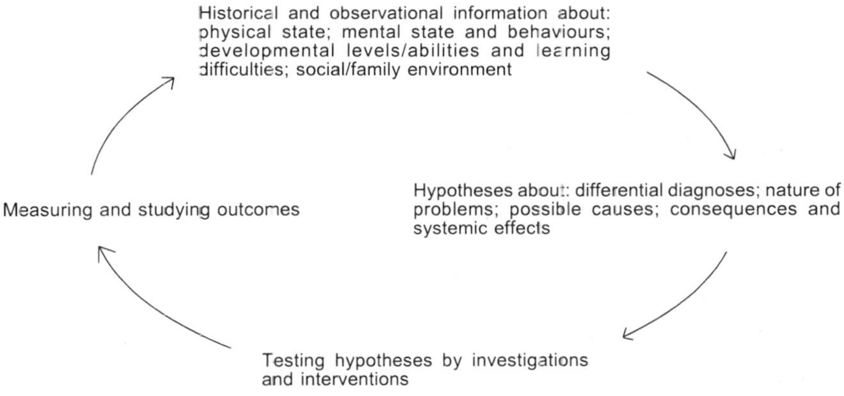

Historical and observational information about:
physical state; mental state and behaviours;
developmental levels/abilities and learning
difficulties; social/family environment

Hypotheses about: differential diagnoses; nature of
problems; possible causes; consequences and
systemic effects

Measuring and studying outcomes

Testing hypotheses by investigations
and interventions

Fig. 6.3 The assessment process.

of the child (such as a change of teacher or depression in a parent) that
has affected tolerance levels or expectations. It is frequently the case that
a knowledge of the carers' perception of the problems, and their
interpretation of the significance and the meaning of such problems, is
the key to successful intervention.

The pattern and duration of the behaviours is also of importance.
Withdrawn and asocial behaviours can, for example, be a symptom of
unhappiness or of depression in a previously sociable child, or a symptom
of the autistic syndrome if associated with the other characteristics. It is
important to make the diagnosis of an underlying impairment such as autism.

Formulation

The formulation should include an analysis of the presenting problems
not only in terms of the possible psychiatric, medical, learning disability
and psychosocial diagnoses, but also in terms of their effects on the systems
within which the child functions. An attempt should be made to
understand the reason why the child needs to behave in this way. Tantrums
in a non-verbal autistic child, for example, may occur because of the
difficulty the child has in understanding and coping with complex social
demands due to the handicap, but are also a reaction that can
communicate distress, reduce the demands made on the child and
increase the child's control of the situation. They may be precipitated
because carers believe that a confrontational approach is the key to
change. Detailed interactional analyses are therefore central to recent
approaches to behaviour modification and such an assessment of
behavioural problems is valuable.

Prevention

It is probable that some of the emotional problems of children with learning disabilities can be prevented by effective counselling to carers and by programmes designed to facilitate recognition of, and response to, the emotional needs of the child. The excellent work on early intervention programmes has been focused on teaching and educating the child, with little attention to emotional maturation and needs within the family. Nevertheless there are undoubtedly gains from these programmes in terms of the skills and confidence of parents and child.

Early detection followed by effective interventions can prevent behaviour problems becoming entrenched and the cycle of parental stress, scapegoating and rejection that can often follow (Fig. 6.2). To achieve this there must be effective screening and readily available psychiatric and psychological services.

Practical and emotional support for the child and family may be available from informal or statutory sources. The use of respite care can be very important in reducing stress, although too frequent or unplanned use can be disruptive to the child and prevent the family from finding more appropriate solutions to behaviour problems.

If a child can no longer be cared for by the natural family, the potential emotional damage from institutionalisation can be prevented by a family placement, usually through schemes that specialise in fostering and adoption for disabled children. The success of such schemes has demonstrated that no child is too disabled to be placed in a family.

Interventions

Very little can be achieved without obtaining a commitment from the carers and, if possible, a relationship with the child. A positive relationship is central to this process.

Psychotherapies

Individual therapies with a child such as play therapy, art therapy, and psychotherapy may be indicated and can be effective, especially if carried out alongside other approaches such as family therapy, marital therapy and network interventions. Psychotherapy and play therapy have been used with children with severe learning disabilities but obviously have to take the developmental level of the child into account. The ability to develop empathy with the child in a nurturing relationship is basic to this approach. Holding therapy and gentle teaching are also based on the carers establishing a close relationship with the child and using this to his or her benefit. In 'holding' this is achieved by confronting and containing the child, whereas in gentle teaching a more indirect approach is used. In both, the attitude of the carer is crucial if it is to remain a positive, constructive and non-punitive interaction. It appears that in some children at least, there is a reduction in behaviour problems when carers start to behave in a different way toward the child.

Very often parents or other carers have a poor understanding of the significance of the learning disability and the nature of associated problems such as autism. Once they are better able to understand the difficulties faced by the child or adolescent, they are then able to make changes to the environment, demands and/or routines to prevent some of the problems arising. They may also need help to understand their own reactions and perceptions and to deal with underlying grief or frustration.

Behaviour modification

Behavioural approaches are very effective interventions for many behaviour problems in children with learning difficulties. There are three important prerequisites. Firstly, underlying organic and psychiatric illness must be excluded or treated. Secondly, carers must be committed to this approach and work together to implement it. Parents will not successfully follow approaches that are alien to their beliefs and usual methods of parenting, and this must be taken into account. The best approach is to build on their strengths rather than to highlight their faults. Finally it is essential to emphasise the importance of respect and dignity for the person who is the subject of the intervention. Behavioural approaches are discussed in chapter 11.

Medication

The use of psychotropic medication has been extensive and often for general tranquillisation rather than as treatment for a specific diagnosis. The major tranquillisers have often been prescribed for antisocial and self-injurious behaviours, usually as a last resort response sometimes necessary because of unsuitable environments and care regimes. It is usually considered good practice that psychotropic medication should only be used for the treatment of a diagnosed psychiatric disorder. Stimulants such as methylphenidate have occasionally been used for hyperactive children with variable success. The use of medication for autistic children is controversial and sometimes recommended on the basis of the suspected biochemical abnormalities in these children. Studies have produced conflicting results and there is no clear evidence that any one drug is beneficial. Haloperidol is probably one of the drugs used most commonly in this group, but side-effects are common and dyskinesias are easily confused with existing stereotypies. The use of naltrexone for severe self-injurious behaviour is being extensively researched with some promising results.

Management of epilepsy

Many children with learning disabilities have epilepsy, and both seizure activity and anti-epileptic medication can be associated with behaviour problems. Good seizure control with appropriate medication at optimal drug levels is therefore an important goal. Phenobarbitone, sodium valproate, clonazepam, vigabatrin and clobazam have all been reported to cause irritability in some children, and sometimes an idiosyncratic reaction can occur in a particular child with a particular drug.

Services

Health and social services

In most areas there are community learning disability teams that consist of psychiatrists, registered nurses in mental handicap (RNMH), clinical psychologists, social workers, occupational therapists, physiotherapists and speech therapists. Although nurses who hold the RNMH qualification are likely to have had some training in behaviour modification, few will have trained in general psychiatry. These teams usually deal with all but the most severe problems for which they may bring in extra expertise from a challenging behaviour team. Not all teams for people with learning disabilities deal with children, and in some areas community paediatricians and district handicap teams take on this responsibility. Behavioural and psychiatric problems may then be referred to the child psychiatric services.

There is also considerable variation in the availability and types of respite care. In most areas family-based respite care is now available and is generally considered preferable to institutional provision in hostels or hospitals. There are often, however, difficulties in finding suitable families in the right locality, especially if a child has very challenging behaviours.

Shortage of resources and failure of early intervention can unfortunately lead to a family deciding that they cannot cope with the problems and to a request for alternative care. Once a family have made that difficult decision it is hard to effect a change of attitude and it is common for professionals to see it as a good solution. It is socially acceptable for a family to reject a handicapped child especially if a 'professional' solution can be found, such as a boarding school or other institutional placement. Many families find fostering or adoption unacceptable because of the social stigma and their feelings of failure, and professionals often collude with this attitude as it may be difficult to find a suitable family placement.

There are very few in-patient beds suitable for this group of patients as mental handicap hospitals rarely admit children, and child psychiatric units and paediatric wards are not equipped to meet the needs of the child with more severe learning disabilities. In some areas specialist local authority residential units may offer respite care or crisis admissions, and a few specialist boarding schools also offer an educational approach to behaviour problems.

Education services

Any child thought to have learning disabilities that will necessitate the provision of extra educational resources requires, under the 1981 Education Act, a Statement of Special Educational Need. This involves a detailed multiprofessional assessment to identify the needs, followed by a statement of all the special services that will be required. Parents are fully involved in this process. The local authority is, at the end of this procedure, legally obliged to provide the necessary services so long as this is within their resources.

Nationally and internationally there has been a move away from segregated education in schools for children with learning disabilities, and many more children and adolescents, especially those with less severe disabilities, are now integrated into mainstream schools. This can be advantageous, especially in terms of social integration, but the benefits very much depend on the quality of support and education available and the attitudes of key people in the school.

Some children, especially those with associated behavioural or psychiatric problems, require a very well planned and specialised approach to their care and this may be provided most easily in segregated schooling. Most schools for children with learning disabilities have classes which specialise in dealing with behavioural or emotional problems and also work closely with families so that there is consistency in home and school.

Some areas make use of residential schooling which has the advantage of consistency and the 24-hour availability of expertise. Such schools often advocate admission at an early age to increase the prospect of improving the child. This has to be weighed against the risks of emotional damage to the child from too early separation from the family, and from institutionalisation. The family may also develop a coping strategy based on enduring the school holidays, when respite care is heavily used; it is then unlikely that other strategies will be established. Most of the behaviourally disturbed children who go to boarding schools for social as well as educational reasons move on to a full-time residential setting when they leave. It may well be the case that a residential school is the only place available to help or cope with the child but the potential long-term benefits and consequences of such a placement must be carefully considered.

Networks

There are often several professionals from different agencies involved with a family. This provides scope for conflicting advice, professional rivalries and confusion. When problems are not being solved, tensions increase and more professionals become involved. A common example is that in which the family blame the school for the behaviour problems of the child and the school blames the family. The professionals often then decide that the family needs therapy. The psychiatrist is usually one of the last to join the fray and can frequently have a role in resolving such network problems. Sometimes it is a simple matter of clarifying misunderstandings and encouraging a joint approach. It may be necessary, however, to convene a meeting of all the professionals and family in which it is essential to avoid any scapegoating and to work with the processes which are taking place. A systemic approach, as used in family therapy, is generally helpful in these situations.

References

American Association on Mental Retardation (1992) *Mental Retardation: Definition, Classification, and Systems of Supports*. Washington, DC: AAMR.

American Psychiatric Association (1994) *Diagnostic and Statistical Manual of Mental Disorders* (4th edn) (DSM–IV). Washington, DC: APA.

Buckley, S. & Sacks, B. (1987) *The Adolescent with Down's Syndrome*. Portsmouth: Portsmouth Polytechnic.

Carr, J. (1990) Supporting the families of people with behavioural/psychiatric difficulties. *International Review of Psychiatry*, **2**, 33–42.

—— (1995) *Down's Syndrome Children Growing Up*. Cambridge: Cambridge University Press.

Corbett, J. A. (1985) Mental retardation: psychiatric aspects. In *Child and Adolescent Psychiatry* (2nd edn) (eds M. Rutter & L. Hersov), pp. 661–678. Oxford: Blackwell Scientific.

——, Harris, R., Taylor, E., *et al* (1977) Progressive disintegrative psychosis of childhood. *Journal of Child Psychology and Psychiatry*, **18**, 211–219.

Einfeld, S. L. & Tonge, B. J. (1991) Psychometric and clinical assessment of psychopathology in developmentally disabled children. *Australian and New Zealand Journal of Developmental Disorders*, **17**, 147–154.

—— & —— (1996*a*) Population prevalence of psychopathology in children and adolescents with intellectual disability: I. Rationale and methods. *Journal of Intellectual Disability Research*, **40**, 91–98.

—— & —— (1996*b*) Population prevalence of psychopathology in children and adolescents with intellectual disability: II. Epidemiological findings. *Journal of Intellectual Disability Research*, **40**, 99–109.

Flint, J. (1996) Behavioural phenotypes: a window onto the biology of behaviour. *Journal of Child Psychology and Psychiatry*, **37**, 355–368.

Fraser, W. I. & Rao, J. M. (1991) Recent studies of mentally handicapped young people's behaviour. *Journal of Child Psychology and Psychiatry*, **32**, 79–108.

Gath, A. & Gumley, D. (1986) Behaviour problems in children with special reference to Down's syndrome. *British Journal of Psychiatry*, **149**, 156–161.

Gillberg, C. (1990) Autism and pervasive developmental disorders. *Journal of Child Psychology and Psychiatry*, **31**, 99–119.

——, Persson, E., Grufman, M., *et al* (1986) Psychiatric disorders in mildly and severely mentally retarded urban children and adolescents: epidemiological aspects. *British Journal of Psychiatry*, **149**, 68–74.

Graham, P. (1991) *Child Psychiatry – A Developmental Approach* (2nd edn). Oxford: Oxford University Press.

Hagberg, B. (ed.) (1993) *Rett's Syndrome – Clinical and Biological Aspects*. Clinics in Developmental Medicine, No.127. Cambridge: Cambridge University Press.

Lord, C. & Rutter, M. (1994) Autism and pervasive developmental disorders. In *Child and Adolescent Psychiatry: Modern Approaches* (3rd edn) (eds M. Rutter, E. Taylor & L. Hersov). pp. 569–593. Oxford: Blackwell Scientific.

McArdle, P., O'Brien, G. & Kolvin, I. (1995) Hyperactivity: prevalence and relationship with conduct disorder. *Journal of Child Psychology and Psychiatry*, **36**, 279–303.

Nihira, K., Foster, R., Shellhaas, M., *et al* (1974) *AAMD Adaptive Behavior Schedule, Revision*. Washington, DC: American Association on Mental Deficiency.

Rutter, M. (1989) Child psychiatric disorders in ICD–10. *Journal of Child Psychology and Psychiatry*, **30**, 499–513.

——, Tizard, J. & Whitmore, K. (1970) *Education, Health and Behaviour*. London: Longman.

Taylor, E. (1991) Developmental neuropsychiatry. *Journal of Child Psychology and Psychiatry*, **32**, 3–47.

——, Sandberg, S., Thorley, G., *et al* (1991) *The Epidemiology of Childhood Hyperactivity*. Maudsley Monograph No 33. Oxford: Oxford University Press.

Tharinger, D., Horton, C. B. & Millea, S. (1990) Sexual abuse and exploitation of children and adults with mental retardation and other handicaps. *Child Abuse and Neglect*, **14**, 301–312.

Trevarthen, C., Aitken, K., Papoudi, D., *et al* (1996) *Children with Autism: Diagnosis and Interventions to Meet their Needs*. London: Jessica Kingsley.

Turner, S. & Sloper, P. (1996) Behaviour problems among children with Down's syndrome: prevalence, persistence and parental appraisal. *Journal of Applied Research in Intellectual Disabilities*, **9**, 129–144.

Wing, L. (1981) A schedule for deriving profiles of handicaps in mentally retarded children. In *Assessing the Handicaps and Needs of Mentally Retarded Children* (ed. B. Cooper), pp 134–141. London: Academic Press.

—— (1991) The relationship between Asperger's syndrome and Kanner's autism. In *Autism and Asperger Syndrome* (ed. U. Frith). Cambridge: Cambridge University Press.

—— (1996) *The Autistic Spectrum: A Guide for Parents and Professionals*. London: Constable.

World Health Organization (1992) *The ICD–10 Classification of Mental and Behavioural Disorders: Clinical Descriptions and Diagnostic Guidelines*. Geneva: WHO.

Additional reading

Gillberg, C. (1995) *Clinical Child Neuropsychiatry*. Cambridge: Cambridge University Press.

Rutter, M. (ed.) (1984) *Developmental Neuropsychiatry*. Edinburgh: Churchill Livingstone.

7 Autism

Michael Cooper

Diagnostic criteria • Assessment • Epidemiology • Biological considerations • Treatment

---

Autism is proving to be the ultimate in biological jigsaws. The picture to be completed and the number of pieces required are still undetermined. It seems likely that no single cause will be found for autism but it could be the final common pathway of a number of different biological disorders.

In 1943 Leo Kanner, working in the US, published his paper on 'Autistic disturbance of affective contact'. This was followed a year later by a thesis by a fellow Austrian, Hans Asperger, a paediatrician practicing in Vienna. Asperger's thesis on 'Autistic Psychopathy' was published in German and then relatively ignored (recently translated and reprinted in Frith, 1991). While these first two descriptions have a considerable overlap, the term *Asperger's syndrome* (perhaps because of his own more optimistic prognostic view) has traditionally been used to describe 'milder' or 'higher functioning' types of autism, while *Kanner's autism* has tended to be used where there is more severe intellectual impairment. The debate over the validity of this differentiation continues (Wing, 1991).

Thirteen years earlier Melanie Klein had described a boy, Dick, whom she thought suffered from a constitutional disorder, characterised by an early affective disorganisation, including disruptions in normal linkages between the child's feelings and objects and people in the world. The child was apparently unable to apprehend people as people.

Other accounts of autistic disorders have come down to us from the late 18th century. Victor, the wild boy of Aveyron (1775–1828) has received, albeit a little posthumously, a diagnosis of autistic disorder. Kasper Hauser, born in 1812 and brought up in a dark dungeon where he was fed opium to keep him quiet, had some behavioural features of autism, although whether these were sufficient to warrant a formal diagnosis of autistic disorder remains open to question.

In presenting his findings Kanner had proposed a psychogenic aetiology, and in the late 1940s and '50s psychotherapy with autistic children and their parents flourished. Although falling out of favour thereafter, it would be unwise to underestimate some of the insights derived from psycho-analytical approaches (Hobson, 1990, 1995; Mayes *et al*, 1993). These require reappraisal and interpretation based on later biological work (and vice versa).

Diagnostic criteria

Although autism was once viewed as a psychotic illness (indeed the term childhood schizophrenia was used to describe such conditions), there is now general agreement that autism and related conditions are distinct from schizophrenia. Autism is now included within the category of pervasive developmental disorders (Lord & Rutter, 1994).

Kanner believed that a diagnosis of autism could be made on the presence of two features: *autistic aloneness* and *obsessive insistence on sameness*. Unfortunately these clinical criteria have not proved to be sufficient to make reliable diagnoses. In recent years Lorna Wing and her colleagues, through their research fieldwork, have drawn up three behavioural criteria for the diagnosis of autistic disorder (Box 7.1). Wing's triad of impairments are: qualitative impairment in reciprocal social interaction; qualitative impairment in verbal and non-verbal commun-ication and in imaginative activity; and a markedly restricted repertoire of activities and interests (Frith, 1989).

Wing's triad of impairments provide the basic building blocks for diagnosis of the condition. These impairments are found in autistic persons throughout the IQ range and in all clinical subtypes.

The diagnostic criteria for autistic disorder included in DSM–IV are shown in Box 7.2.

Assessment

The initial presentation is variable, but all too frequently, despite a mother's intuitive feelings that all is not well, it can be a struggle to convince professionals that something serious is amiss. Detection of autism is too often delayed. This is not surprising as routine developmental checks only screen motor, intellectual and perceptual development, all of which may seem normal in autism. Early detection is possible, and Baron-Cohen *et al* (1992) have developed the Checklist for Autism in Toddlers (CHAT) to assist early diagnosis. Their preliminary conclusion is that the key predictors of autism at 30 months are showing two or more of the following

---

Box 7.1 Behavioural criteria for the diagnosis of autistic disorder: Wing's triad of impairments

Qualitative impairment in reciprocal social interaction

Qualitative impairment in verbal and non-verbal communication and in imaginative activity

A markedly restricted repertoire of activities and interests

at 18 months: (a) lack of pretend play; (b) lack of protodeclarative pointing; (c) lack of social interest; and (d) lack of joint-attention (Baron-Cohen *et al*, 1996).

If a child aged two or three is unusually shy or withdrawn then it is advisable for the doctor to be worried when the parents are worried. A diagnostic evaluation can draw on a variety of assessment schedules such as the Childhood Autism Rating Scale, a 15-item rating scale which is felt to be a valid and reliable tool for children and adolescents (Schopler *et al*, 1986). The Autism Diagnostic Observational Schedule (Lord *et al*, 1989) is also useful for screening. The Autism Diagnostic Interview, a standard instrument based on ICD–10, can be used with the principal care-giver (Le Couteur *et al*, 1989).

Diagnostic evaluation should also include tests of intellectual and communicative abilities. For more able subjects a Wechsler (WAIS or WISC) should be used, whereas the Merrill-Palmer may be more suitable for the assessment of younger, more disabled subjects. British Picture Vocabulary Scales, Reynell Developmental Language Tests and Ravens matrices may also be administered.

Assessment should include a history of the pregnancy, and a detailed family history, looking particularly for learning disabilities and language problems in other family members. The difficult differentiation of autistic disorder from developmental expressive language disorder usually becomes clearer with the years. Parents of a child with the latter often sense the child's desire to communicate and socialise, sadly lacking in those with autistic disorder.

The question of what medical investigations need to be undertaken as a routine in autism has to be considered in the light of the potential yield of new information (Rutter *et al*, 1994). An assessment of vision and hearing should be routine. This is mainly because visual and hearing loss may add to the existing handicaps. Screening blood and urine for metabolic disorders can be useful. Chromosomes should be examined to detect fragile X and other abnormalities. An electroencephalogram may be diagnostic of certain progressive neurological disorders but is unlikely to produce results which are useful in the differential diagnosis. A CAT scan should be performed if there is a clinical indication. The routine use of lumbar puncture to examine the cerebrospinal fluid and the use of brain imaging techniques are not indicated.

Epidemiology

Before the triad concept was established in the 1980s, epidemiological studies reported prevalence rates of around 4–6 per 10 000 population. However, Wing & Gould's (1979) study in Camberwell found that while 21 per 10 000 had the triad, only 4.9 per 10 000 met all the criteria for

Box 7.2 DSM–IV diagnostic criteria for autistic disorder

(A) A total of six or more items from (1) (2) or (3), with at least two from (1) and one each from (2) and (3)

(1) Qualitative impairment in social interaction, as manifested by at least two of the following:

(a) marked impairment in the use of multiple non-verbal behaviours such as eye-to-eye gaze, facial expression, body postures, and gestures to regulate social interaction

(b) failure to develop peer relationships appropriate to developmental level

(c) a lack of spontaneous seeking to share enjoyment, interests, or achievements with other people

(d) lack of social or emotional reciprocity

(2) Qualitative impairments in communication as manifested by at least one of the following:

(a) delay in, or total lack of, the development of spoken language (not accompanied by an attempt to compensate through alternative modes of communication such as gesture or mime)

(b) in individuals with adequate speech, marked impairment in the ability to initiate or sustain a conversation with others

(c) stereotyped and repetitive use of language or idiosyncratic language

(d) lack of varied, spontaneous make-believe play or social imitative play appropriate to developmental level

(3) Restricted repetitive and stereotyped patterns of behaviour, interests and activities, as manifested by at least one of the following:

(a) encompassing preoccupation with one or more stereotyped and restricted patterns of interest that is abnormal either in intensity or focus

(b) apparently inflexible adherence to specific, non-functional routines or rituals

(c) stereotyped and repetitive motor mannerisms (e.g. hand or finger flapping or twisting, or complex whole-body movements)

(d) persistent preoccupation with parts of objects

(B) Delays or abnormal functioning in at least one of the following areas, with onset prior to the age of three years:

(1) social interaction

(2) language as used in social communication

(3) symbolic or imaginative play

(C) The disturbance is not better accounted for by Rett's Disorder or Childhood Disintegrative Disorder

With permission from the American Psychiatric Association.

autism and only 2.0 per 10 000 could be said to have classical Kannerian autism. Gillberg found autistic traits in 35 per 10 000 children who did not meet diagnostic criteria for autism or Asperger's syndrome (Gillberg, 1993). Epidemiological studies thus provide data on a spectrum of autistic disorder, ranging from classical Kannerian autism to children who have autistic traits.

Sex ratios

All studies report an excess of boys. The ratios are lowest among those with severe and profound learning disabilities. The relative paucity of girls in the higher IQ ranges suggests the possibility of a sex-linked genetic mechanism.

Social class and seasonal influence

Early studies suggested a bias towards higher social class. Such conclusions were flawed by self-referral or self-selection to centres of excellence by knowledgeable, motivated and mobile parents. To emphasise this point, in eight out of Kanner's 11 cases, family members have appeared in *Who's Who* or in *Men of Science*. Most recent studies from Europe, North America and Japan conclude that suffering from autism has no connection with social class. This may be an oversimplification; a Swedish study indicated an excess of March births characterised by low social class, urban dwelling while *in utero*, and psychosocial disadvantage, suggesting perhaps that epidemics of influenza which are known to occur in crowded urban regions of Sweden during January and March could cause viral damage during late foetal life (Gillberg, 1990).

Psychological theories

During the past 15 years developmental psychologists have struggled to understand how social behaviour, interpersonal relationships, and language and communication develop in young children with autism. These studies have generated a rich and complex set of data which has stimulated a rewarding debate on the nature of autism. There are now a number of excellent books which enable the non-specialist reader to understand the central issues. Frith (1989) and Happe (1994*a, b*) have both written concise and easy to follow accounts of the various debates; Baron-Cohen *et al* (1993) have edited a comprehensive selection of papers by the main participants; and Hobson (1993) has written a closely argued monograph in which he sets his ideas alongside those of others.

The debate among developmental psychologists has focused on three main issues:

Impairment of affective response

In 1981 Hobson proposed that the primary problem for children with autism was an interpersonal impairment. This could not be defined without regard to the child's relationship to care-givers. He postulated an innate impairment in the child's ability to become emotionally engaged with others and because of this deficit, the autistic child does not receive the necessary social experiences in infancy to develop the cognitive structures for understanding (Happe 1994*b*; Hobson, 1995).

A primary cognitive impairment

In 1985 Baron-Cohen and colleagues outlined their view that the key issue for the autistic child was primarily a cognitive deficit. They argued that the triad of impairments resulted from a deficit in the ability of the autistic child to 'mind read'. Their *theory of mind* hypothesis is based on the idea that in autism there is a failure to develop a normal understanding that people have minds and mental states, and that mental states relate to behaviour (see Baron-Cohen, 1993).

A failure in the development of language, communication and social skills

The third focus for debate started from the view that the fundamental impairment in autism lies in the failure by the autistic child to develop an understanding of the nature of language as communication. It is argued that unlike normal children or children with Down's syndrome, children with autism do not develop an understanding that communication and language exist for the exchange of information. The use of language is inextricably linked to our understanding of minds. Children with autism do not develop an understanding of mind because they have suffered a fundamental impairment in their acquisition of language (Tager-Flusberg, 1993).

Imagination and play

Research has shown that most normal children will, by the age of two, have begun to engage in imaginative play in which experiment and pretence play an increasing role. In order to maintain some separation between reality and the pretend world, young children appear to develop two modes for representing the world around them. These have been called primary representations, representing aspects of the world in an accurate, faithful and literal way, and metarepresentations, which are psychological devices used by children to capture the special world of pretence or in other words representations of representations (see Perner, 1993, for more discussion of these issues). When children involve themselves in pretend play they engage in metarepresentations. In pretend play the normal child develops the ability to keep primary representations and metarepresentations in separate compartments of the mind. The process by which the child does this has been called "decoupling".

Observations of autistic children show that autistic children do not spontaneously engage in pretend play. This is either because they cannot form metarepresentations, or because they are unable to decouple the metarepresentation from the primary representation. It seems likely that the ability to decouple is the process which allows the young child to become involved in imagination and fantasy, and ultimately to develop the ability to reflect on his or her own thoughts.

The theory of mind hypothesis

By *theory of mind* is meant the ability of normal children to attribute mental states such as beliefs, desires, intentions to themselves and other people, as a way of making sense and predicting behaviour (Baron-Cohen *et al*, 1993). During the last ten years the theory of mind hypothesis has provided a common thread linking much of the psychological research into autism.

The hypothesis that autistic children are unable to form meta-representations led to the suggestion that autism might constitute a specific impairment in the cognitive mechanism necessary for representing mental states, or 'mentalising' (Happe, 1994*b*). It was suggested that the impairments seen in autistic children arise because they lack a 'theory of mind'. This deficit, felt to be specific to autism, is well illustrated in the now famous Sally Anne experiment.

> "We used two dolls, Sally and Anne, and acted out a little scenario: Sally has a basket and Anne has a box. Sally has a marble and she puts it in her basket. She then goes out. Anne takes out Sally's marble and puts it into her box while Sally is away. Now Sally comes back and wants to play with her marble. At this point we ask the critical question: where will Sally look for her marble ? The answer is of course in the basket. This answer is correct because Sally has put the marble into the basket and has not seen it being moved. She believes the marble is still where she put it. Therefore she will look in the basket even though the marble is not there any more. Most of the non-autistic children gave the correct answer, that is they pointed to the basket. In contrast, all but a few of the autistic children got it wrong. They pointed to the box. This is where the marble really was, but where of course Sally did not know it was. They did not take Sally's own belief into account." (Quoted from Frith, 1989)

The failure of the autistic children to understand Sally's belief was all the more remarkable because they had a much higher mental age than the other children. Further studies suggest that children with autism are unimpaired in other social cognitive tasks, such as peer recognition and visual self-recognition.

Although the theory of mind hypothesis has provided many useful insights on psychological function in people with autism, it has not provided the complete answer. Recent work has suggested that there may be more fundamental deficits, for example in the child's capacity to visualise relationships between objects. Baron-Cohen has postulated that autistic children do not use eye contact as a source of information (Happe, 1994*b*). A greater understanding of the biological deficits which disrupt psychological function in autistic individuals should provide more insights into the autistic spectrum of disorders (Rutter & Bailey, 1993).

Intellectual performance

In their classic study in Camberwell, Wing & Gould (1979) found that there was a marked association between IQ and the severity of social impairment. The majority of autistic children had IQs in the range 20–49, even using tests based on visuospatial skills and avoiding language-based tests. Follow-up of these children into adulthood showed that the IQ on testing tended to remain the same or fall (Wing, 1988).

Tests performed using the Wechsler Intelligence Scale for Children (WISC) show a highly characteristic pattern of sub-test performance throughout the IQ range. The lowest performance is associated with the comprehension subtest and the highest with block design, considered to test spatial ability. In autism competence in the latter is misleading and pathological. Normally when faced with an array of stimuli, non-autistic people create a particular form of coherence or overall mental imagery, but this is diminished in autistic children. They generally perform poorly on tasks requiring connection of stimuli while a high performance is seen on tasks requiring isolation of stimuli, also leading to their enhanced ability to spot embedded figures more easily than non-autistic peers. An enhanced memory for stimuli without coherence creating meaning and comprehension is socially disastrous, but it may be linked to special abilities to recall single unusual facts or rote memory. Thus islands of ability (e.g. calendrical calculators) are really a sign of extreme cognitive dysfunction.

Psychometric tests have variously described dysfunctions in both left and right hemispheres and frontal lobes, with a previous emphasis on pure left hemisphere dysfunction, predominantly because of the language abnormalities. Recent psychometric studies have failed to substantiate the latter, indicating that there may be bilateral hemispheric dysfunction. There is increasing evidence that dysfunction of frontal lobes may reflect abnormalities at a lower cortical or subcortical level.

Biological considerations

There is now general agreement that autism is a neurodevelopmental disorder arising as a consequence of organic brain disorder. But there is little agreement about the role of coexisting medical conditions in the genesis of the disorder. A Swedish population-based study of 35 subjects found clear indications of severe brain dysfunction in nearly 90% of those studied (Steffenberg, 1991). Half the children had an abnormal EEG; a quarter had an abnormal CAT scan; a third had abnormal auditory brain-stem responses. In the population under study there were children with a variety of genetic syndromes including two with Moebius syndrome, two with fragile X, and others with tuberose sclerosis and Laurence-Moon Biedl syndrome. The authors concluded that autism has multiple biological aetiologies.

Similar findings came from the UCLA–University of Utah epidemiological survey of autism (Ritvo *et al*, 1990). This study also supported the hypothesis that different diseases producing different types of damage to the central nervous system may play an aetiological role in autism. Out of a total of 233 autistic subjects, 26 had medical conditions known to cause central nervous system pathology (11% of the group). The authors commented that despite the fact that these central nervous conditions were rare, there was a high probability against random co-occurrence with autism and that these disorders probably caused autism by acting through a final common pathway.

The UCLA–University of Utah study was unable to associate any specific potentially pathological prenatal, perinatal or postnatal event with autism (Mason-Brothers *et al*, 1990). In view of the lack of a clear-cut result, the study concluded that any pathological factor leading to autism must be subtle, act in combination, and be present at the time of conception (genetic) or very early in neural tube or foetal brain development. As now seems the case in cerebral palsy, complications in the prenatal and perinatal periods, if they occur at all, are more likely to be secondary to the autistic foetus rather than causal (Goodman, 1990).

Although approximately 50 different medical conditions have been associated with autism, only a relatively small proportion of autistic people have a clearly identifiable medical disorder. Rutter *et al* (1994) suggested that the rate of known medical conditions in autism is probably about 10%, but it may be higher when the autistic disorder is accompanied by profound learning disability. They also noted that medical conditions are more frequently found in atypical autism. Gillberg disagrees with this view and has reported that 37% of cases of autism are linked with known medical conditions (Gillberg & Coleman, 1992).

Genetic influences

Until the late 1970s it was considered that genetic factors were unlikely to play a substantial role in autism. The situation has changed and there is now strong support for the view that genetic factors play an important role in autism. However, there are still those who have not been convinced by the genetic argument and who see the autistic spectrum of disorders as a final common pathway for a number of diseases which cause damage to the developing brain.

The evidence for genetic influences comes from four main sources.

Autism in siblings

By the 1980s studies of the families of autistic children had begun to suggest that genetic factors probably play a significant role in the manifestation of autism. Pooled data from a number of studies gave a frequency of autism among the siblings of autistic children of 2.7%. Using the narrower definition of 2–4 per 10 000 population this gives a rate which is over 50 times higher than the prevalence in the general population, and using the broader definition based on Wing's triad the prevalence was 10 times that found in the general population. However, some of these studies were criticised because the assessments were considered to be not sufficiently standardised.

A recent US/UK collaborative study examined the family history of 99 autistic and 36 Down's syndrome subjects (Bolton *et al*, 1994). In the siblings of the autistic subjects researchers found autism in 2.9%, and a further 2.9% when the broader diagnosis of pervasive developmental disorder was used. In the siblings of the Down's syndrome subjects the prevalence rates were zero in both cases.

Cognitive disability in siblings

It is estimated that about 15% of the siblings of people with autism have developmental disorders of speech, language or reading skills. It has been suggested that it is these psychological characteristics or defects rather than a global cognitive defect which is inherited. Even in a study of Kanner's original cases (most of whom were not severely handicapped) a familial loading for cognitive disabilities, mostly involving specific speech and language impairment, has been found.

The collaborative study of Bolton *et al* (1994) also explored the incidence rates among siblings of a lesser variant of autism comprising more subtle communication problems, social impairments or stereotypical behaviours. This revealed that between 12% and 20% of the siblings of the autistic subjects exhibited this lesser variant, but only 1.6% to 3.2% of the Down's siblings.

Twin studies

The first major study of same-sex autistic twins reported a concordance rate of 36% among 11 monozygotic pairs, but a zero concordance rate among the dizygotic pairs (Folstein & Rutter, 1977). Most of the non-autistic co-twins had some form of cognitive impairment, usually a speech or language impairment. The concordance rates for these lesser impairments was 82% in the monozygotic twins but only 10% in the dizygotic pairs. The authors of the study concluded that the cognitive impairments were part of an inherited phenotype which could include autism.

A Scandinavian study of twins found that 10 of their 11 monozygotic pairs (and a monozygotic set of triplets) were concordant for autism. There was zero concordance for autism among their 10 dizygotic pairs. In respect to cognitive disorder they found 10 out of the 11 (89%) monozygotic pairs were concordant, compared with 30% of the dizygotic pairs (Steffenburg *et al*, 1989).

The third twin study comprised a follow-up of 19 twin pairs from the earlier sample of Folstein and Rutter and a new sample of 28 twin pairs. The twins were all examined or re-examined and concordance rates recalculated. Sixty-nine per cent of the monozygotic twins were concordant for autism whereas there was zero concordance in the dizygous twin pairs. Concordance for cognitive deficits was 88% in the monozygotic pairs and 9% in the dizygotic pairs (Bailey *et al*, 1995).

There were some important differences between the results of these twin studies, but in general all three found a high concordance rate for autism in monozygotic pairs and a zero concordance rate in dizygotic pairs. In none of the three studies has concordance for autism been attributable to obstetric damage. On the basis of this evidence it seems that the liability to autism is largely genetically determined, but it is unlikely to be inherited as a Mendelian disorder.

Combining the results of family and twin studies suggests that the autism phenotype extends beyond autism as traditionally diagnosed; that the aetiology may involve several genes; and that autism is genetically heterogeneous (Bolton *et al*, 1994).

The parents of autistic children

The parents of autistic individuals have also been studied to test the hypothesis that there is a genetic basis for autism. In a recent study the personality characteristics of 87 parents of autistic individuals and 38 parents of people with Down's syndrome were examined using a standardised personality interview (Piven *et al*, 1994). The hypothesis was that the parents of autistic individuals would have high ratings on the characteristics *aloof, undemonstrative*, and *unresponsive*. The researchers were not blind to the parental grouping and the study had other methodological problems, but using the best estimate ratings of personality, significant differences were found among the parents of the autistic individuals for the characteristics *aloof* and *untactful*. For the characteristics *undemonstrative* and *unresponsive* there was a difference which tended to support the hypothesis.

The authors suggest that while these characteristics may result from having an autistic individual in the home, it may be that these personality characteristics are expressions of the underlying genetic abnormality in autism.

Autism and the fragile X syndrome

Fragile X syndrome is now considered to be the second most common known cause of learning disability after Down's syndrome. Early studies indicated, incorrectly, a high rate of autism in affected males in the region of 20–25%. There is now accumulating evidence that only 2–3% of people with autism have the fragile X syndrome (Turk, 1992, 1995). There are also some doubts over the validity of describing the range of behaviours seen in fragile X as embodying Wing's triad; instead they may reflect a degree of social anxiety and shyness with associated poor eye contact, qualitatively different from that seen in autism. It seems that fragile X children who have autistic-like disturbance have more communicatory and ritualistic disorder, in particular a form of gaze aversion, delayed echolalia, repetitive speech and hand-flapping, whereas autistic children who do not have the fragile X syndrome have more social and symbolic disturbance. Fragile X children engage in 'torso-turning', most noticeable when engaging in a handshake. Early studies may have misconstrued this as a sign of being autistic.

Neurobiology

Postmortem studies

In general postmortem studies have shown little evidence of any gross pathology in the brains of autistic individuals. Subtle alterations in cell packing have been noted in the hippocampus and related limbic structures, and decreased Purkinje cell counts have been found in the cerebellar hemispheres and vermis. However, the limbic and cerebellar abnormalities may be secondary to abnormal innervation from other areas of the brain (Bailey, 1993).

Computer assisted tomography and magnetic resonance imaging

A variety of structural abnormalities have been reported on CAT scans. Reversed cerebral asymmetries, enlargement of the lateral and third ventricles, decreased cerebellar vermis (VI–VII) and a decrease in the radiodensity of the nuclear caudate have been described. There have been problems in reproducing these results and to date there has been a failure to find a consistent picture. In a recent MRI study, 13 male autistic subjects were compared with 13 male non-autistic controls, matched for age and non-verbal IQ (Piven *et al*, 1990). MRI scans were performed and rated for the presence of cortical malformations. Developmental cortical malformations were found in seven of the autistic subjects and none of the controls. Five had polymicrogyria (an excessive number of diffuse or local cerebral convolutions). Abnormal neuronal migration occurring perhaps in the first six months of gestation could account for the cerebral cortical defects (and cerebral hypoplasia). The underlying cause of the failed cell migration remains unknown, but viral and immunological theories need to be considered.

Neuroimaging studies

Functional brain imaging studies using positron emission tomography (PET) or single photon emission computed tomography (SPECT) have failed to detect consistent abnormalities in autistic adults and school-age children. It may be that the abnormalities in the brain of the autistic person are too subtle to be detected by current methods. The hypothesis has been advanced that abnormalities which may be transiently detectable may occur in the brain during postnatal development. Studies of cerebral blood flow to test this hypothesis have been carried out in five autistic children and in five controls. The results are consistent with a delayed maturation of the frontal lobes in autistic children (Zilbovicius *et al*, 1995).

Neurochemistry

If autistic spectrum disorder, or the 'autisms', are regarded as a biological jigsaw or even jigsaws, then many of the pieces yet to be sorted out and put in place are likely to be found at a neurochemical level. Abnormalities have been described in monoamine chemistry, peptides, amino acids and neuroendocrine functioning, but the identification of specific defects crucial to the development of the core triad remains elusive.

Platelet serotonin has been shown to be consistently elevated in 30% of autistic people, a finding which correlates with levels found in first-degree relatives. Levels of 5-hydroxy-tryptamine (5HT) in people with autism with affected siblings have been found to be significantly higher than in autistic people without affected relatives, levels in both groups being higher than in controls. Perhaps levels of 5HT in platelet-rich plasma may be used as a test for autism associated with genetic inheritance rather than those linked to other causes. The dopamine system may also be abnormal. Low levels of dopa hydroxylase have been found in probands and first-degree relatives compared with controls. Elevated urinary and cerebrospinal fluid levels of homovanillic acid as well as elevated plasma noradrenaline have been described. Elevated cerebrospinal fluid opioid levels and reduced plasma endorphin have been described in several studies. Most of the opioid theories have usually included some reference to self-injurious behaviour and diminished sensitivity to pain, but the opioid hypothesis has produced little of clinical relevance (Gillberg, 1995). Involvement of monoamine oxidase and indoleamine abnormalities is suggested by a growing body of evidence indicating abnormalities in the hypothalamic–pituitary axis. A variety of neuroendocrine probes indicate a high rate of nonsuppression to dexamethasone, blunted responses to thyroid stimulating hormone, and abnormalities in growth hormone response to L-dopa, but not to clonidine.

Disturbance in any given chemical system could greatly interfere with normal cognitive processes. Disruptions of perceptual pathways, be they concerned with touch, vision, hearing, and so on, are all mediated by neurotransmitters and homeostatic neuroregulators (for example B endorphin). In a few people who have 'emerged' from autism, their perception of the world is sometimes compared to listening to and watching an untuned television receiver. The often variable and conflicting neurochemical findings are fully reviewed by Cook (1990).

Treatment

There is no cure for autism. Each autistic person has a unique array of needs requiring a range of facilities, professionals and treatments (Trevarthen *et al*, 1996). Repeated assessment of these needs should be undertaken primarily by the person's local services, increasingly using a system such as the IPP (Individual Personal Profile) complemented by clinical centres specialising in the disorder. Assessment and therapy should rapidly move from a surgery or clinic-based setting to the parental home, educational, residential, or work environment. It should be the basic remit of a service for people with learning disabilities to provide this within the person's own health district. Wherever possible professionals should complement and support therapy generated by other carers in any given environment. Easy access to professions and their sustained clinical input will help implement any therapeutic regime and may prevent the need for permanent admission to units for people with challenging behaviour, simply because of a crisis at home. The same can be said about the excessive need to use respite care, although its sensible and regular use can be of benefit to the autistic person and family alike.

Education

Attendance at nursery or play-school is increasingly common and permits early assessment of social and behavioural difficulties as well as early intervention, often based on operant behaviour techniques and development of preverbal communication skills. It is not known if attendance at such nursery schools influences long-term outcome, but they are exceptionally helpful to exhausted and harassed young mothers who are predominantly expected to take on the burden of handling emotional and behavioural problems in their children. The majority proceed to local special schools or less frequently to residential special schools. The National Curriculum, while encouraging a breadth of educational experience, acknowledges the special difficulties in meeting the needs of these individuals and provides an excellent code of practice to help teachers establish structure and introduce planned and gradual change.

Some more able children may move on to participate in main-stream education, including Colleges of Further Education. More able people may present for the first time at their local secondary school because of mental health problems or behavioural difficulties. A minority of exceptionally gifted people with Asperger's syndrome will proceed to study at university level.

Behavioural therapies

These are often the most important therapies in modifying challenging behaviours, including acts of aggression to self or others, but are also helpful in effecting the successful handling of gradual change in routine or environment (Matson *et al*, 1996).

One of the essential features of treatment is the provision of opportunities for children to learn how to communicate and how to develop social relationships. Left to their own devices children with autism tend to isolate themselves and engage in obsessional rituals and stereotypical behaviour. In their case–control study of the treatment of autistic children, Howlin & Rutter (1987) devised a treatment programme which took place in the family home. Much of their therapeutic input was concerned with shaping behavioural responses and encouraging language development.

Operant techniques are often the basis of behaviour modification programmes. In a study of its intense use (40 hours per week for several years) in people's homes, it was shown to be successful in the long-term reduction of a wide range of problems, especially in those who were more able and had a fair overall prognosis (Lovaas, 1987). In normal practice assessments should occur in all main daily living environments, thereby addressing problems of consistency of recording and implementation of policies, but most importantly generalising therapeutic success from one environment to another. Insufficient support for carers invariably causes even simple programmes to lapse quickly.

Drug therapy

The rational use of medication depends possibly more than all other therapies on precise identification of the biological defects which are responsible for the core triad of impairments. Early therapeutic trials focused on lowering levels of serotonin using fenfluramine, but enthusiasm diminished for the 5HT excess theory as it became clear that this drug was no better than placebo. This may be more a reflection on fenfluramine or study methodology than proof that 5HT is no longer of essential importance. Interest has been rekindled with the use of the potent 5HT uptake inhibitors fluvoxamine and fluoxetine, albeit in a handful of autistic people with normal intelligence (McDougle *et al*, 1990). The former caused a significant reduction in a coexisting obsessive–compulsive disorder, and the latter reduced rituals and increased tolerance to changes in routine. Clomipramine, a selective serotonin reuptake inhibitor, has been shown to be effective in a double-blind placebo-controlled trial (Gordon *et al*, 1993). In this study obsessive–compulsive symptoms improved but, against expectation, autistic symptoms such as abnormal reciprocal interaction and motor stereotypy also improved.

It seems possible that the opioid hypothesis will assume the role of mediator for core symptoms. Although early open trials using naltrexone given orally (in a dose of 0.5 mg/kg every third day) showed a reduction in hyperactivity, aggressiveness, self-injurious behaviour and stereotypies after an hour, and increased social exploration and contact (Panskepp *et al*, 1991), but the results of controlled studies have not confirmed the effectiveness of the drug (Campbell *et al*, 1993; see Gillberg, 1995, for a review of the opioid hypothesis).

Neuroleptics in low doses, for example haloperidol, can reduce stereotypies and aggression as well as increase peer relations without adversely affecting learning. However, haloperidol is associated with the emergence of tardive dyskinesia, especially in the more intellectually disabled.

Claims have been made for the use of casein and gluten-restricted diets, and several groups have successfully used megavitamin therapy in a minority of children (for example vitamin B6 in combination with magnesium lactate).

Non-drug therapies

Research to date strongly suggests that a range of living and work environments is required and should be tailored to match the needs of a individual. Traditional concepts of large country mansions with on-site occupational therapy, teamwork, and extensive grounds to roam in may be perfect for some young adults, yet a four-bedroom house in a city and attendance at a local Adult Opportunity Centre may be equally well suited for a middle-aged man. Therapeutic choice is too often limited by what is available rather than what might be best suited for that individual.

Regular music therapy can help with the range of different behavioural challenges. Holding therapy, massage, pet therapy, ethologically orientated family therapy, individual psychotherapy, regular aerobic exercise, low social intrusion teaching and social empathy, to name but a few, all have their advocates and enthusiasts.

Speech therapy for children should build on the child's existing abilities and motivational factors with an emphasis on developing social communication. Adults who are unable to communicate by speech should be encouraged to use signing and symbols as well as technology. The use of facilitated communication has become controversial.

Outlook

The majority of autistic individuals will be handicapped throughout their lives. They are likely to require a variety of social and therapeutic interventions. In particular they will need continuing help to develop spontaneous and reciprocal communication with others and help to modify repetitive behaviours. Underlying medical conditions will need to be attended to. But, above all, the parents and carers who look after them will need understanding and support (Wing, 1996).

References

American Psychiatric Association (1995) *Diagnostic and Statistical Manual of Mental Disorders* (4th edn), International Version. Washington, DC: APA.

Asperger, H. (1944) "Autistic psychopathy" in childhood. In *Autism and Asperger Syndrome* (1991) (ed. U. Frith). Cambridge: Cambridge University Press.

Bailey, A. J. (1993) The biology of autism. *Psychological Medicine*, **23**, 7–11.

——, Le Couteur, A., Gottesman, I., *et al* (1995) Autism as a strongly genetic disorder: evidence from a British twin study. *Psychological Medicine*, **25**, 63–77.

Baron-Cohen, S. (1993) From attention-goal psychology to belief-desire psychology: the development of a theory of mind and its dysfunction. In *Understanding other Minds: Perspectives from Autism* (eds S. Baron-Cohen, H. Tager-Flusberg & D. J. Cohen). Oxford: Oxford University Press.

——, Allen, J. & Gillberg, C. (1992) Can autism be detected at 18 months? *British Journal of Psychiatry*, **161**, 839–843.

——, Tager-Flusberg, H. & Cohen, D. J. (1993) *Understanding Other Minds: Perspectives from Autism*. Oxford: Oxford University Press.

——, Cox, A., Baird, G., *et al* (1996) Psychological markers in the detection of autism in infancy in a large population. *British Journal of Psychiatry*, **168**, 158–163.

Bolton, P., Macdonald, H., Pickles, A., *et al* (1994) A case-control family history study of autism. *Journal of Child Psychology and Psychiatry*, **35**, 877–900.

Campbell, M., Anderson, L., Small, A., *et al* (1993) Naltrexone in autistic children: behavioural symptoms and attentional learning. *Journal of the American Academy of Child and Adolescent Psychiatry*, **32**, 1282–1291.

Cook, E. (1990) Autism; review of neurochemical investigation. *Synapse*, **6**, 292–308.

Corbett, J., Harris, R., Taylor, E., *et al* (1977) Progressive disintegrative psychosis of childhood. *Journal of Child Psychology and Psychiatry*, **18**, 211–219.

Folstein, S. & Rutter, M. (1977) Infantile autism: a genetic study of 21 twin pairs. *Journal of Child Psychology and Psychiatry*, **18**, 291–321.

—— & Piven, J. (1991) Etiology of autism: genetic influences. *Pediatrics*, 767–773.

Frith, U. (1989) *Autism: Explaining the Enigma*. Oxford : Blackwell.

—— (ed.) (1991) *Autism and Asperger Syndrome*. Cambridge: Cambridge University Press.

Gillberg, C. (1988) Autism and pervasive developmental disorders. *Journal of Child Psychology and Psychiatry*, **31**, 99–119.

—— (1990) Infantile autism: diagnosis and treatment. *Acta Psychiatrica Scandinavica*, **82**, 209–215.

—— (1993) Autism and related behaviours. *Journal of Intellectual Disability Research*, **37**, 343–372.

—— (1995) Endogenous opioids and opiate antagonists in autism: brief review of empirical findings and implications for clinicians. *Developmental Medicine and Child Neurology*, **37**, 239–245.

—— & Coleman, M. (1992) *The Biology of the Autistic Syndrome* (2nd edn). *Clinics in Developmental Medicine*, No. 126. London: McKeith Press.

Goodman, R. (1990) Technical note: Are perinatal complications causes or consequences of autism? *Journal of Child Psychology and Psychiatry*, **31**, 809–812.

Gordon, C. T., State, R. C., Nelson, J. E., *et al* (1993) Double-blind comparison of clomipramine, desipramine and placebo in the treatment of autistic disorder. *Archives of General Psychiatry*, **50**, 441–447.

Happe, F. G. E. (1994*a*) Current psychological theories of autism: the "theory of mind" account and rival theories. *Journal of Child Psychology and Psychiatry*, **35**, 215–229.

—— (1994*b*) *Autism: an Introduction to Psychological Theory*. London: UCL Press.

Hobson, R. (1990) On psychoanalytic approaches to autism. *American Journal of Orthopsychiatry*, **60**, 324–336.

—— (1995) *Autism and the Development of Mind*. Hove: Lawrence Erlbaum.

Howlin, P. & Rutter, M. (1987) *Treatment of Autistic Children*. Chichester: John Wiley.

Kanner, L. (1943) Autistic disturbances of affective contact. *The Nervous Child*, **2**, 217–250.

Le Couteur, A., Rutter, M., Lord, C., *et al* (1989) Autism Diagnostic Interview; a semi-structured interview for parents and care-givers of autistic persons. *Journal of Autism and Developmental Disorders*, **19**, 363–387.

Lord, C., Rutter, M., Goode, S., *et al* (1989) Autism diagnostic information schedule: a standardized observation of communicative and social behaviour. *Journal of Autism and Developmental Disorder*, **19**, 185–212.

—— & —— (1994) Autism and pervasive developmental disorders. In *Child and Adolescent Psychiatry: Modern Approaches* (3rd edn) (eds M. Gutter, E. Taylor & L. Hersov), pp. 569–593.

Lovaas, O. (1987) Behavioural treatment and normal educational and intellectual functioning in young autistic children. *Journal of Consulting and Clinical Psychology*, **55**, 3–9.

McDougle, C., Price, L. & Goodman, W. K. (1990) Fluvoxamine treatment of coincident autistic disorder and obsessive compulsive disorder: a case report. *Journal of Autism and Developmental Disorders*, **20**, 537–543.

Mason-Brothers, A., Ritvo, E., *et al* (1990) The UCLA–University of Utah epidemiologic survey of autism: prenatal, perinatal and postnatal factors. *Paediatrics*, **86**, 514–519.

Matson, J. L., Benavidez, D. A., Compton, L. S., *et al* (1996) Behavioural treatment of autistic persons: a review of research from 1980 to the present. *Research in Developmental Disabilities*, **17**, 433–466.

Mayes, L., Cohen, D. & Klin, A. (1993) Desire and fantasy: a psychoanalytic perspective on theory of mind and autism. In *Understanding Other Minds: Perspectives from Autism* (eds S. Baron-Cohen, H. Tager-Flushberg & D. J. Cohen). Oxford: Oxford Medical Publications.

Panskepp, J. & Lensing, P. (1991) A synopsis of an open trial of naltrexone treatment of autism with four children. *Journal of Autism and Developmental Disorders*, **21**, 243–249.

Perner, J. (1993) The theory of mind deficit in autism: rethinking the metarepresentation theory. In *Understanding other Minds: Perspectives from Autism* (eds S. Baron-Cohen, H. Tager-Flushberg & D. J. Cohen). Oxford: Oxford Medical Publications.

Piven, J., Berthier, M., Startstein, S., *et al* (1990) Magnetic resonance imaging evidence for a defect of cerebral cortical development in autism. *American Journal of Psychiatry*, **146**, 734–739.

——, Wzorek, M., Landa, R., *et al* (1994) Personality characteristics of the parents of autistic individuals. *Psychological Medicine*, **24**, 783–795.

Ritvo, B., Mason-Brothers, A., Freeman, B. J., *et al* (1990) The UCLA–University of Utah epidemiologic survey of autism: the etiologic role of rare diseases. *American Journal of Psychiatry*, **147**, 1614–1621.

Rutter, M. & Bailey, A. (1993) Thinking and relationships: mind and brain (some reflections on theory of mind and autism). In *Understanding Other Minds: Perspectives from Autism* (eds S. Baron-Cohen, H. Tager-Flushberg & D. J. Cohen). Oxford: Oxford Medical Publications.

——, ——, Bolton, P., *et al* (1994) Autism and known medical conditions: myth and substance. *Journal of Child Psychology and Psychiatry*, **35**, 311–322.

Schopler, E., Reichler, R. J. & Renner, B. R. (1986) *The Childhood Autism Rating Scale*. New York: Irvington.

Steffenburg, S. (1991) Neuropsychiatric assessment of children with autism: a population study. *Developmental Medicine and Child Neurology*, **33**, 495–511.

——, Gillberg, C., Hellgren, L., *et al* (1989) A twin study of autism in Denmark, Finland, Iceland, Norway and Sweden. *Journal of Child Psychology and Psychiatry*, **30**, 405–416.

Tager-Flusberg, H. (1993) What language reveals about the understanding of minds in children with autism. In *Understanding Other Minds: Perspectives from Autism* (eds S. Baron-Cohen, H. Tager-Flushberg & D. J. Cohen). Oxford: Oxford Medical Publications.

Trevarthen, C., Aitken, K., Papoudi, D., *et al* (1996) *Children with Autism: Diagnosis and Interventions to Meet their Needs*. London: Jessica Kingsley.

Turk, J. (1992) The fragile X syndrome: on the way to a behavioural phenotype. *British Journal of Psychiatry*, **160**, 24–35.

—— (1995) Fragile X syndrome. *Archives of Disease in Childhood*, **72**, 4–5.

Wing, L. (ed.) (1988) *Aspects of Autism: Biological Research.* London: Gaskell/ The National Autistic Society.

—— (1991) The relationship between Asperger's syndrome and Kanner's autism. In *Autism and Asperger Syndrome* (ed. U. Frith). Cambridge: Cambridge University Press.

—— (1996) *The Autistic Spectrum: A Guide for Parents and Professionals.* London: Constable.

—— & Gould, J. (1979) Severe impairments of social interaction and associated abnormalities in children: epidemiology and classification. *Journal of Autism and Childhood Schizophrenia*, **9**, 11–29.

Zilbovicius, M., Garreau, B., Samson, Y., *et al* (1995) Delayed maturation of the frontal cortex in childhood autism. *American Journal of Psychiatry*, **152**, 248–252.

8 Psychiatric disorders and mild learning disability

David Wilson

Prevalence data ● *Assessment* ● *Conclusions*

"So the desperate search for self-esteem continues. The ex-patients strive to cover themselves with a protective cloak of competence. To their own satisfaction they locate such coverings, but the cloaks that they think protect them are in reality such tattered and transparent garments that they reveal their wearers in all their naked incompetence." (Edgerton, 1993)

The psychiatrist working with people with mild learning disabilities needs to understand that this group of people are not a homogeneous group in intellectual, physical, social or cultural characteristics. A person with mild learning disabilities is a thinking and feeling individual who, like everyone else, has emotional problems and social difficulties

There is no easy way to define this population of people, and intellectual ability is just one of many variables which act together to determine the social functioning of an individual at a particular time in their lives. There are enormous difficulties in identifying this group of people. Specialist learning disability services will connect with some of these people, but general psychiatrists will also treat many people with mild learning disabilities almost without realising it.

There is probably another sizeable group who fail to receive any service at all because the particular characteristics of their presentation are not fully understood.

Little literature is available to help us understand what it is like to have a mild learning disability. However, Edgerton's work in California has provided valuable insights. His book *The Cloak of Competence* (Edgerton, 1967; revised in 1993) describes in some detail the behaviour of 48 men and women who were discharged from a State hospital in California in the early 1960s. He astutely observed how people developed the skill of 'passing for normal' and of 'denying their handicap' as a way of coping with the social isolation and rejection. A key factor in a successful strategy for survival was the ability to locate a 'benefactor' – an individual who would give help and support and be contactable if a crisis arose. Ten years later Edgerton managed to follow up 30 of the original cohort. For most of the group 'passing for normal' had become less of a central issue, as had paid work. The group were now more interested in leisure, friends, hobbies and having a good time (Edgerton & Bercovici, 1976). In a third study in 1982 he was only able to trace 21 of the original group. In this admittedly unrepresentative group his overwhelming impression was of a set of people with 'unshakeable optimism' who had kept going against the odds over the previous 20 years (Edgerton *et al*, 1993).

There is a growing body of evidence that people with mild learning disabilities are aware of stigmatisation. Szivos has suggested that denial or 'passing' may not be the most useful strategy for people with mild learning disabilities. She uses the paradigm of "loss" and "consciousness raising" in attempting to construct a more positive group identity based on being different. Other stigmatised groups have found it useful to 'own' the stigma, whether it be gender, colour or sexual orientation. Although the early aims of consciousness-raising were political and involved bringing attention to the ways in which stigmatised people were subjected to prejudice and exploitation, the approach can also be therapeutic (Szivos & Griffiths, 1992).

What is so different about people with mild learning disabilities who present with psychiatric disorders? Firstly, because they may be more dependent, it may well be that they are brought to services, rather than seeking help themselves. Parents or carers may bring them to services expecting "something to be done". The attitudes of the family or carers may be angry due to the extra burden of care that an already somewhat dependent person creates when they are further disabled by mental disorder. Because the person with mild learning disabilities is very likely to have unsophisticated communication skills, the family or carers may have great difficulty in understanding the changes produced by the mental disorder and see the individual as stubborn or uncooperative. The person with mild learning disabilities may be quite incapable of communicating their pain and distress without acting-out behaviour, which may further anger their carers. Because of this communication problem it is quite usual for psychiatric disorder to present very late in people with mild learning disabilities.

Prevalence data

Holland & Murphy (1990) have reviewed the literature in a thoughtful way and have pointed out the many pitfalls in attempting to assess the prevalence of psychiatric and behaviour disorder in people with mild learning disabilities. Many studies have reported rates of psychiatric disorder as 25–50% (Ballinger & Reid, 1977; Lund, 1985; Reiss, 1990). Even studies based on population registers are unlikely to be able to ascertain the base rate in people with mild learning disabilities because the true prevalence of this group is unlikely to be known. Rutter *et al*

(1970) in their Isle of Wight study did use a total population and reported rates of nearly 40% in a brain-damaged group of children, compared with just under 7% in their control group. Corbett (1979) found comparable rates of psychiatric disorder in a Camberwell population of people with mild and severe learning disabilities, although the true number of people with mild learning disabilities was not known because of the difficulties of ascertainment after school leaving age. Other studies suggest that the people with mild learning disabilities who remain in touch with services are those who have other disabilities and needs, implying that this may cause an overestimate of the prevalence in this group if only an administrative prevalence is known. Other methodological difficulties arise in studies, either because of their failure to use clearly defined diagnostic criteria, or when appropriate criteria are used, many of the subjects lack the sophisticated language ability to describe abnormal mental phenomena.

Given these difficulties the lifetime prevalence of schizophrenia has been reported to be 2–3% compared with the lifetime prevalence of 1% in the general population (Reid, 1972*b*). The lifetime rates for manic–depressive psychosis have been reported to be 1–2% (Reid, 1972*a*).

Many different terms have been used to refer to disordered behaviour in people with mild learning disabilities. Many of these terms imply a difference between the behaviour of people with mild learning disabilities and the general population. The term that has found some favour is 'challenging behaviour' which is based more on a social constructionist framework. This locates the problem more within a system, than in an individual with mild mental learning disabilities (Emerson *et al*, 1988; see chapter 4).

Reported rates of behaviour disorder have ranged between 3% and 27%, which again highlights the difficulties of definition of behaviour disorder and an inability to study the whole population.

The reasons for the apparent increased prevalence rates in people with mild learning disabilities are unclear. Underlying abnormalities of brain structure and function are probably important, as are the high rates of seizure disorder as well as social and psychological factors.

There are few discussions in the literature about the degree of overlap between psychiatric and behavioural disorders. However, it is clear that people with mild learning disabilities may present with a behaviour problem as a result of a psychiatric disorder such as depression. Equally they could present with a behaviour disorder without being psychiatrically ill.

Assessment

The assessment of psychiatric disorder in people with mild learning disabilities makes high demands on the interviewer's communication skills.

Not only must the interviewer be a good listener but they must also be empathic and intuitive. It is always helpful to begin by meeting the person who has been referred for assessment. They may have little to say for themselves and may come with others such as carers or family members. Although it may be tempting to allow the carers to voice their opinions first, it is usually best to enable the person with learning disabilities to start by telling their own story. However, it is often difficult to capture the attention of a person with learning disabilities who may be frightened or alarmed by the situation. It is helpful if the interview can be conducted in a quiet room where there are no distractions. On occasions a person will arrive for an interview in a distressed state and it is important to ensure that they are not thirsty or wanting to go to the toilet. It is best to sit opposite the person, so that the interviewer is on the same level and each party can see the other's face. If they usually wear glasses or have a hearing aid it is important that they have such aids available.

The interview should begin with brief introductions and the interviewer should make some personal contribution to the interchange. It is wise for the interviewer to give some idea about the intended purpose of the interview. The interviewer should speak clearly, slowly and precisely, avoiding complex words. Once the interviewer has established some degree of rapport more detailed questioning can begin. Open questions are usually best for eliciting accurate responses, but if the person is shy or reluctant they may not respond at all. If open questions are unsuccessful the next stage is to use closed questions providing two or three options for reply. If these fail to elicit a response, neutral comments and general statements may do so. Leading questions should be avoided.

The interviewer may need to meet the person several times before they feel comfortable in the interview situation. It is often useful to have paper and pencil available for the person's use. Drawing or writing a word they have difficulty articulating may help shared understanding. After taking the history and making a mental state examination it will then be important to take collateral histories from others who know the person well. Having done this the nature of the problem may still not be clear, and it may be helpful to observe the person in their natural environment. Watching them interacting with others in their own home or in their workshop often opens a new dimension. Because a person with learning disabilities may not be able to give a coherent account of their thoughts and feelings there is always a high chance that they will be misunderstood and that their problems will be poorly diagnosed. Good interviewing techniques are therefore important (Duckworth *et al*, 1993).

Neurotic, personality and behaviour disorders

It is extremely difficult to separate neurotic, personality and behaviour disorders in people with mild learning disabilities. An individual will often show features of all three. It is known that many of this group of people have early lives often marked by abuse, poverty, poor housing, stigmatisation, poor family organisation, and a poor quality of parental care, which sometimes even leads to removal of a child from their family.

Many people with mild learning disabilities acquire reasonably adequate skills in self-care (washing, dressing, cooking and road safety) and have good basic communication skills, but they are sadly lacking in the skills for fostering good interpersonal relationships. They find it extremely difficult to control and express their emotions and have major problems with temper control. They tend to have poor tolerance of frustration and often lack the coping strategies for finding their way round social obstacles.

Psychiatric assessment and management in this group starts with careful exclusion of any other psychotic or organic disorder, and then aims to help the person to learn to make better interpersonal relationships. Many of the issues raised in individuals will relate to extremely low self-esteem. This has its roots in stigma, abuse, poverty, and poor family organisation. Hence starting to provide some structure in someone's life may be helpful. The importance of skills training and sheltered work cannot be over-emphasised.

There is growing interest in the use of various psychotherapeutic interventions when working with people with mild learning disabilities (Black *et al*, 1988; Goldstein, 1988; Sinason, 1992; Waitman & Conboy-Hill, 1992). Behaviour modification techniques so popular 20 years ago have given way to more eclectic packages drawing on both behavioural and cognitive schools of psychology. For example, the issues of stigma have been addressed in group work by Szivos & Griffiths (1992). Anger management techniques have been used and evaluated by Novaco (1975) (see also Benson, 1994). Social skills training has been used with this group of people and found to be helpful. A constant theme in reports of all this work is the poverty of language which people with mild learning disabilities have to describe their emotions, and most interventions will usually need to start by attempting to increase their repertoire of words to describe feelings and emotions.

Case example

John, an 18-year-old man, was excluded from the school for children with mild learning difficulties because of recurrent physical aggression to staff and other pupils. After he was excluded from school he returned home and smashed doors and windows in the family home, and threatened his GP with a bread knife when he visited the house. John is the illegitimate child of a woman with mild learning disabilities. She married a man with temper control and alcohol problems and produced a further five children who all live in the family home. John was developmentally delayed but no specific cause was ever established for this; from the time of school entry he had major problems with temper control. After an initial period of assessment in a therapeutic living unit he took part in a package which included skills training, anger management training, social skills training and individual psychotherapy. After two years he moved on to a supported lodging house but is unable to find paid work.

Pervasive developmental disorders

Chapter 5 examines these disorders and the issues they raise. However, there are a number of issues which are important to consider in people with mild learning disabilities. Arguments in the literature about the spectrum concept apart, clinicians will come across people with peculiar disorders of social interaction who are mildly learning disabled. These are probably the people who Asperger first described. Gillberg (1990) has suggested research criteria for Asperger's syndrome: social impairment (extreme egocentricity), narrow interest, repetitive routines, speech and language peculiarities, non-verbal communication problems, and motor clumsiness. It has been suggested that the basic deficit might be the lack of 'theory of mind', i.e. people with pervasive developmental disorder cannot conceive of other people having minds. They would therefore be expected to show low concern for the thoughts and feelings of other people, be lacking in their capacity to reciprocate social interaction, have poor language skills, and to rely on rote memory skills and a set of predictable routines.

People with Asperger's syndrome have the deficits described above, but they also seem to be at high risk of developing additional emotional disorders. This fact is rarely grasped by clinicians, and lack of knowledge of this association can cause confusion in clinicians' minds. The apparently high prevalence of people with schizophrenia in many studies may well be due to the fact that people with disorders of social interaction with a mental disorder superimposed have been misdiagnosed as schizophrenic.

The management of this group requires a particular kind of empathy from staff who must be capable of accepting the devastating and incurable central deficit, and working to adapt their own behaviour and the environment to make the world a more hospitable place for this group of people. Work and living environments need to provide a predictable shape to the day. People also need a chance to withdraw when interpersonal interaction becomes too arousing.

Case example

Pat presented to psychiatric services because she was exhibiting acting-out behaviour at the residential setting where she lived. This was a small staffed house which provided support for people with autism. She had started to abscond into the town and had been reported to the police for shouting at strangers, undressing in a lorry park, and pulling up flowers from local gardens. Pat was the seventh child of a poor but very close-knit and caring family. She had been diagnosed as having autism at the age of three years and had attended specialist schools, but had progressed very well with acquisition of extremely good communication skills. Although her academic progress at school had been good she had had recurrent interpersonal problems which often resulted in physical aggression to other people. Pat's mother had died three months before her presentation. After a period of in-patient assessment she was felt to have many unresolved feelings about her mother's death. Individual sessions using guided mourning techniques helped her to feel better and dramatically reduced the frequency of her acting-out behaviours.

Affective disorders

There is little doubt that the symptoms of depression are often not recognised in people with mild learning disabilities. It is therefore necessary to have a high index of suspicion for the disorder in all people with mild learning disabilities presenting with changes in behaviour. With careful investigation the symptoms of increasing social withdrawal, loss of interests, slowing of psychomotor activity, loss of appetite and sleep disturbance can usually be identified. Uncharacteristic 'acting-out' behaviour should always alert a clinician to the possibility of depression.

Mania is best recognised by comparing the person's normal behaviour with that which they exhibit during a period of instability. A rise in motor activity and intrusiveness, assaultiveness, destructiveness and self-abuse are usually seen. Confusion, cognitive impairment and hallucinations may occur in mania. Some authors have commented that family and staff working with people with mild learning disabilities often overlook mania, particularly if the person is likeable and not aggressive.

Treatment of affective disorders in people with mild learning disabilities should follow similar lines to those used in the general population. In people with brain damage drugs should be started in small dosages and increased slowly. There are no contraindications to the use of lithium or electroconvulsive therapy in people with mild learning disabilities. Reassurance and supportive psychotherapy are particularly.

Case example

Heather is a 23-year-old woman with mild learning disabilities due to Sotos syndrome. She lived with her parents with whom she had a good relationship. She had a good social network, both near her home and at work in a sheltered workshop. She had a good work record and was highly valued by her colleagues at work. Heather presented to psychiatric services as an emergency having attacked her mother with a frying pan and pinned her to the floor. She exhibited uncontrollable screaming and crying. Careful history-taking revealed that she had become slowly and insidiously more withdrawn over the previous six months. She still attended work but was less outgoing. She had stopped calling on friends on the way home, and she had stopped knitting, which was a hobby. She also admitted to early morning waking for the previous six weeks. All these changes probably started shortly after the marriage of her older sister who then moved to another town 60 miles away. A period of in-patient treatment with supportive psychotherapy tempered with recurrent reassurance and tricyclic antidepressants led to a slow recovery of mood and agitation. Within three months she was markedly improved, but it took 12 months for her to return to her premorbid level of functioning and come to terms with the 'loss' of her sister.

Schizophrenia and paranoid psychosis

The interrelationship between schizophrenia and mild learning disabilities has always been of interest to clinicians. Kraepelin originally held the view that mental retardation might form the basis for the development of other psychoses, but later changed his mind and agreed with Bleuler that the association between schizophrenia and mental retardation was random.

The diagnosis of schizophrenia in people with mild learning disabilities can be difficult because of their inability to describe their internal world. Diagnosis of the condition is, however, based upon the discovery of first-rank symptoms such as primary delusions, passivity experiences, and hallucinations. People who have a schizophrenic illness are also likely to show changes in energy, volition, social interaction and mood. These changes occur in a state of clear consciousness. Meadows *et al* (1991) compared 25 people with mild learning disabilities with 26 people of average intelligence who also suffered with schizophrenia. The people with mild learning disabilities had an earlier onset and were less likely to have been married or employed. However, the clinical phenomena exhibited by the two groups, as elicited by a SADS-L interview, were very similar.

Paranoid psychosis is characterised more by an affect of anger, grievance and irritability. There is often a marked depressive component. Delusions tend to be persecutory and involve family, neighbours and staff. Delusions may have a sexual or erotic content. Auditory hallucinations are common and voices accuse, sneer and criticise. The person's behaviour can often be disturbed and aggressive.

The management of schizophrenia in people with mild learning disabilities is no different than in the general population. Neuroleptic drugs should be used in small doses to start with and built up depending upon response. People with mild learning disabilities may have difficulty reporting side-effects of drugs and these should be monitored carefully. It is difficult to know whether movement disorders are more common in people with mild learning disabilities. Attempts to manipulate the person's environment would also be similar to those in the general population, aiming at reduction of expressed emotion in their carers.

Organic psychosis

Organic psychosis of any type can occur in people with mild learning disabilities. Structural brain damage is probably common so that one might expect a high prevalence of delirium, dementia and epilepsy.

There is nothing distinctive about delirious reactions in people with mild learning disabilities. People with mild learning disabilities are particularly susceptible to drugs, alcohol and biochemical change. Delirium is characterised by clouding of consciousness, particularly at night, disorientation, impairment of memory, illusions, visual hallucinations, and fearfulness. Attention and concentration are impaired, with paranoid misrepresentations and fleeting delusions. Behaviour is often very disturbed with impulsive aggression.

Dementias of all types can occur in people with mild learning disabilities. The presentation is essentially similar to that in people of normal intelligence. However, cognitive testing can sometimes present dilemmas; is the apparent cognitive defect a loss, or did the person never have that ability in the first place? For example, a person may never have known the days of the week or the name of the Queen, or they may have lost the ability to recall the memory because of some dementing process. If a person is being seen for the first time it may be quite impossible to decide from an interview, but taking a collateral history may be helpful. It is also extremely important that the results of a clinician's attempts to examine the cognitive state are clearly recorded, to provide useful information when reassessment takes place at a later date, when it may be possible to show evidence of deterioration.

The medical and psychiatric investigation of dementia in people with mild learning disabilities is no different from that in the general population. The association between Down's syndrome and dementia is covered in chapter six; epilepsy in people with learning disabilities in chapter 12.

Conclusion

Working with people with mild learning disabilities who have emotional disorders provides the psychiatrist with particular challenges. Booth & Booth (1996) point out that although people with learning disabilities often lack verbal fluency their inarticulateness goes beyond shyness, anxiety or natural reserve. While their difficulties in communication may originate in their restricted language skills, their inability to make themselves understood is made more difficult by their low self-esteem, learned habits of compliance (Sigelman *et al*, 1981), social isolation, loneliness and sense of being oppressed. Psychiatrists need to pay special attention to their own communication skills if they are to engage in fruitful dialogue. They will need the time to gain insight and information from a variety of other people as well as the patient. Above all they will need tenacity, as the situation is often complex and confusing at the beginning of an intervention.

References

Ballinger, B. R. & Reid, A. H. (1977) Psychiatric disorder in an adult training centre and a hospital for the mentally handicapped. *Psychological Medicine*, **7**, 525–528.

Benson, B. A. (1994) Anger management training: a self control programme for persons with mild mental retardation. In *Mental Health in Mental Retardation* (ed. N. Bouras), pp. 224–232. Cambridge: Cambridge University Press.

Black, L., Cullen, C., Dickens, P., *et al* (1988) Anger control. *British Journal of Hospital Medicine*, **133**, 1124–1128.

Booth, T. & Booth, W. (1996) Sounds of silence: narrative research with inarticulate subjects. *Disability and Society*, **11**, 55–69.

Corbett, J. (1979) Psychiatric morbidity and mental retardation. In *Psychiatric Illness and Mental Handicap* (eds F. E. James & R. P. Snaith), pp. 11–25. London: Gaskell.

Duckworth, M. S., Radhakrishnan, G., Nolan, M. E., *et al* (1993) Initial encounters between people with a mild mental handicap and psychiatrist: an investigation of a method of evaluating interview skills. *Journal of Intellectual Disability Research*, **37**, 263–276.

Edgerton, R. B. (1993) *The Cloak of Competence: Revised and Updated.* Berkeley: University of California Press.

—— & Bercovici, S. M. (1976) The Cloak of Competence: years later. *American Journal of Mental Deficiency*, **80**, 485–497.

Emerson, E., Cummings, R., Barrett, S., *et al* (1988) Challenging behaviour and community services: who are the people who challenge services. *Mental Handicap*, **16**, 16–19.

Gillberg, C. (1990) What is autism? *International Review of Psychiatry*, **2**, 61–66.

Goldstein, A. P. (1988) *The Prepare Curriculum: Teaching Pro-Social Competences.* Champaign, Illinois: Research Press.

Holland, T. & Murphy, G. (1990) Behavioural and psychiatric disorder in adults with mild learning difficulties. *International Review of Psychiatry*, **2**, 117–136.

Lund, J. (1985) Prevalence of psychiatric morbidity in mentally retarded. *Acta Psychiatrica Scandinavica*, **72**, 563–570.

Meadows, G., Turner, T., Campbell, L., *et al* (1991) Assessing schizophrenia in adults with mental retardation: a comparative study. *British Journal of Psychiatry*, **158**, 103–105.

Novaco, R. W. (1975) *Anger Control: the Development and Evaluation of an Experimental Treatment.* Lexington, MA: Lexington Books.

Reid, A. (1972*a*) Psychoses in mental defectives. I. Manic depressive psychosis. *British Journal of Psychiatry*, **120**, 205–212.

—— (1972*b*) Psychoses in mental defectives. II. Schizophrenic and paranoid psychoses. *British Journal of Psychiatry*, **120**, 213–218.

Reiss, S. (1990) Prevalence of dual diagnosis in community based day programs in the Chicago Metropolitan Area. *American Journal on Mental Retardation*, **94**, 578–585.

Rutter, M., Graham, P. & Yule, W. (1970) *A Neuropsychiatric Study in Childhood*. Clinics in Developmental Medicine No. 35/36. London: Spastics International Medical Publications/Heinemann.

Sigelman, C., Budd, E., Spanhel, C., *et al* (1981) When in doubt, say 'Yes': acquiescence in interviews with mentally retarded persons. *Mental Retardation*, April, 53–58.

Sinason, V. (1992) *Mental Handicap, the Human Condition: New Approaches from the Tavistock*. London: Free Association Books.

Szivos, S. E. & Griffiths, E. (1992) Coming to terms with learning difficulties: the effects of groupwork and group processes on stigmatized identities. In *Psychotherapy and Mental Handicap* (eds A. Waitman & S. Conboy-Hill). London: Sage.

Waitman, A. & Conboy-Hill, S. (eds) (1992) *Psychotherapy and Mental Handicap*. London: Sage.

Additional reading

Reid, A. (1982) *The Psychiatry of Mental Handicap*. Oxford: Blackwell Scientific.

Russell, O. (1985) *Mental Handicap*. Edinburgh: Churchill Livingstone.

9 Psychiatric problems in elderly people with learning disabilities

Richard Collacott

Epidemiology ● *Dementia* ● *Differential diagnosis* ● *Dependency needs and service provision*

The increasing proportion of elderly people in the general population has been reflected in those with learning disabilities, as a result of their increased longevity. It would appear that early mortality is a feature of those who are more severely disabled, while those who are less impaired have a life expectancy approaching that of the general population. In the older age ranges, the overall prevalence of psychiatric disorder diminishes. This is largely because in this group behaviour disorders are seen less frequently, behaviour disorder being more prevalent in those with severe learning disabilities.

However, because of the absolute increase in the number of elderly people with learning disabilities, the psychiatrist's work is concerned increasingly with the diagnosis and management of mental disorders in this group. In addition, individuals with Down's syndrome, which is the most common genetically determined condition giving rise to a severe learning disability, are particularly vulnerable to dementing conditions, predominantly Alzheimer's disease. However, while a diagnosis of Alzheimer's disease may currently preclude the opportunity for cure (rather than care), such individuals are also susceptible to other disorders, such as depression and hypothyroidism, which may mimic a dementing process but are eminently treatable.

The care of the elderly person with a learning disability requires input from the primary and secondary healthcare services. Such care will be concerned with maintaining an individual's physical and mental health as well as their social well-being. It must take into account their needs for appropriate residential placement, vocational, leisure, social and recreational opportunities.

Epidemiology

The provision of appropriate services for elderly people with learning disabilities requires accurate information. Estimates of the prevalence of older people with learning disability have given rise, however, to widely

136

divergent statistics, as a result of largely unresolved methodological difficulties. To measure the true prevalence of learning disability in relation to age requires a clear and rigorously applied definition of the population under consideration. However, there is unfortunately a lack of a commonly agreed definition of learning disability, which is essentially defined by social criteria. Even where IQ is employed as one criterion for learning disability, as in the American Association on Mental Retardation classification system, some measure of social adaptation is invariably employed. Disagreement is greatest with individuals of mild or borderline degrees of learning disability, who are more numerous than those of other categories. Studies that focus on individuals with severe or profound learning disability, as opposed to borderline or mild, tend to yield more reliable estimates, since this population is more readily recognised.

Another difficulty in estimating the prevalence of older people with learning disability is that of surveying the client population in such a way that no group of individuals who should be included is overlooked. This represents a particular logistical difficulty when surveying individuals who live in the community.

A third major difficulty is more semantic and refers to the difficulty of defining 'elderly' or 'old' for this population. Many service providers consider that a lower age of entry should be employed in the case of people with a learning disability than in the general population. Accordingly, while some studies have used the traditional demarcation line of 65 years for defining this group, others have employed 55, 50, 45 and even 40 years as the definitive age. However, philosophically it must be borne in mind that in the absence of a universally accepted index of ageing, any age criterion is essentially arbitrary. Great caution must, therefore, be employed in using or comparing statistical data of this kind.

The life expectancy of individuals who have a learning disability appears to have increased considerably over the past 50 years, although their longevity is not, in general, as great as that of the rest of the population. It should be recognised, however, that many studies on longevity in people with learning disabilities are drawn from studies of institutional populations, which may not reflect the true situation. Additionally, the indices employed have frequently included crude death rates, median age or mean age at death. These measures of mortality, although useful, are affected by the age distribution of the institutional population, and provide a false indication of mortality or life expectancy. Administrative practices that reduce the admission of young children into an institution, and the recent decline in the size of the institutional population through the selective de-institutionalisation of the younger and less seriously handicapped individuals, makes the interpretation of such data extremely difficult.

Carter & Jancar (1983) studied deaths in learning disability hospitals in Bristol, UK, between 1930 and 1980. They showed that the average age at death had increased from 15 to 58 years for men and from 22 to 60 years for women during this period. During the first 25-year period, 99% of men and 93% of women died before the age of 50. During the period 1955–1980, only 57% of men and 40% of women died before this age.

Wolf & Wright (1987) studied the life expectancy of institutionalised people with learning disabilities in Canada between 1966 and 1978. A 17% reduction in the number of people resident in institutions occurred over this period. However, the proportion of residents who were more severely handicapped increased, as did the mean age of the institutional population. The crude death rate fell for the institutional population, and this was associated with an increase in the mean age at death from 32 to 37 years for men, and from 33 to 38 years for women. Nevertheless, the crude death rate for residents with learning disabilities was still twice that of the general population. After the age of five years had been reached, the additional number of years that a person with learning disabilities could expect to live had increased from 44 to 46 years over this 12-year period.

Life expectancy is influenced by the severity of learning disability. Having reached the age of five years, a profoundly handicapped individual can expect to live a further 35 years, whereas a person with borderline learning disability can expect to live a further 53 years. Studies in the UK have demonstrated that two-thirds of people with learning disabilities who survive to 65 years of age have a mild or moderate disability, compared with only a third of those aged between 15 and 64 years. Additionally, in the over-65-year-old age group there are twice as many women compared with men (Day, 1987).

Mortality data for individuals with Down's syndrome indicate a shorter lifespan than for other people with learning disabilities. As a result of changed practices in the management of congenital heart disease and infection, 80% now survive to the age of five years. While the death rate in Down's syndrome is still high in early childhood, it falls to a lower level in early adulthood, only to rise rapidly in the middle years. The death rate at age 10 years is 2.65 times that of the general population; by the age of 50 years, however, the comparative death rate is 40 times greater. Relatively few people with Down's syndrome survive into the seventh and subsequent decades.

Prevalence of psychiatric disorders

In the general adult population, the use of and need for mental health services increases with advancing years. However, the take-up rate for psychiatric services by people with learning disabilities is paradoxically low. A study from Northumberland (Day, 1985) showed that there is a progressive fall in the proportion of long-stay hospital in-patients with psychiatric disorders, as a function of age; prevalence rates for age-related cohorts 40–49, 50–59, 60–69, and 70+ years, were found to be 48.7%, 30.3%, 25.2% and 16.7% respectively. This was particularly the case for behaviour disorders, where the prevalence was 29%, 18.2%, 9.1%, and 4.2% respectively. A similar decline was seen in neurotic disorders, with prevalence rates of 2.3%, 2.0%, 1% and 0%. Since behaviour disorders are more associated with severe learning disability and male sex, this finding may be explained on the basis of the observed differential mortality of this group. Overall prevalence rates of paranoid psychoses and affective disorders appear to remain constant throughout such age-related cohorts. The prevalence of dementia increases with age, particularly in individuals with Down's syndrome.

Among acute admissions of psychiatrically disturbed people with learning disabilities to hospital, three-quarters have a mild disability. Two-thirds of acute admissions consist equally of individuals with either behaviour/personality disorders or with neurotic disorders. A fifth of admissions represent functional psychosis, and 10% organic states. This is in contrast to prevalence studies among hospital long-stay patients. Sixty per cent of admissions show evidence of cerebral pathology. In individuals admitted with behaviour disorders, the problem usually dates from adolescence, and the antisocial conduct occurs on the basis of a longstanding personality disorder, usually associated with gross psychosocial deprivation during childhood. It is believed that in people with learning disabilities, brain damage and a failure of maturation, as well as environmental factors such as a lack of suitable learning opportunities, inappropriate models and faulty management, play an important sustaining role.

The high prevalence of neurotic disorders among acute admissions for psychiatric treatment lends support to the belief that people with learning disabilities resident in the community, far from living a stress-free life, are subject to the normal stresses and strains experienced by others. In addition, they may have to cope with the stigma and social consequences of their handicap.

Dementia

Diagnostic criteria

In individuals with a mild or borderline learning disability, dementia may be diagnosed using standard diagnostic criteria, for example those employed by ICD–10 or DSM–IV. However, in individuals with greater degrees of learning disability, such classification systems may be less useful, since many of the characteristic symptoms and signs of such systems are a feature of learning disability itself. In addition, people with learning disabilities frequently possess deficits in communication, which make formal standardised psychiatric interview techniques inappropriate. In individuals with severe learning disability, the diagnosis of mental disorder has perforce to be made on the accurate observation of behaviour, taking particular account of changes that may have occurred over a determined time-scale from a pre-existing state. Based on DSM–IV criteria, dementia in individuals with learning disability may be operatively defined when the conditions listed in Box 9.1 are met.

Alzheimer's disease

Alzheimer's disease occurs in ageing people with learning disabilities at the same rate as in the general population, with the exception of individuals with Down's syndrome. Several authors have demonstrated that all individuals with Down's syndrome who come to autopsy after the age of 40 years demonstrate Alzheimer's disease. In several instances such changes have also been reported during the second decade. The pathological changes seen in the general population – lowering of brain weight, enlargement of cerebral ventricles, neuronal loss, senile plaques, neurofibrillary change, and granulovacuolar degeneration are seen in individuals with Down's syndrome. Similar neurotransmitter changes including reduced activities of acetylcholine, acetylcholinesterase and choline acetyl-transferase, together with widespread monoamine deficits, have also been reported in such individuals. However, such studies, being

---

Box 9.1 Criteria for a diagnosis of dementia in people with learning disabilities

(a) A global deterioration in self-care skills
(b) A change in personality (for example, the development of apathy, social withdrawal, hostility, etc.)
(c) The disturbance in (a) or (b) has led to a significant deterioration in work, social activities, or relationships with others
(d) Such changes do not occur exclusively during the course of delirium
(e) Either (i) or (ii):
(i) There is evidence from the history, physical examination or laboratory tests of a specific organic factor, that is judged to be aetiologically related to the disturbance
(ii) In the absence of such evidence, an aetiological factor can be presumed, if the change cannot be accounted for by any non-organic mental disorder (for example, depression, schizophrenia, etc.)

based on post-mortem material, may exaggerate the risks of developing Alzheimer's disease, since Alzheimer's disease is itself associated with increased mortality. Only a third of elderly individuals with Down's syndrome show clinical evidence of a dementing process.

Aetiology in Down's syndrome

Our understanding of the aetiology of Alzheimer's disease in individuals with Down's syndrome is currently fragmentary. It is believed that Alzheimer's disease represents the outcome of both inherited and environmental or exogenous factors. The nature of such exogenous factors is unclear, while evidence supports, to a limited extent, the implication of aluminium toxicity or viral components. The genes that code for familial Alzheimer's disease and for b-amyloid have been localised to a region on the long arm of chromosome 21. However, such sites lie some distance from the area of chromosome 21 which represents the obligatory Down's syndrome site. The distal segment of the long arm of chromosome 21 also encodes the gene for cytoplasmic superoxide dismutase (SOD). Whether the elevated levels of SOD found in Down's syndrome contribute to accelerated ageing is unknown. The intracellular concentrations of peroxide and SOD are potentially capable of pathological interaction with many structural cell elements such as proteins, lipids and polynucleotides, and have been implicated in premature ageing.

Clinical findings in demented individuals with Down's syndrome

Serial examinations of dementing Down's syndrome individuals demonstrate a progressive decline in short- and long-term memory and orientation comparable with changes seen in the general population (Das & Mishra, 1995). Personality change is a frequent presenting symptom, and while not uniformly found, apathy, withdrawal and irritability may be seen. Examinations of older individuals compared with young individuals with Down's syndrome have demonstrated significant impairments in language, visuospatial skills, visual recognition and attention-span – which have been attributed to Alzheimer's disease. Large cross-sectional cohort studies have demonstrated global deterioration in self-care skills and IQ score with age. However, such changes have not become apparent until after 50 years of age. It is believed that, in spite of the histopathological studies, clinical evidence of a dementing process occurs in only a third of individuals with Down's syndrome. The age of onset of clinical dementia is thought to be variable, as is its rate of progression. The changes that are recognised frequently represent advanced stages of Alzheimer's disease, the earliest stages passing unnoticed. The cryptic nature of such early stages has been attributed to the fact that relatively few demands are placed on individuals with Down's syndrome. Their lives tend to be organised in a repetitive and ordinary basis, which may not permit the early stages of Alzheimer's disease to be demonstrated.

As in the general population, the terminal stages of Alzheimer's disease may be associated with abnormal neurological signs. In this group, increased muscle tone, hyper-reflexia and the emergence of snout, palmomental and Hoffman reflexes may be seen. Epilepsy developing for the first time in Down's syndrome individuals over 35 years of age is usually associated with Alzheimer's disease. It is important that such seizures are managed appropriately, since many anticonvulsants, and particularly phenytoin, may be associated with cognitive decline. Such adverse effects are less apparent with sodium valproate and carbamazepine.

Investigations

There are no simple laboratory investigations that are diagnostic of Alzheimer's disease in people with learning disabilities. However, all individuals in whom a dementing process is suspected should receive a full physical examination. Venous blood should be taken for full blood count and indices, biochemistry, thyroid function tests, vitamin B12 and folic acid levels. A urine specimen should be sent for microscopy and culture. Macrocytosis, due to abnormal erythrocyte membrane components, is frequently seen in Down's syndrome, in the presence of normal vitamin B12 and folic acid levels. An elevated TSH concentration in the presence of normal T3 and T4 levels may represent borderline hypothyroidism. However, in the elderly general population such a pattern of thyroid function test results has been shown to be associated with Alzheimer's disease (Christie *et al*, 1987). There is some evidence that a similar pattern of thyroid function occurs in dementing individuals with Down's syndrome.

Differential diagnosis

Multi-infarct dementia

While there is an extensive range of possible causes for dementing processes in the general adult population, overwhelmingly most cases are due to Alzheimer's disease, multi-infarct dementia, or a combination of both. While other people with learning disabilities may be at risk of multi-infarct dementia, this is rare in those with Down's syndrome. The reasons for this are obscure. It is possible that this is because even now, relatively few reach the age group at risk. Vascular disease is uncommon in those with Down's syndrome, which has been considered an atheroma-free model (Murdoch *et al*, 1977*b*). Few individuals with Down's syndrome have hypertension, and population studies show that blood pressures are significantly reduced in this group (Richards & Enver, 1979). People with Down's syndrome may smoke fewer cigarettes than the general population. However, they have an increased prevalence of embolic sources, owing to congenital heart disease, and they are frequently overweight.

Hypothyroidism

Hypothyroidism is frequently associated with Down's syndrome but is also found in other people with learning disabilities. As part of a constellation of congenital defects, the thyroid gland in Down's syndrome individuals is small. Thyroid autoantibodies are common in Down's syndrome children (and indeed in their mothers). Approximately 20% of Down's syndrome adults aged over 40 years show evidence of abnormal thyroid function tests. It is considered that the congenitally hypoplastic thyroid gland is able to maintain T3 and T4 levels within the low normal range during early life. However, the emergence of additional factors such as thyroid autoimmunity in those with precarious thyroid function leads to gross thyroid failure more readily than in subjects with normal thyroid reserve (Murdoch *et al*, 1977*a*).

The clinical features of hypothyroidism such as slow reflexes, puffy dry skin, brittle nails, sparse hair, increased body weight and brachycardia are found as part of Down's syndrome. Investigation has shown that the evaluation of hypothyroidism in this group, based solely on clinical grounds, is unreliable (Mani, 1988). Accordingly individuals with Down's syndrome should be screened regularly for hypothyroidism (Prasher, 1995). Such a screening programme can be assisted through the development of a local learning disability register.

Hypothyroidism is associated with mental lethargy, dulling of the personality and slowing of cognitive function. Memory is affected at an early stage with failure to register events, and forgetfulness for day-to-day happenings. Further progress of hypothyroidism leads to an inability to sustain mental exertion, with slowness of uptake and grasp. Loss of interest and initiative and the emergence of apathy occur. Self-care and other skills are lost. Some individuals become markedly agitated or aggressive.

In the general population the response to treatment has been considered to be good if treatment is commenced within two years of the onset of hypothyroidism. Thereafter, measurable deficits in intellect and memory may remain, even after the patient has been rendered euthyroid. Functional mental illness in association with hypothyroidism has a less certain outcome with replacement therapy.

Outcome studies of the effect of thyroid replacement therapy in hypothyroid individuals with Down's syndrome are limited. While some studies have shown no benefit, when individuals have been assessed on IQ tests, most individuals described have demonstrated increased alertness, reduced apathy and the regaining of self-care skills which had been lost. Presumably such mixed results may be attributed to either coexistent Alzheimer's disease or diagnostic delay.

Depression

Over 10% of individuals with Down's syndrome experience one or more episodes of depressive illness during their lives, and appear to be between two and three times as vulnerable to affective disorders as other people with learning disabilities. People with learning disability have difficulty in reporting their cognitive experiences due to their limited communication skills. Whereas low mood may often be observed or reported, depressive disorders in this group frequently present with pseudodementia. Loss of self-care skills occur in half of Down's syndrome individuals with depression, while apathy and social withdrawal may occur in two-thirds. A third of depressed individuals show evidence of personality change such as the emergence of aggression or agitation. Thought retardation may be misinterpreted as a loss of grasp. Impaired concentration may give rise to apparent memory deficits. Independent life events may precede nearly 40% of depressive episodes. Such affective disorders require supportive psychotherapy and energetic treatment with antidepressant medication.

Eighty per cent of individuals with Down's syndrome who develop depressive illnesses sustain a single episode. This may be of prolonged duration, with half continuing for over two years. In Down's syndrome individuals who sustain recurrent depressive episodes, the duration of each episode is shorter, with 70% resolving within six months. Additionally, at follow-up Down's syndrome individuals who have sustained depressive episodes function less well than their non-depressed peers on measures of adaptive behaviour.

Dependency needs and service provision

In addition to their psychiatric morbidity, older people with learning disabilities are vulnerable to increased physical morbidity. Several studies have demonstrated increased rates of sensory loss, particularly visual and auditory handicaps, with age. Musculoskeletal and associated mobility difficulties increase in frequency and severity. Cardiovascular disease becomes more prominent, with 25% of those aged over 65 years affected. Epilepsy becomes less common in older people with learning disabilities. Presumably this is due to the differential mortality of more severely handicapped people. Apart from epilepsy, neurological disorders are more frequently seen among the elderly. Much physical morbidity is unreported by people with learning disabilities as a result of their poor communication skills and their inability to seek appropriate services for themselves. Additionally, the need for such intervention may be unrecognised by carers. The Royal College of General Practitioners has recently drawn attention to the needs of this group for primary medical care and has suggested that some aspects of screening need to be undertaken proactively.

In the general population it is the informal support system – primarily the family – that provides the bulk of services for the elderly. Because of the efforts of family members, as many as 60% of the extremely impaired elderly live outside institutions. In most cases support is provided by a spouse, or by adult daughters, daughters-in-law or sons. Unlike most elderly, however, ageing individuals with learning disabilities often do not have children or a spouse on whom they can depend for support. In some cases, there are very old parents who still provide some support to the already elderly handicapped person. However, in most cases the family network of a person with learning disability consists of siblings and the children of siblings. Some research on families has suggested that siblings of people with learning disabilities may be at risk of adjustment problems which may impair their ability to provide informal support in adulthood and old age. A common finding is that the percentage of older people with learning disabilities who live with family members is lower in the older age groups.

The increasing life expectancy of people with learning disabilities, and their need for care on account of physical, psychological and psychiatric disabilities, has major implications for the provision of services catering for them. There is a crossflow of policy perspectives affecting older people with learning disabilities. Proponents for services for nonhandicapped elderly people favour the benefits of age-specialised programmes to concentrate professional expertise, and to respond to the well-documented preferences of older people to interact with others of similar age. On the other hand, proponents for services for people with learning disabilities favour the use of community-based learning disability services in order to achieve maximum social, physical and functional integration.

Studies have identified two distinct groups of elderly people with learning disabilities. The first, smaller group, consists mainly of people over the age of 75 years, who have shown significant physical and mental deterioration with age, have high dependency needs, and make considerable demands upon health services (Janicki *et al*, 1996). Their difficulties as an older person completely overshadow the problem of learning disability, and their needs are practically identical to those of the elderly population as a whole. It is considered that this group would probably be more appropriately catered for within services for the elderly (Day, 1987). The second and larger group consists of older people with learning disabilities who are more mentally alert, and who have not developed such mental and physical deterioration. This group may be misplaced in old peoples' homes, alongside much older and incontinent, physically incapacitated, dementing patients. The majority require more support and specialist care (because of their learning disability rather than their age) and should probably continue to be provided for from within the learning disability services. Their needs are for a comprehensive package of residential care, with occupational and recreational activities, which takes account of the process of ageing, but which would enable them to remain as active and engaged as possible.

Nearly 90% of older people with learning disabilities reside in learning disability hospitals, having been admitted many years previously when different care policies for people with learning disabilities were current. It is questionable to what extent the present policy of deinstitutionalisation should apply to them. The majority have remained in this form of care for most of their lives, and have made longstanding relationships with other residents and staff. They may respond badly to the breakdown of established social networks and may be rendered liable to psychiatric disorders as a consequence (James, 1986). Their ability to make an informed choice about future accommodation is unclear. They may respond poorly to the inevitable breakdown of established social networks. Many studies have pointed to the transitional shock that elderly people with learning disabilities experience during the process of deinstitution-alisation.

References

Carter, G. & Jancar, J. (1983) Mortality in the mentally handicapped: a fifty year survey at the Stoke Park Group of Hospitals (1930–1980). *Journal of Mental Deficiency Research*, **27**, 143–156.

Christie, J. E., Whalley, J., Bennie, J., *et al* (1987) Characteristic plasma hormonal changes in Alzheimer's disease. *British Journal of Psychiatry*, **150**, 674–681.

Das, J. P. & Mishra, R. K. (1995) Assessment of cognitive decline associated with aging: a comparison of individuals with Down syndrome and other etiologies. *Research in Developmental Disabilities*, **16**, 11–25.

Day, K. A. (1985) Psychiatric disorder in the middle-aged and elderly mentally handicapped. *British Journal of Psychiatry*, **147**, 660–670.

—— (1987) The elderly mentally handicapped in hospital – a clinical study. *Journal of Mental Deficiency Research*, **31**, 131–146.

James, D. H. (1986) Psychiatric and behavioural disorders amongst older severely mentally handicapped inpatients. *Journal of Mental Deficiency Research*, **30**, 341–345.

Janicki, M. P., Heller, T., Seltzer, G. B., *et al* (1996) Practice guidelines for the clinical assessment and care management of Alzheimer's disease and other dementias among adults with intellectual disability. *Journal of Intellectual Disability Research*, **40**, 374–382.

Mani, C. (1988) Hypothyroidism in Down's syndrome. *British Journal of Psychiatry*, **153**, 102–104.

Murdoch, J. C., Ratcliffe, W. A., McLarty, D. G., *et al* (1977*a*) Thyroid function in adults with Down's syndrome. *Journal of Clinical Endocrinology and Metabolism*, **44**, 453–458.

——, Rodger, J. C., Rao, S. S., *et al* (1977*b*) Down's syndrome – an atheroma-free model. *British Medical Journal*, *ii*, 226.

Prasher, V. P. (1995) Reliability of diagnosing clinical hypothyroidism in adults with Down syndrome. *Australia and New Zealand Journal of Developmental Disabilities*, **20**, 223–233.

Richards, B. W. & Enver, F. (1979) Blood pressure in Down's syndrome. *Journal of Mental Deficiency Research*, **23**, 123–135.

Wolf, L. C. & Wright, R. E. (1987) Changes in life-expectancy of mentally retarded persons in Canadian institutions – a 12 year comparison. *Journal of Mental Deficiency Research*, **31**, 41–59.

Additional reading

Berg, J. M., Holland, A. J. & Karlinsky, H. (eds) (1993) *Alzheimer's Disease, Down's Syndrome and their Relationship*. Oxford: Oxford University Press.

Day, K. & Jancar, J. (1994) Mental and physical health and ageing in mental handicap: a review. *Journal of Intellectual Disability Research*, **38**, 241–256.

Hogg, J. M., Moss, S. & Cooke, D. (1988) *Ageing and Mental Handicap*. London: Croom Helm.

Holland, A. J. & Oliver, C. (1995) Down's syndrome and the links with Alzheimer's disease. *Journal of Neurology, Neurosurgery and Psychiatry*, **59**, 111–114.

Royal College of General Practitioners (1990) *Primary Care for People with a Mental Handicap*. Occasional Paper 47. London: RCGP.

Wisniewski, K. E. & Wisniewski, H. M. (1983) Age associated changes and dementia in Down's syndrome. In *Alzheimer's Disease: The Standard Reference* (ed. B. Reisberg), pp. 319–326. London: Collier MacMillan.

10 Psychiatric problems in people with multiple handicaps and severe disabilities

Andrew H. Reid

Clinical syndromes ● *Psychopharmacological treatment* ● *Alternative treatments* ● *Conclusion*

Multiple handicaps are common in people with severe learning disabilities: for example, problems of deafness, blindness, mobility disorders, epilepsy and incontinence. The prevalence of these disabilities rises with increasing degrees of retardation; Lund (1985) found a lifetime prevalence rate for epilepsy of 40% of 324 such people selected at random from the register of the Danish National Services for the Mentally Retarded.

Deafness and blindness do not *per se* preclude the presence of mental illness, and in the normally intelligent population there is some association between impaired hearing and paranoid syndromes. Deafness, even more than blindness, tends to lead to social isolation, and it is understandable that it should be accompanied by a tendency to misinterpretation which might progress in time to frank mental illness. Kiernan & Moss (1990), however, found no specific associations between psychiatric disorder and deficiencies of vision and hearing among people with learning disabilities.

The relationship of epilepsy to mental disorder is controversial. Concepts of epileptic personality, epileptic psychosis and epileptic dementia have been called into question, but clinicians still encounter cases which meet the original descriptions of these syndromes. Certainly there does seem to be an association between epilepsy and suicide in the general population and between epilepsy and psychiatric disorder in people with learning disabilities. In so far as epilepsy is a reflection of abnormal brain structure or electrophysiological function, it is perhaps not surprising that this should be so.

Language function is also progressively impaired with increasing degrees of learning disability, and people with the most severe degrees of retardation are non-verbal and have very limited powers of communication. Language is the substrate of mental illness and central to such psychopathological phenomena as delusional beliefs, ideas of influence, 'made' experiences and hallucinations. As such it is not possible to confirm the presence of any mental illness in non-verbal people where the diagnostic features are entirely or very substantially dependent on language. Where a diagnosis can be based on observable phenomena, however, this problem can be partially overcome.

The issue is further complicated by the need to distinguish items of maladaptive behaviour from psychiatric disorder. Psychiatric and behavioural indices are not necessarily coterminous. Jacobson (1990) suggested that differences in reported prevalence rates for diagnosed psychiatric disorder in people with learning disabilities may be due to the non-syndromic occurrence of isolated problem behaviours. Certainly many behavioural treatment approaches are, quite correctly, targeted on isolated symptoms.

In general terms, therefore, the presence of brain damage or abnormality, whether reflected in epilepsy, disorders of mobility or language, impairments of communication, levels of activity or social and emotional control, does tend to render people with learning disabilities more vulnerable to psychiatric disorders. These predisposing organic factors summate with social and family issues such as failure to achieve, disappointment, prolonged dependency and stress on carers. It seems likely that, as a result, psychiatric disorder is common in people with learning disabilities, and more common than in the general population. The bulk of the psychopathology, however, consists of neurotic and personality disorders, and challenging behaviour (Reid & Ballinger, 1987), which are often more difficult to classify than the major categories of functional and organic psychosis (see chapter 4).

Clinical syndromes

Affective psychoses

The cardinal diagnostic features of manic and depressive psychoses are alterations in mood in the direction of elation or depression, which are pathological in intensity and duration, and accompanied by mood-related changes in the level of psychomotor activity. These changes in mood and activity levels are not dependent on intelligence, and carers or relatives who know the patient well will be able to identify them, even in patients who are non-verbal. Patients who are verbally competent may be able to describe feelings of sadness or the opposite, and perhaps ideas of guilt or failure, and mood-related delusions and hallucinations. Depression of mood may present with aggressiveness, irritability, or hysterical conversion phenomena, and somatic or hypochondriacal symptoms may be prominent features (Reid, 1972). Suicide and attempted suicide are by no means unknown.

Patients who are manic may present with excitement or impulsivity rather than elation of mood, and it is important to identify the underlying mood change and not dismiss it as a behavioural problem.

In many patients there will be accompanying changes in patterns of sleep, levels of activity, appetite and social responsiveness. These can be a pointer to an underlying affective disorder. Additional evidence for the diagnosis can sometimes be obtained from family histories of mental illness patterns.

Case example 1
Linda is aged 45 with an IQ of around 40. She was sexually abused as a child and has spent long periods in care. In her middle 30s she started to show alterations of mood accompanied by changes in behaviour. She had periods of excitement accompanied by severe restlessness and sleep disturbance in which she was impulsively aggressive, noisy and disinhibited. At such times there would be no peace in her. At other times she became severely socially withdrawn, her eyes lacklustre and her hair limp and lifeless. She appeared depressed and might moan to herself; her conversation consisted of repetitive hypochondriacal complaints of headache, stomach-ache or not feeling well. On one occasion she attempted to set fire to her nightdress and sustained minor burns. The diagnosis appeared to be one of bipolar affective disorder and was supported by the knowledge of a family history of suicide in a first-degree relative.

In some patients the episodes of affective disorder may be shortlived but frequently recurrent. Glue (1989) has described 10 patients with a rapid cycling affective disorder. In some patients with severe learning disabilities these disorders may follow a regularly repetitive pattern.

Schizophrenic and paranoid psychoses

In the early years of the century there was considerable interest in the complex movement disorders shown by some patients, and a confusion arose between dementia praecox, and people with severe learning disabilities with complex and multiple stereotypies and cataleptic phenomena.

Kraepelin (1896) considered that "certain forms of idiocy with developed mannerisms and stereotypies might be early cases of dementia praecox" and coined the term *Pfropfschizophrenia* to denote "a schizophrenic psychosis of particularly early onset". De Sanctis (1909) referred to *dementia praecocissima*. Critchley & Earl (1932) regarded these mannerisms and stereotypies as "a primitive type of catatonic schizophrenia ... played out upon the psychomotor level rather than the symbolic". An alternative view was put forward by Bleuler (1916) who considered that "the stereotyped movements of many idiots cannot really be mistaken for the stereotyped movements of catatonia if one has seen both forms". Subsequently the term Pfropfschizophrenia came to be used as indicating a particular and distinctive form of schizophrenia grafted on to a learning disability, but as the term started to mean different things to different investigators it dropped into disuse.

There is now some consensus that schizophrenic and paranoid syndromes are language-dependent and a certain level of verbal competence is required to describe the pathognomonic clinical features of primary delusional phenomena, passivity experiences and true hallucinations. As such it is not feasible to diagnose these psychoses in people with an IQ below around 45 (Reid, 1972; Meadows *et al*, 1991). The complex stereotypical phenomena seen in some people with severe learning disabilities may bear a relationship to childhood psychosis, or be a pleasurable, self-stimulatory phenomenon, or even at times be related to boredom. Some of them undoubtedly have an origin in organic neurological disorder (Rogers *et al*, 1991). They are an ill-understood group of phenomena, and would benefit from much more detailed and consistent study than they have received in the past. Turner (1989) has produced a detailed and scholarly review of the relationship of mental retardation and schizophrenia.

Case example 2

Peter is aged 55 with an IQ of around 60. He comes from an itinerant family, and his early life and upbringing was deprived, and his educational opportunities curtailed. There is a family history of schizophrenia and in his early 20s Peter was noted to be facile, irrational and tangential in his replies and conversation. Over the years he has gone on to develop a frank schizophrenic psychosis with grandiose delusional beliefs, auditory hallucinations and increasing incoherence of language. In his 40s he suffered a brain-stem ischaemic episode which triggered epilepsy and a water intoxication syndrome which has led on to chronic dilutional hyponatraemia. He is now managed on an anticonvulsant and a depot neuroleptic with careful monitoring of fluid intake.

Psychoses of senescence

Senile and multi-infarct dementias do occur in elderly people with learning disabilities, but it is difficult to establish their presence with any degree of certainty since the clinical diagnosis is based on evidence of change and deterioration in personality, self-care skills and cognitive functions. For this it is necessary to have detailed and accurate records of premorbid levels of performance and achievement, and these are rarely available. Down's syndrome adults do, however, almost universally show the neuropathological changes of Alzheimer's disease with increasing age (see chapter 9), but these changes are accompanied by deterioration in cognitive function in only around 25% of cases. The discrepancy appears to be real and casts an intriguing doubt on the assumed linear association between density of senile plaques and tangles, and degree of cognitive impairment, which has become accepted as received wisdom for some years now.

The issue of dementia in elderly people with learning disabilities should not be overstated, however. Prevalence rates for dementia are no higher than in the general population, and most of these elderly people are remarkable more for their good health and state of preservation, than for any excess of age-related dementias in them (Day & Jancar, 1994). Studying prevalence rates for dementia in the over-65s, Reid & Aungle (1974) found rates of 13.6% in the population of an adult learning disabled hospital in Dundee, while Tait (1983) found rates of 7% (definite) and 10% (possible) in a hospital and community survey of learning disabled people. These can be compared with a general population survey by Kay *et al* (1964), who found rates of 5.6–5.7% (severe–mild) in their institutional and community sample in Newcastle-upon-Tyne.

Childhood psychoses

Childhood autism (discussed fully in chapter 7) is now regarded as a pervasive developmental disorder, present from infancy, often associated with organic abnormality of the central nervous system, and usually with severe learning disabilities. The condition continues through adolescence into adult life, and whereas some of the secondary symptoms such as restlessness, noisiness, self-injury or insomnia may fade with time, the social isolation, language abnormalities and stereotypical behaviour persist into adult life and on into old age. Sometimes an affective disorder may be superimposed on a syndrome of grown-up childhood psychosis, and the condition may then be very difficult to diagnose.

> **Case example 3**
> Joyce is aged 32, with an IQ of around 30, and shows features of childhood psychosis. She has virtually no language. Normally she leads a quiet life at home, keeping herself to herself and spending her days in stereotypical play with a piece of wood. She is gentle, undemanding and non-aggressive. From time to time she has periods of sustained, intense animation when she is more active, seeks contact, and touches female staff at the day centre she attends, in a sexually familiar way. At such times her eyes sparkle and she is almost amusing. At other times she can have periods when she is even more actively withdrawn than usual, goes off her food, appears disinterested, forgoes her stereotypical play and indicates by gesture that she has a sore stomach. These episodes last a few weeks to two or three months and appear to have an affective basis. In depressed phases she derives some benefit from antidepressant medication.

As the life expectancy of people with learning disabilities has increased, the identification of these grown-up cases of childhood psychosis has assumed increasing importance. The symptomatology is persistent (Reid

& Ballinger, 1995) and they form one of the behavioural groupings which may require continuing care in hospital as opposed to the community (Ballinger *et al*, 1991).

Neurotic disorders

Neurotic disorders are usually divided into hysterical, anxiety/phobic, obsessive–compulsive, depressive and hypochondriacal syndromes. These conditions have not been systematically studied in people with learning disabilities, although they do certainly experience the gamut of anxiety and neurotic reactions, states of panic, human unhappiness, loss and bereavement. It does become progressively harder to identify the symptomatology with increasing degrees of retardation. For example, there is a tendency to classify much of the repetitive, stereotypical behaviour as obsessional. In true obsessions, however, there are components of subjective compulsion, the retention of insight, and the struggle against giving in to the compulsion. The repetitive, stereotypical behaviours seen in people with learning disabilities are, on the contrary, pleasurable, often actively sought after, and should not be incorrectly classified as true obsessional phenomena. It is doubtful, therefore, whether obsessive–compulsive neurosis as such can be diagnosed in people with severe learning disabilities.

Personality disorders

Personality disorders have been defined as "deeply engrained and enduring behaviour patterns, manifesting themselves as inflexible responses to a broad range of personal and social situations. They represent either extreme or significant deviations from the way the average individual in a given culture perceives, thinks, feels, and particularly relates to others. Such behaviour patterns tend to be stable and to encompass multiple domains of behaviour and psychological functioning. They are frequently, but not always, associated with various degrees of subjective distress and problems in social functioning and performance." (ICD–10; World Health Organization, 1992).

Corbett (1979) reported a prevalence rate of around 25% for behaviour/personality disorder in his epidemiological survey of people with learning disabilities in Camberwell. He commented that whereas paranoid, schizoid, anxious and explosive personality types could all be identified, the largest categories consisted of people with impulsive or immature behaviour patterns. In a subsequent systematic study, Reid & Ballinger (1987) reported on the applicability of the ICD–9 categories of personality disorder with the addition of anxious and self-conscious personality types, using a Standardised Assessment of Personality. Reid & Ballinger found a prevalence rate for significant personality disorder of 22% for the population studied. The disorders identified were predominantly of mood in females, and of explosiveness and aggressiveness in males. The study was, however, carried out on a population resident in hospital, and was confined to people with mild or moderate degrees of learning disability. The authors commented that in people with more severe learning disabilities a personality typology rooted more in developmental concepts would be more appropriate.

There is little doubt that personality disorders are important in the field of learning disability, contribute much to management problems, and may be the determining factors in a retarded person's acceptability in a non-hospital environment.

Finally, problems of sexuality and sexual behaviour occur and can be very persistent in adults with learning disabilities. Again the problem is predominantly encountered among people with mild learning disabilities, but it does occasionally occur in people with more severe disabilities. It is usually stated that prostitution and paedophilia are the two aspects of deviant sexual activity most frequently found, but exploitation and an inability to find appropriate adult sexual partners are often relevant factors (Day, 1990). Even so, some deviant sexual activity in people with learning disability can be very persistent and resistant to treatment.

Case example 4

George is aged 35 and has an IQ of around 40. For many years now he has talked freely of his sadistic sexual fantasies to female carers, such as sticking a knife in them, undressing and cutting off their breasts and trying to touch their feet in a fetishistic fashion while sexually aroused. There have been incidents of sexual aggressiveness, and his condition has proved unresponsive to behavioural approaches, sex education and libidinal-reducing drugs.

In most people with learning disability, however, and in many grown-up childhood psychotics, problems of sexual behaviour are more correctly seen as developmental phenomena and socially inappropriate, rather than as driven by deviant or aberrant sexuality. Examples of developmentally determined and sexually inappropriate sexual behaviour might be touching, excessive physical affection, or masturbating in public. These expressions of sexuality are more appropriately treated through an educational, counselling or behavioural approach.

Challenging behaviour

In addition to the above psychosyndromes one encounters a wide range of challenging behaviour in people with learning disability of any degree. In a few people with very severe learning disability the behavioural repertoire is so limited as to preclude any disorder, and the presentation is dominated by their total dependency needs (Kiernan & Moss, 1990).

Some of the problem behaviours consist of individual symptoms only, such as stereotypies and mannerisms, restlessness, noisiness, self-injury, or aggressiveness. Self-injury, for example, seems an almost ubiquitous phenomenon, and reported prevalence rates remain remarkably uninfluenced by geography, and by pharmacological or behavioural interventions (Emerson, 1992). Oliver *et al* (1987) carried out a total screening for self-injurious behaviour in one health region in England, identifying cases both in hospital and in the community. They described examples of head-banging; hand, lip and digit-biting; skin-picking and scratching; eye-poking; poking of other orifices; teeth-banging; hair-removing; and cutting and banging with instruments. The prevalence rate of self-injurious behaviour in the hospital population was around 12%, and in the community around 3%. Rates of self-injury were higher in the younger groups with more severe degrees of learning disability. The authors concluded that self-injurious behaviour posed one of the most pressing management problems in people with learning disabilities, and was usually the cause – and not the effect – of admission to hospital.

Self-injury can serve as a paradigm for challenging behaviour in people with learning disabilities. The impetus to self-injury remains obscure. In some cases boredom may be a factor, or alternatively there may be a component of attention-seeking from staff or carers. Excitement, anger, irritability and over-arousal may all be factors in individual cases. In some people with learning disabilities who perpetrate terrible injuries on themselves – for example, enucleating an eye, picking away the nasal septum, cutting the nail beds with slivers of glass – there seems to be a component of altered pain sensation and analgesia. There are no universally applicable explanatory theories.

More usually, however, problem behaviours coexist and in most cases there is a combination of multiple behavioural problems. These behavioural 'syndromes' tend to manifest at an early age, persist over the years, and are extraordinarily difficult to classify.

Psychopharmacological treatment

Psychopharmacological treatments are reviewed in chapter 14. The subject, including the ethical issues raised by the Coldwater Studies in the US, has also been reviewed by Aman (1987) and Sovner (1988). Sovner in particular has drawn attention to the importance of behavioural psychopharmacology. In general terms, however, similar guidelines apply for the treatment with psychopharmacological agents of mental disorder in people with learning disabilities, as in the general population.

Affective psychosis

There are several reports of cases of affective disorder responding to antidepressant and antimanic treatment, but there is no scientifically convincing drug trial.

From clinical experience the main tricyclic antidepressants appear to be no more, and not much less, effective in patients with depressive psychoses, and side-effects are comparable to those in people of normal intelligence. First-line drugs are now probably the selective serotonin reuptake inhibitors (SSRIs), with the tricyclics and other preparations as second-line drugs. Mania is treated with the phenothiazine or butyrophenone groups of drugs, with or without lithium, and the risks of adverse interactions between haloperidol and lithium have probably been overstated; even so it is sensible to proceed cautiously and to use modest doses. Prophylaxis with lithium is of use in some cases, although the results may be disappointing with rapid cycling disorders. Carbamazepine has found a place as a second-line drug in the treatment of mania.

Schizophrenic and paranoid psychoses

Schizophrenia in people with learning disability usually responds in some degree to treatment with phenothiazines. Those most commonly in use are probably chlorpromazine and thioridazine, the longer-acting oral preparations such as pimozide, and depot preparations such as fluphenazine decanoate and flupenthixol. For a while depot preparations were considered contraindicated on the grounds of toxicity, but this fear is now believed to have been overstated. Chlorpromazine and thioridazine are being rapidly superseded by the newer neuroleptics such as risperidone, clozapine, sertindole and olanzapine, which have a more specific antipsychotic effect and which are also less neurotoxic.

Childhood psychoses

There is no reliably effective medical treatment for childhood psychosis. Hyperkinesis, screaming or self-injury may respond partially to phenothiazines or butyrophenones, and a few patients seem to derive benefit from treatment with lithium. Stimulants are contraindicated for the treatment of associated hyperactivity, however, as they may promote stereotypies. Insomnia may require night sedation but paradoxical reactions to sedatives have been reported. Good control of fits is essential, and there is some evidence to suggest that the newer anticonvulsants such as carbamazepine can exert a beneficial effect on symptoms such as aggressiveness and overactivity. Depressive episodes may respond to antidepressant medication. Overall, however, in the educational setting treatment approaches draw more on behavioural techniques (see chapter 7).

Neurotic disorders

Neurotic disorders characterised by a state of disproportionate anxiety, fearfulness, depression and phobias, may respond to treatment with drugs of the benzodiazepine group, although the benzodiazepines can generate dependency problems and it is prudent to use them in small doses and for limited periods of time. We should also remember that benzodiazepines in patients with brain damage may cause paradoxical reactions. Where phobias are situation-specific and circumscribed, they may respond more readily to a behaviour therapy approach using anxiety management and relaxation techniques.

Challenging behaviour

The treatment of challenging behaviour with psychopharmacological drugs is still at an empirical stage. Many of these people live in conditions of social and environmental disadvantage, both in the community and in the residential setting, and there is always the temptation to resort to neuroleptic drugs to control behaviour problems which are basically related to boredom, a deprived and unstimulating environment, and the frustrations of congregate living. While in such circumstances the first and main thrust of treatment is towards a better and more normal lifestyle, for example, in the small, staffed house setting (Emerson & Hatton, 1994), that is not the only answer. Many of these challenging behaviours are persistent, intrusive and disruptive, even in an optimal environment, and it may sometimes be legitimate to use drugs, usually of the phenothiazine or butyrophenone groups, or lithium, to modify symptoms of aggressiveness and irritability, for example.

Psychopharmacological agents are widely used in people with learning disabilities associated with challenging behaviour. The problems are pressing and real, no treatment approaches have a monopoly of solutions, and there is an urgent need to develop new behaviour-modifying drugs and to inject a greater degree of scientific knowledge into this field of clinical work.

Alternative treatments

The limitations in the presently available psychopharmacological treatments for mental illness and challenging behaviour, particularly in people with more severe learning disabilities, mean that the practitioner needs to keep an open mind and be prepared to consider alternative treatment approaches. One such approach lies in the further study of the effects of dietary treatments and restrictions. Additive-free diets, and fruit-free diets, have both been suggested as possible treatments for the symptom of restlessness. Harper & Reid (1987) have reported on the successful treatment with a reduced protein diet of a very severe behaviour disorder in an adult phenylketonuric woman with severe learning disabilities.

The field of behavioural treatment is of great importance and is considered specifically in chapter 11.

Conclusion

Diagnostic clarity is maximal with the major functional and organic psychoses, becoming less with neurotic and personality problems, and minimal in the area of challenging behaviour. Throughout, the role of structural, functional and neurophysiological brain abnormality has to be emphasised, and there is enormous scope for further fundamental research linking behavioural patterns to neuropathological processes. Treatment approaches derive largely from mainstream psychiatry, but need to be flexible and imaginative, and based on an open mind and a multidisciplinary pattern of working. Alternative approaches should always be considered.

References

Aman, M. G. (1987) Overview of pharmacotherapy: current status and future directions. *Journal of Mental Deficiency Research*, **31**, 121–130.

Ballinger, B. R., Ballinger, C. B., Reid, A. H., *et al* (1991) The psychiatric symptoms, diagnoses and care needs of 100 mentally handicapped patients. *British Journal of Psychiatry*, **158**, 251–254.

Bleuler, E. (1916) *Lehrbuch der Psychiatrie*. Translated (1924) *Textbook of Psychiatry* (A. A. Brill). New York: Dover Publications.

Corbett, J. A. (1979) Psychiatric morbidity and mental retardation. In *Psychiatric Illness and Mental Handicap* (eds F. E. James & R. P. Snaith), pp. 11–25. London: Gaskell.

Critchley, M. & Earl, C. J. C. (1932) Tuberous sclerosis and allied conditions. *Brain*, **55**, 311–346.

Day, K. A. (1990) Mental retardation: clinical aspects and management. In *Principles and Practice of Forensic Psychiatry* (eds R. Bluglass & P. Bowden), pp. 399–418. Edinburgh: Churchill Livingstone.

—— & Jancar, J. (1994) Mental and physical health and ageing in mental handicap: a review. *Journal of Intellectual Disability Research*, **38**, 241–256.

de Sanctis, S. (1909) Dementia praecocissima catatonica. Fol. Neurobiol. 2. Cited by A. von Glaus (1936) Uber Pfropfschizophrenie und schizophrene Frühdemenz. *Schweizer Archiv für Neurologie und Psychiatrie*, **38**, 37–68.

Emerson, E. (1992) Self-injurious behaviour: an overview of recent trends in epidemiological and behavioural research. *Mental Handicap Research*, **5**, 49–81.

—— & Hatton, C. (1994) *Moving Out. The Impact of Relocation from Hospital to Community on the Quality of Life of People with Learning Disabilities*. London: HMSO.

Glue, P. (1989) Rapid cycling affective disorders in the mentally retarded. *Biological Psychiatry*, **26**, 250–256.

Harper, M. & Reid, A. H. (1987) Use of a restricted protein diet in the treatment of behaviour disorder in a severely mentally retarded adult female phenylketonuric patient. *Journal of Mental Deficiency Research*, **31**, 202–212.

Jacobson, J. W. (1990) Assessing the prevalence of psychiatric disorders in a developmentally disabled population. In *Assessment of Behaviour Problems in Persons with Mental Retardation Living in the Community: Report on a Workshop* (eds E. Dibble & D. B. Gray), pp. 19–70. Maryland: NIMH.

Kanner, L. (1943) Autistic disturbances of affect contact. *Nervous Child*, **2**, 217–250.

Kay, D. W. K., Beamish, P. & Roth, M. (1964) Old age mental disorders in Newcastle-upon-Tyne. I. A study of prevalence. *British Journal of Psychiatry*, **110**, 146–158.

Kiernan, C. & Moss, S. (1990) Behaviour disorders and other characteristics of the population of a mental handicap hospital. *Mental Handicap Research*, **3**, 3–20.

Kraepelin, E. (1896) *Psychiatrie*. Translated (1902) *Clinical Psychiatry* (A. R. Deferndorf). New York.

Lund, J. (1985) Epilepsy and psychiatric disorder in the mentally retarded adult. *Acta Psychiatrica Scandinavica*, **72**, 557–562.

Meadows, G., Turner, T., Campbell, L., *et al* (1991) Assessing schizophrenia in adults with mental retardation. A comparative study. *British Journal of Psychiatry*, **158**, 103–105.

Oliver, C., Murphy, G. H. & Corbett, J. A. (1987) Self-injurious behaviour in people with mental handicap: a total population survey. *Journal of Mental Deficiency Research*, **31**, 147–162.

Reid, A. H. (1972) Psychoses in adult mental defectives. I. Manic depressive psychosis. II. Schizophrenic and paranoid psychoses. *British Journal of Psychiatry*, **120**, 205–212 & 213–218.

—— & Aungle, P. G. (1974) Dementia in ageing mental defectives: a clinical psychiatric study. *Journal of Mental Deficiency Research*, **18**, 15–23.

—— & Ballinger, B. R. (1987) Personality disorder in mental handicap. *Psychological Medicine*, **17**, 983–987.

—— & —— (1995) Behaviour symptoms among severe and profoundly mentally retarded patients. A 16 to 18 year follow-up study. *British Journal of Psychiatry*, **167**, 452–455.

Rogers, D., Karki, C., Bartlett, C., *et al* (1991) The motor disorders of mental handicap. An overlap with the motor disorders of severe psychiatric illness. *British Journal of Psychiatry*, **158**, 97–102.

Sovner, R. (1988) Behavioural psychopharmacology: a new psychiatric subspecialty. In *Mental Retardation and Mental Health: Classification, Diagnosis, Treatment, Services* (eds J. A. Stark, F. J. Menolascino, M. H. Albarelli, *et al*), pp. 229–242. Berlin: Springer-Verlag.

Tait, D. (1983) Mortality and dementia among ageing defectives. *Journal of Mental Deficiency Research*, **27**, 133–142.

Turner, T. H. (1989) Schizophrenia and mental handicap: an historical review. *Psychological Medicine*, **19**, 301–314.

World Health Organization (1992) *The ICD–10 Classification of Mental and Behavioural Disorders*. Geneva: WHO.

Additional reading

Bouras, N. (1994) *Mental Health in Mental Retardation*. Cambridge: Cambridge University Press.

Fletcher, R. J. & Dosen, A. (1993) *Mental Health Aspects of Mental Retardation*. New York: Lexington Books.

Reid, A. H. (1982) *The Psychiatry of Mental Handicap*. London: Blackwell Scientific.

11 Behavioural interventions

Eric Emerson & Chris Kiernan

The behavioural model • *Behavioural assessment* • *Constructional intervention* • *Challenging behaviours as conditioned responses* • *Programme design and implementation*

This chapter presents an overview of what could be considered the 'most promising practices' in applying behavioural methods to the remediation of severely challenging behaviours shown by people with learning disabilities. More details of this extremely extensive field can be found in Carr *et al* (1993), Emerson (1995) and Kiernan (1993).

Behaviours such as severe aggression, self-injury and destructiveness (among others) constitute a significant social challenge. They are often associated with a number of undesirable outcomes including, for example, secondary infections; physical malformation; loss of sight or hearing; additional neurological damage; stress for parents and carers; exclusion from community placements; institutionalisation; neglect and abuse.

Despite advances in knowledge, however, people with challenging behaviours in the UK are unlikely to receive effective behavioural support. Unfortunately, this remains true despite the increased attention which has been paid over the last decade to the development of community based services for people with seriously challenging behaviours (Blunden & Allen, 1987; Department of Health, 1989, 1993; Emerson *et al*, 1994).

The behavioural model

Most commonly, behavioural approaches to intervention conceptualise challenging behaviour as being an example of operant behaviour; that is, it is seen as behaviour which is shaped and maintained by its environmental consequences. Thus it is seen as functional and (at least in the short-term) adaptive. It is behaviour which has been 'selected' or shaped through the person's interaction with their physical and, perhaps more importantly, social world. In lay terms it can be thought of as behaviour through which the person exercises control over key aspects of their environment.

Basic concepts of behavioural models include the following terms. Consequences which shape or maintain behaviour are termed reinforcers. Two types of reinforcement contingencies may be important in establishing and maintaining challenging behaviour. *Positive reinforcement* refers to an increase in the rate of a behaviour as a result of the contingent *presentation* of a reinforcing stimulus (positive reinforcer). *Negative reinforcement* refers to an increase in the rate of a behaviour as a result of the contingent *withdrawal* (or prevention of occurrence) of a reinforcing stimulus (negative reinforcer).

Common examples of positive reinforcement include pressing a light switch to activate the lights in a room (positive reinforcer: light), smiling and saying hello to a colleague to initiate further conversation (positive reinforcer: conversation) and requesting a drink when thirsty (positive reinforcer: drink). Similarly, common examples of negative reinforcement include completion of a piece of work to *escape* from the demands of your manager (withdrawal of negative reinforcer: demands), and the *avoidance* of potential crashes and fines by stopping at red lights when driving (negative reinforcer: fines and/or crashes).

Two characteristics of the behavioural approach, its focus upon *function* and the *context* of behaviour, are particularly relevant to understanding challenging behaviour. In a behavioural analysis, our concern is to determine the effect (or *function*) that a person's behaviour may have upon their environment, rather than to study the particular form (or topography) of behaviour. For example, a behaviour analyst would be interested in understanding the consequences of self-injury (its function) and the conditions under which it occurred, rather than its specific topographical form (e.g. face-slapping v. lip-biting).

Consideration of the *context* in which behaviour occurs, including its biological and historical context, is fundamental to the behavioural approach. Contextual factors may establish the motivational bases which underlie behaviour; and the context in which behaviour occurs may provide important information or cues to the individual concerning the probability of particular behaviours being reinforced.

The behavioural approach makes no assumptions regarding the capacity of a particular stimulus to act as a reinforcer. Indeed, behavioural theory would suggest that the reinforcing power of any stimulus needs to be established by historical and/or contextual variables. Thus, for example, food will only operate as a positive reinforcer if the person is denied free access to it and also if, among other things, they have not recently eaten. Indeed, in a different context (e.g. immediately after a very large meal or during a stomach upset) food could operate as a negative reinforcer (increasing behaviours which lead to the withdrawal or postponement of food).

Similarly, a particular classroom task may only become aversive (and consequently become established as a negative reinforcer) for a child when repeated many times over a short period or when presented in a noisy or stressful setting. Social contact with adults may become aversive (and hence act as a negative reinforcer) after the experience of sexual abuse. That is, personal, biological, historical and environmental contexts influence the motivational basis of behaviour by determining or establishing the reinforcing and punishing potential of otherwise neutral stimuli. The behavioural terminology for dealing with such operations is currently evolving but includes the concepts of setting events, establishing operations and establishing stimuli.

In addition to this motivational influence, aspects of contexts may gain 'informational value' as a result of their previous association with variations in the probability with which particular behaviours have been reinforced. That is, contextual *discriminative stimuli* distinguish between situations in which specific consequences for a given behaviour are more or less likely. So, for example, an 'out of order' notice on a lift provides information regarding the operation (or not) of a particular contingency, i.e. the probability of pressing the button being followed by the appearance of a lift. The difference between these two general classes of antecedent or contextual stimuli is crucial. In lay terms, establishing operations and stimuli change "people's behaviour by changing what they want ... [as opposed to discriminative or conditional stimuli, which change] ... their chances of getting something that they already want" (Michael, 1982, p.154).

Behavioural approaches to intervention

It appears that the most promising behavioural approaches to intervention are those which would be described by the term positive behavioural support (see Carr *et al*, 1993, for a description of these methods). This includes a series of techniques which are based on the assumptions that:

(a) challenging behaviour usually serves a purpose for the person who displays it (i.e. challenging behaviour is functional);

(b) prior to intervention, functional assessment should be used to try to identify the purpose of challenging behaviour;

(c) the goal of intervention is to educate and teach new skills, not simply to reduce challenging behaviour (also known as the constructional approach);

(d) challenging behaviour often serves many purposes and therefore requires many interventions;

(e) intervention involves changing social systems such as schools or the way families interact, rather than just changing the person with challenging behaviour;

(f) the ultimate goal of intervention is to improve a person's quality of life or lifestyle, not just to reduce challenging behaviour.

As we have seen above, a behavioural analysis draws attention to the functions served by behaviour, rather than to external form or topography of behaviour. Dissimilar-looking behaviours may, in some instances, be maintained by similar processes. Behaviours which look similar may, in other instances, be maintained by very different processes. Indeed, it could well be the case that the same behaviour shown by the same individual could serve different functions in different settings (Emerson *et al*, 1995). These observations have important implications.

Selecting treatments on the basis of the appearance of behaviour is likely to be inefficient. Consider, for example, the use of 'time-out' to treat the tantrum behaviours of a child with severe learning difficulties. Time-out is a behavioural treatment which involves reducing the person's access to potential reinforcing events or activities for a brief period following the occurrence of the target challenging behaviour. This may involve either removing the person to a less reinforcing environment or removing potential reinforcers from the vicinity of the person (e.g. by removing preferred objects and others turning away). The logic of the procedure is that, if the person's challenging behaviour reliably results in an overall reduction in general levels of positive reinforcement, over time the behaviour should become less frequent and eventually disappear.

Indeed, this would be the most likely outcome if time-out were applied to episodes of the child's aggression *if* it had previously been maintained by a process of positive reinforcement (e.g. attention elicited from carers). In this case, instead of the child's aggression leading to reinforcing consequences (adult attention) it would now result in a temporary loss of access to that particular reinforcer and a number of other potential reinforcers (e.g. preferred activities). But what would happen if the child's aggression was maintained by a process of negative reinforcement, e.g. escape from aversive school tasks? In this case time-out would guarantee that each episode of aggression was (negatively) reinforced by the contingent removal of materials and attention (demands). At best this would be ineffective, at worst it could lead to a strengthening of the aggression.

Intervention, therefore, needs to be based upon an analysis of the behavioural processes underlying the person's challenging behaviours. This may be termed a *functional approach* to analysis and intervention. The only alternative to such an approach is one in which intervention techniques are employed which may be effective regardless of the processes underlying the behaviour. A number of approaches fall within this category including *punishment* and the *differential reinforcement of other* (DRO) or *incompatible* (DRI) behaviours. While punishment techniques are undoubtedly effective, their use does raise ethical questions, especially if less intrusive methods are available (Repp & Singh, 1990). While techniques based upon differential reinforcement do not raise such immediate ethical concerns, the available evidence indicates that, on their own, they are not particularly effective (Carr *et al*, 1990).

A functional approach to analysis and intervention is complementary to what has been termed the *constructional approach*. The constructional approach to intervention seeks to establish new behaviours as alternatives to the challenging behaviours shown by individuals. This may be contrasted with a pathological approach which simply focuses upon the elimination of behaviour. Thus, while a constructional approach would posit the question "what should the person be doing in this situation instead of engaging in challenging behaviours?", a pathological approach would simply ask "how can we stop him doing this?". While it is possible to develop constructional interventions in ignorance of the behavioural processes underlying the person's challenging behaviours (as it is to develop functionally based 'pathological' treatment plans), evidence does indicate that the combination of these two approaches may be less intrusive and more effective than more traditional behavioural approaches to treatment.

Behavioural assessment

The aim of a behavioural assessment is to identify the relationships that exist between behaviour (what people actually do), the context in which the behaviour occurs and the environmental consequences of the behaviour. These three components of the person–environment interaction (behaviour, context, consequence) constitute what has been termed the three-term contingency which underlies the study of operant behaviour.

Behavioural assessment can be conceptualised as a three stage process (Carr *et al*, 1993) consisting of: describing the behaviour(s) of interest; developing hypotheses about their maintaining variables; testing these hypotheses.

Describing behaviour

Behavioural assessment commences with developing detailed descriptions of the behaviour(s) of concern, the environmental and personal conditions under which these behaviours occur, and the environmental consequences of the behaviour. Useful suggestions of ways of going about this task are provided by, among many others, Bailey & Pyles (1989), Meyer & Evans (1989), O'Neill *et al* (1990), Carr *et al* (1993), and Zarkowska & Clements (1994).

Typically, this stage of a behavioural assessment will seek information from multiple sources including (where practicable) self-report, interviews with parents and carers and, most importantly, direct observation of the person in their normal situation.

The outcome of this process will consist of:

(a) a description of the range of adaptive, communicative and challenging behaviours shown by the person across different settings;

(b) a detailed description of the person's challenging behaviours in terms of the specific forms they take, the sequence in which they occur, their frequency, intensity and duration;

(c) the social and material contexts in which the challenging behaviours occur in terms of the patterns of interaction and activity taking place in the person's current and preceding settings, physical aspects of the environment (e.g. materials present, ambient noise, lighting, temperature and humidity) and the physical state of the individual (e.g. fatigue, illness);

(d) the impact of the person's challenging behaviours upon the social and material context in which they occur, especially with regard to their impact upon ongoing patterns of interaction and activity.

Generating hypotheses

On the basis of such descriptions, tentative hypotheses can be developed regarding the function of the person's challenging behaviours. As noted above, it is possible that challenging behaviours may be maintained by different processes in different contexts. It is necessary, therefore, to attempt to identify the processes underlying each form of the person's challenging behaviours in each of the social contexts in which they occur.

Four general processes may underlie challenging behaviours: positive social reinforcement; negative social reinforcement; positive automatic reinforcement; and negative automatic reinforcement. Box 11.1 (Emerson, 1995) illustrates the types of context–behaviour–consequence relationships that may be indicative of these processes.

Testing hypotheses: functional analysis

In many instances clinicians will proceed from tentatively identifying hypotheses to intervention. The functional analysis of challenging behaviours goes one step further by empirically testing these hypotheses prior to intervention. There are obvious ethical and practical arguments in support of such an approach. For suggestions regarding specific procedures see Carr *et al* (1993), Durand (1990), and O'Neill *et al* (1990).

Recently attention has been paid to the use of 'analogue assessment' procedures, an approach involving observations of the person's reaction to brief, artificially structured situations. For example, behaviours maintained by carer attention (positive social reinforcement) would be more likely to occur under conditions in which a carer is in close proximity to the individual but attending to some other task (e.g. reading a magazine). Challenging behaviours maintained by escape from social demands (negative reinforcement) would be more likely to occur under conditions under which the person is expected to perform a novel task. Challenging behaviours maintained by their arousing sensory

Box 11.1 Relationships between antecedents, challenging behaviours and consequent events which may suggest particular underlying processes

Socially mediated positive reinforcement

Does the person's challenging behaviour sometimes result in them receiving more or different forms of contact with others (e.g. while the episode is being managed or while they are being 'calmed down') or having access to new activities?

Is the behaviour more likely when contact or activities are potentially available but not being provided, e.g. situations in which carers are around but are attending to others?

Is the behaviour less likely in situations involving high levels of contact or during preferred activities?

Is the behaviour more likely when contact or activities are terminated?

Socially mediated negative reinforcement (escape or avoidance)

Do people respond to the behaviour by terminating interaction or activities?

Is the behaviour more likely in situations in which demands are placed upon the person or they are engaged in interactions or activities they appear to dislike?

Is the behaviour less likely when disliked interactions or activities are stopped?

Is the behaviour less likely in situations involving participation in preferred activities?

Is the behaviour more likely in those situations in which they may be asked to participate in interactions or activities they appear to dislike?

Positive automatic reinforcement (sensory stimulation, perceptual reinforcement or opioid release)

Is the behaviour more likely when there is little external stimulation?

Is the behaviour less likely when the person is participating in a preferred activity?

Does the behaviour appear to have no effect on subsequent events?

Negative automatic reinforcement (de-arousal)

Is the behaviour more likely when there is excessive external stimulation or when the individual is visibly excited or aroused?

Is the behaviour less likely when the individual is calm or in a quiet, peaceful environment?

Does the behaviour appear to have no effect upon subsequent events?

(Emerson, 1995)

consequences may be more likely to occur under conditions incorporating low levels of external stimulation (e.g. being alone in a rather barren room). Repeated brief exposure to such scenarios can be used to examine the hypotheses developed concerning the processes underlying a person's challenging behaviour.

Figure 11.1 gives an example of such an assessment of two forms of self-injury shown by a 13-year-old girl. As can be seen, one form of self-injury (back-poking) occurred with much greater frequency under conditions of demand, while the other (body-digging) was much more frequent when she was alone. These observations suggest that the two forms of self-injury served different functions: her back-poking was being maintained by negative social reinforcement, while her body-digging was maintained by positive automatic reinforcement.

These approaches are most suitable for examining the processes underlying challenging behaviours that occur fairly frequently.

Constructional intervention

There exist ethical and practical arguments in support of taking a constructional approach to intervention, based upon a thorough analysis of the processes underlying a person's challenging behaviours. Specific behavioural techniques which may form the constituent parts of intervention are outlined below.

The goal of constructional intervention is to help the person to develop socially appropriate ways of acting as *alternatives* to challenging behaviours. If we simply eliminate behaviour we can be sure that other behaviours will take their place. Rather than leave the nature of this process of behavioural substitution to chance, a constructional approach makes this the target of intervention.

For example, consider approaches to intervention for a young woman's self-injurious behaviour which occurs most frequently while waiting for lunch and appears to be maintained by the attention of carers. A constructional approach would begin by identifying alternative responses the person could make while waiting. These would include engaging in currently available activities (e.g. helping with lunch preparation) or participating in a different activity (e.g. a favourite leisure activity, talking to a friend). Once a socially appropriate alternative response has been selected from among the alternatives, intervention would proceed by ensuring that the alternative behaviour became a firmly established response in this context (waiting for lunch) and thereby replaced the woman's self-injury.

In doing so it would be necessary to ensure that the target behaviour (e.g. lunch preparation) resulted in significantly more frequent or powerful reinforcement than the existing self-injury. In general, people distribute

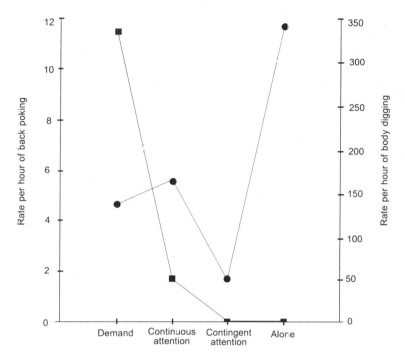

Fig. 11.1 Rate per hour of two types of self-injurious behaviour (■,back poking; ●, body digging) under four 'analogue' conditions.

their time between concurrently available activities in the same proportions as the relative frequency or magnitude of reinforcement contingent upon those activities. Thus, if helping with lunch and self-injury resulted in the same consequences (i.e. similar rates and durations of carer attention) we would expect the young woman to distribute her time equally between these two activities. Clinically effective treatment would require that the new behaviour actually replaces self-injury. In order to achieve this it would be necessary to ensure that the rate/magnitude of reinforcement for self-injury was nil, or as low as possible, while the rate of reinforcement for helping with lunch was as high as possible.

One variant of the constructional approach is known as *functional displacement* (Carr, 1988), the *differential reinforcement of communication* or DRC (Carr *et al*, 1993). These terms refer to intervention strategies based upon establishing a new (often communicative) behaviour which results in the *same* consequences as the challenging behaviour. Thus, at a metaphorical level, challenging behaviours may be conceptualised as powerful forms of non-verbal communication (Durand, 1990; Carr *et al*, 1993). The goal of intervention then becomes one of substituting equally powerful but more appropriate modes of communication for the person's challenging behaviour.

A communication-based approach to intervention (Carr *et al*, 1990) would proceed along similar lines, with the important exception that the target behaviour would be a response which elicited the same consequence as the challenging behaviour. In this case an appropriate communicative response could be requesting the carer to talk to her. Again, the success of the intervention would depend on ensuring that the differences in the rate or magnitude of reinforcement for the two responses were sufficiently different that the new communicative response replaced, rather than coexisted alongside, the young woman's self-injury.

The logic underlying this example could also be applied to challenging behaviours maintained by a process of negative reinforcement (e.g. aggression maintained by escape from demands). A constructional approach would focus upon replacing the aggression, say, with a more appropriate response to demanding situations (e.g. self-control of anger), while a communication-based intervention would provide the individual with an alternative communicative response which resulted in the same consequences as those maintaining the aggression (e.g. asking for a break). Again, the effectiveness of either intervention would depend upon the relative rates of reinforcement of the two alternative responses.

Thus, constructional approaches most often consist of two distinct components. Firstly, socially appropriate behaviours are established as possible alternatives in situations that elicit episodes of challenging behaviour; then, the new behaviours are strengthened and the challenging behaviours weakened so that the challenging behaviours are replaced by more appropriate alternatives.

Establishing alternative behaviours

A constructional intervention must ensure that either the person already possesses the skills required for the target behaviour (e.g. lunch preparation in the above example), is taught the required skills, or is provided with whatever additional support (carer assistance, prostheses) that is necessary for them to participate in the target behaviour.

It is beyond the scope of this chapter to summarise the vast literature on behavioural techniques for teaching new behaviours (Kiernan, 1985; Yule & Carr, 1987; Matson, 1990). Effective teaching procedures are likely to involve a number of processes including:

(a) breaking complex tasks down into their constituent components through a process of *task analysis;*
(b) providing additional assistance in the form of instructions or *prompts* (which may be verbal, gestural or physical, e.g. guiding the person's hands), demonstration or *modelling*, examples, templates or other prostheses, so that the person accurately performs the task;

(c) *repeated practice* of the task during which the additional assistance is gradually withdrawn (*faded*) over time;

(d) *repeated training* across a number of examples of the types of conditions under which the new skill will be performed (i.e. settings, trainers, materials) to facilitate the generalisation of the skill to novel settings.

Strengthening alternative behaviours

The second component of a constructional approach is to ensure that the new behaviour is established at such a strength that it replaces the challenging behaviour. This may involve a number of techniques including: differential reinforcement of the alternative behaviour; changing the contexts within which behaviours occur; and the weakening of the challenging behaviours.

Differential reinforcement of alternative behaviours

Simply establishing an alternative response may not lead to the replacement of challenging behaviours. While we are far from understanding the precise processes by which behavioural substitution occurs, one powerful determinant will be the degree to which the two alternative responses (the selected alternative or target behaviour and the challenging behaviour) are differentially reinforced. Treatment effectiveness can be improved if we combine maximising reinforcement for the alternative with minimising reinforcement for the challenging behaviour (Carr *et al*, 1990, 1993). In general, these procedures for *differentially reinforcing alternative behaviours* (DRA) arrange for the individual to receive *additional programmed reinforcers* while engaged in the target behaviour, these reinforcers being withheld during and/or immediately following episodes of challenging behaviours. For example, individually determined reinforcers (praise, food, specific activities) could be made available for each component correctly assembled in a workshop (target behaviour), as long as no self-injury had occurred during construction. A number of variants on this procedure have been used to reduce challenging behaviours:

(a) the *differential reinforcement of incompatible behaviour* (DRI) refers to the application of the procedures to target behaviours physically incompatible with the challenging behaviours;

(b) the *differential reinforcement of communication* (DRC) refers to establishing alternative methods of communication which result in the same consequences (reinforcers) as the person's challenging behaviours, a procedure in which the form of the target behaviour (communicative response) and reinforcer (identity with maintaining reinforcer) are specific;

(c) compliance training in which the target behaviours consist of generalised compliance with carer requests.

Changing the context of behaviour

In addition to intervention techniques that seek to change the consequences of behaviour, a number of intervention strategies seek to either strengthen or weaken the probability of behaviours occurring by changing the context of behaviour. Thus, for example, if we know that participation in a vocational task is more likely if the person is allowed to select the nature of the task (Bannerman *et al*, 1990) then we can increase the time the person spends in constructive activity by giving them greater control over task selection and scheduling, that is, by changing the context rather than the consequences of behaviour. Examples of stimulus-based procedures, i.e. intervention procedures which alter the context of behaviour, to make alternative responses more likely, include:

(a) introducing into situations stimuli that elicit high rates of occurrence of the target behaviour, e.g. choice over task scheduling;

(b) introducing into situations stimuli that result in low rates of occurrence of the challenging behaviour, e.g. high levels of external stimulation which may suppress behaviours maintained by their arousing sensory properties;

(c) removing from situations stimuli that set the occasion for high rates of the challenging behaviours, e.g. excessive noise in a workshop under which task-related demands may become significantly more aversive or under which stereotypical behaviours maintained by their arousal-reducing feedback functions may be elicited;

(d) embedding stimuli which elicit the challenging behaviours (e.g. carer request) in a different context (e.g. following on from a number of requests which usually elicit compliance, making requests in a joking fashion).

Behaviours may also be seen as challenging when they occur in the wrong context; that is, the behaviours have failed to come under the control of appropriate discrimination stimuli. A number of sexual deviations and atypical social behaviours can be considered in this light. It is not the behaviours themselves which are inappropriate (e.g. masturbation) but the social contexts in which they occur (e.g. at the lunch table).

It is important to distinguish between two distinct types of failure in the contextual control of behaviour. Firstly, the behaviour may occur rather indiscriminately in a wide range of situations – some appropriate, some not. Examples of the failure to establish stimulus control would include masturbation in public and private settings, and the indiscriminate use of very warm and friendly ways of greeting people (e.g. throwing your arms around someone). A constructional approach to intervention in these instances would focus upon the development of appropriate stimulus control through a combination of instruction, modelling, role-play and programming for the differential reinforcement of the behaviour in its appropriate context, and extinguishing (withholding reinforcement) from episodes of the behaviour occurring in inappropriate contexts. This treatment package when applied to social behaviours would normally be termed social skills training (Marchetti & Campbell, 1990). This general approach can, of course, prove problematic for behaviours which are under the control of powerful non-social reinforcers (e.g. masturbation). Here a combination of redirection to appropriate settings once the behaviour has started, the provision in the socially appropriate context of sexually stimulating materials to facilitate masturbation, and, if necessary, mild punishment (e.g. verbal reprimands) may be required.

An alternative type of failure of stimulus control occurs when stimulus control has been established to inappropriate stimuli. A number of sexual deviations can be considered in this light, in that the sexual acts are powerfully elicited by socially inappropriate stimuli (e.g. public places, in the presence of young children). In these cases a constructional approach to intervention would be likely to proceed upon two fronts. Firstly, the establishment of appropriate stimulus control would be attempted by the procedures noted above. If necessary a second strand to the intervention may attempt to abolish the conditioned elicitive powers of the inappropriate discrimination stimuli. This could be approached in a number of ways, including *aversion therapy* which pairs the inappropriate discrimination stimuli with overt aversive stimuli (e.g. noxious smells, electric shock), *covert sensitisation* which pairs covert representations of the inappropriate discrimination stimuli (e.g. fantasies of young children) with covert aversive stimuli (e.g. thoughts of nausea), or *orgasmic reconditioning* which involves the use of the inappropriate discrimination stimuli to initiate sexual activity but involves a switch to appropriate discrimination stimuli prior to orgasm.

Weakening challenging behaviours

A number of techniques have been developed which directly change the reinforcing consequences of the challenging behaviours themselves. They include:

(a) *extinction*: the withholding of the specific reinforcers which maintain the challenging behaviour, e.g. if a person's self-injury were maintained by the attention it elicited from others (positive reinforcement), an extinction procedure would entail ensuring that the person's self-injury was ignored, i.e. it no longer elicited the maintaining reinforcer;

(b) *escape extinction*: extinction of behaviours maintained by negative reinforcement by the prevention of escape from the aversive situation which elicits the challenging behaviour;

(c) *sensory extinction*: the extinction of behaviours maintained by their arousing sensory qualities by the blocking of the sensory feedback resulting from behaviour, e.g. reducing the sensory feedback from head-banging by replacing hard surfaces in the person's environment with soft surfaces;

(d) *time-out*: the withholding of a range of opportunities for reinforcement;

(e) *response cost*: the removal of specific positive reinforcers following an episode of challenging behaviour, e.g. fines;

(f) *punishment*: the presentation of an aversive stimulus, which may range in severity from a verbal reprimand to electric shock, contingent upon the challenging behaviour.

As we have noted, some challenging behaviours may be maintained by their internal consequences, such as providing additional sensory stimulation at low levels of arousal, or providing 'distraction' under conditions of aversive stimulation. Constructional behavioural interventions for such behaviours would again involve procedures to increase alternative behaviours, while at the same time minimising the 'reinforcing' consequences which are currently maintaining the challenging behaviours. The types of procedures effective in establishing alternative behaviours have been outlined above. In addition, establishing new behaviours which affect the same senses as the challenging behaviour (e.g. substituting horse-riding for stereotypical body-rocking) may be more effective than establishing new behaviours affecting other senses.

There are obvious difficulties in minimising the extent to which behaviours are reinforced when the reinforcers involved are internal events, for example the possible effects of self-injury upon endogenous opiate activity. Two approaches are possible. It may be feasible to alter the motivating conditions (change the context of behaviour) which make certain consequences more or less reinforcing. Eating food is only reinforcing when we are hungry; indeed it can be a powerfully aversive experience when satiated. Similarly, the sensory feedback from stereotypical behaviours may only be reinforcing under low levels of arousal. Thus increasing the background level of stimulation may in effect resolve the deprivational state (low arousal) necessary for the sensory feedback from stereotypical behaviours to become reinforcing. A similar approach could be taken to behaviours maintained by their function in providing distraction under conditions of aversive stimulation. In this case reducing the level of aversive stimulation (e.g. pain or noise) would abolish the state under which a 'distracting' behaviour became reinforcing.

Secondly, it may be possible to block or reduce the internal consequences of such behaviours, either psychopharmacologically (e.g. naltrexone hydrochloride as an endogenous opiate blocker), or behaviourally through the use of *sensory extinction* procedures which involve blocking the sensory feedback emanating from stereotypical mannerisms.

Challenging behaviours as conditioned responses

Some forms of challenging behaviours can be conceptualised as resulting from atypical emotional learning. Thus, for example, for some individuals relatively innocuous stimuli may evoke intense emotional responses. Examples include both simple and complex phobias and the apparent distress elicited by social contact in some individuals with autism.

There is no reason to believe that people with learning disabilities should be immune to the development of the gamut of anxiety-related disorders found among the rest of the population. Indeed, some of the atypical learning processes identified as characteristic of learning disabilities, such as the phenomenon of stimulus overselectivity, would suggest that such learning could be more prevalent among people with learning disabilities or autism. Despite this it is only fairly recently that anxiety-related problems among people with learning disabilities have received much attention.

Fear reduction

There is a vast literature in the mental health field pertaining to fear reduction methods. Readers are directed to one of a number of current sources (Beck *et al*, 1985; Marks, 1987; Rachman, 1990).

Behavioural approaches to fear reduction and anxiety management among people with learning disabilities have, by and large, followed those developed in the mental health field (Benson, 1990). A constructional approach to fear reduction should focus upon establishing appropriate behaviour rather than simply eliminating inappropriate behaviour. Thus, for example, eliminating the fear elicited by a situation (such as going out) is not a sufficient goal of a constructional intervention. Instead we should be focusing upon helping the person develop appropriate and positively reinforcing ways of using their time while outside.

As discussed above, constructional approaches are to be preferred on practical grounds. In this instance a constructional formulation of the goal of treatment corresponds well to the available evidence, which points to the superiority of exposure-based methods of fear reduction, which also involve the modelling or shaping of appropriate ways of acting (such as physically relaxing) in the presence of the feared stimulus (Marks, 1987; Benson, 1990).

Programme design and implementation

The design of an effective intervention package incorporating the techniques described is a complex matter reflecting a number of variables, including judgements regarding the likely effectiveness of intervention techniques and combinations of techniques. These include: the nature of the processes underlying the person's challenging behaviours; the resources available; the urgency of intervention; the personal, social and material costs to the individual, carers and the community of the intervention procedure.

In some situations such decisions may involve difficult judgements in which an individual's right to the least restrictive or aversive treatment has to be balanced against their right to effective help (Meinhold & Mulick, 1990; Repp & Singh, 1990).

The intervention package may often represent a form of *ecological programming* (Donnellan *et al*, 1988; Meyer & Evans, 1989) in which a wide variety of socially valued responses leading to greater personal independence are established by a combination of strategies. The package may also involve components which require the person themselves to monitor, evaluate and reinforce their own actions through a process of self-management (Gardner & Cole, 1989).

In addition to developing an intervention package as outlined above, it is also important to ensure that the changes in behaviour are maintained over time and generalise to new situations (Horner *et al*, 1988). The intervention programme must include procedures by which carers can cope with and effectively manage actual episodes of challenging behaviours in ways which do not jeopardise the aims of the intervention, and the programme needs to be implemented under conditions which will ensure the reliable and accurate application of the procedures specified. Inaccurate or inconsistent treatment can be worse than no treatment at all.

References

Bailey, J. S. & Pyles, A. M. (1989) Behavioral diagnostics. In *The Treatment of Severe Behavior Disorders* (ed. E. Cipani), pp. 85–107. Washington, DC: American Association on Mental Retardation.

Bannerman, D. J., Sheldon, J. B., Sherman, J. A., *et al* (1990) Balancing the right to habilitation with the right to personal liberties: The rights of people with developmental disabilities to eat too many doughnuts and take a nap. *Journal of Applied Behavior Analysis*, **23**, 79–89.

Beck, A. T., Emery, G. & Greenberg, R. L. (1985) *Anxiety Disorders and Phobias*. New York: Basic Books.

Benson, B. A. (1990) Emotional problems. 1. Anxiety and depression. In *Handbook of Behavior Modification with the Mentally Retarded* (ed. J. L. Matson), pp. 391–420. New York: Plenum.

Blunden, R. & Allen, D. (1987) *Facing the Challenge: An Ordinary Life for People with Learning Difficulties and Challenging Behaviours*. London: King's Fund.

Carr, E. G. (1988) Functional equivalence as a mechanism of response generalization. In *Generalization and Maintenance: Life-Style Changes in Applied Settings* (eds R. H. Horner, G. Dunlap & R. L. Koegel), pp. 221–241. Baltimore: Paul H. Brookes.

——, Robinson, S., Taylor, J. C., *et al* (1990) *Positive Approaches to the Treatment of Severe Behavior Problems in Persons with Developmental Disabilities*. Washington. DC: Association for Persons with Severe Handicaps.

——, Levin, L., McConnachie, G., *et al* (1993) *Communication-Based Intervention for Problem Behavior: A User's Guide for Producing Positive Change*. Baltimore: Paul H. Brookes.

Department of Health (1989) *Needs and Responses*. London: DoH.

—— (1993) *Services for People with Learning Disabilities and Challenging Behaviour or Mental Health Needs*. London: HMSO.

Donellan, A. M., La Vigna, G. W., Negri-Shoultz, *et al* (1988) *Progress Without Punishment: Effective Approaches for Learners with Behaviour Problems*. New York: Teachers College Press.

Durand, V. M. (1990) *Severe Behavior Problems: A Functional Communication Training Approach*. New York: Guilford.

Emerson, E. (1995) *Challenging Behaviour: Analysis and Intervention in People with Learning Disabilities*. Cambridge: Cambridge University Press.

——, McGill, P. & Mansell, J. (eds) (1994) *Severe Learning Disabilities and Challenging Behaviours: Designing High Quality Services*. London: Chapman and Hall.

——, Thompson, S., Reeves, D., *et al* (1995) Descriptive analysis of multiple response topographies of challenging behavior across two settings. *Research in Developmental Disabilities*, **16**, 301–329.

Gardner, W. I. & Cole, C. L. (1989) Self-management approaches. In *The Treatment of Severe Behavior Disorders: Applied Behavior Analytic Approaches* (ed. E. Cipani), pp. 19–35. Washington, DC: American Association on Mental Retardation.

Horner, R. H., Dunlap, G. & Koegel, R. L. (1988) *Generalization and Maintenance: Life-Style Changes in Applied Settings*. Baltimore: Paul H. Brookes.

Kiernan, C. C. (1985) Behaviour modification. In *Mental Deficiency. The Changing Outlook* (eds A. M. Clarke, A. B. Clarke & J. M. Berg), pp. 382–456. London: Methuen.

—— (ed.) (1993) *Research to Practice? Implications of Research on the Challenging Behaviour of People with Learning Disability*. Kidderminster: BILD Publications.

Marchetti, A. G. & Campbell, V. A. (1990) Social skills. In *Handbook of Behavior Modification with the Mentally Retarded* (ed. J. L. Matson), pp. 335–355. New York: Plenum.

Marks, I. M. (1987) *Fears, Phobias and Rituals*. Oxford: Oxford University Press.

Matson, J. L. (ed.) (1990) *Handbook of Behavior Modification with the Mentally Retarded*. New York: Plenum.

Meinhold, P. M. & Mulick, J. A. (1990) Risks, choices and behavioral treatment. *Behavioral Residential Treatment*, **5**, 29–44.

Meyer, L. & Evans, I. M. (1989) *Non-aversive Intervention for Behavior Problems: A Manual for Home and Community*. New York: Teachers College Press.

Michael, J. (1982) Distinguishing between discriminative and motivational functions of stimuli. *Journal of the Experimental Analysis of Behavior*, **37**, 149–155.

O'Neill, R. E., Horner, R. H., Albin, R. W., *et al* (1990) *Functional Analysis of Problem Behavior: A Practical Assessment Guide*. Sycamore, IL: Sycamore Publishing Company.

Rachman, S. J. (1990) The determinants and treatment of simple phobias. *Advances in Behaviour Research and Therapy*, **12**, 1–30.

Repp, A. C. & Singh, N. N. (1990) *Perspectives on the Use of Nonaversive and Aversive Interventions for Persons with Developmental Disabilities*. Sycamore, IL: Sycamore Publishing Company.

Yule, W. & Carr, J. (1987) *Behaviour Modification for People with Mental Handicaps*. London: Croom Helm.

Zarkowska, E. & Clements, C. (1994) *Problem Behaviour and People with Severe Learning Disabilities: the STAR Approach* (2nd edn). London: Chapman and Hall.

12 Communicating with people with learning disabilities

Bill Fraser

Early infant communication ● Communication techniques ● Autistic spectrum disorders ● Mild learning disabilities ● Messages and channels

---

Early infant communication

Skilled dialogue with people who have learning disabilities requires first that the stages of normal speech development are understood. The acquisition of language follows distinct milestones (Box 12.1). The child with a learning disability goes through these stages at a slower rate, like a slow-motion film. In some handicapping conditions, there may only be delay in language development, due to cognitive impairment and a relatively unrewarding language environment. However, in most syndromes language development is also asynchronous with other aspects of development, for example in Down's syndrome (disproportionately delayed), or different in quality, as in autistic spectrum disorders.

From birth a child is in interaction with others and is conveying information about states of mind. In the early months, vocalisations communicate feelings of pain and distress or surprise. These signs are aimed to get the attention of adults. After six months, gestures, for example pointing, are combined with vocalisations to influence other people. At 10 months, 'protolanguage' emerges. In protolanguage 'interpersonal functions' influence what others do, and 'ideational functions' convey the child's state of mind. These are conveyed by gestures with vocalisation, and by vocalisations alone respectively. Halliday (1973) rejected the idea that the child is acquiring things such as sounds or words or grammar; rather, he is actively learning to 'mean'. It is therefore necessary to study how the child expresses intentions.

Austin (1962) has mapped the infant's acquisition of semiotic means. Early infant behaviours such as cries, gazes and short reaches which have communicative effects on adults, even if there is no evidence that the infant understands his/her ability to have such effects, are assigned to what Austin terms the 'perlocutionary' stage. As care-givers respond with an assigned meaning to these early infant actions, the child gradually discovers his ability to evoke responses from others. The next, 'illocutionary' stage is characterised by the child's coordinated actions on objects and people related to development of a small set of gestures directed at receivers – give, show, request and point – by which the child indicates an intention in order to have an effect on a receiver. Finally, the 'locutionary' stage arrives when the child produces actual linguistic forms to carry his or her intentions.

The goal of language intervention has shifted to assisting children to acquire the most adaptable, generalisable and acceptable communication skills possible. Thus, from an era in which infants and young children were ignored as appropriate candidates for communication skills training, programmes have been developed for young people with every sort of disability. The professional who works with people with learning disabilities must have some familiarity with augmented and affective communication systems and know basic Makaton sign language (see Stansfield, 1991, for an account of alternative communicative systems).

Mitchell (1987), in a review of parents' interactions with developmentally disabled or at-risk infants, noted that mothers of premature infants tend to be more active and intrusive and less responsive than mothers of

---

Box 12.1 Milestones of speech and language acquisition (at average ages)

Birth	**Vocalisations**
6 months	Babble.
10 months	Reduplications appear: 'ma-ma', 'da-da'.
1 year	One word sentences.
18 months	Two word utterances.
20 months	Telegrammatic speech.
2 years	Pre-sleep monologues.
2.5 years	50-word lexicon, 5-word sentences, use of personal pronoun.
3 years	Plurals established, 250 words.
3.5 years	'p', 'b', 'm', 'w', 'h' pronounced. How and why questions.
4 years	Tells story; still many morphological errors.
4.5 years	't', 'k', 'd', 'ng', 'y' pronounced. Asks what words mean.
5.5 years	'f', 'z', 's', 'v' pronounced.
6.5 years	'sh', 'zh', 'l', 'th' pronounced. Adult morphology complete. Listens to another's standpoint in conversation.
8 years	'ch', 'r', 'wh' pronounced.

full-term infants in joint activities such as playing or feeding. Infants with learning disabilities present similarly as problematic interactive partners for their parents.

As people with learning disabilities are exposed to parent-dominated interventions, they come to develop feelings of ineffectiveness or 'learned helplessness'. The parents similarly 'turn off' as competent interactive partners. There is now considerable literature on room and group management and care-giver variables for facilitating infant development. As Mitchell (1987) pointed out, "Parent/infant interaction is no place for parents to dance to a different drummer. For the most part, the infant should call the tune".

Awareness of the subtleties of the above developmental sequences is a necessary prerequisite to skilled consultations with people who have profound handicaps. The professional must be able to apply the approaches of mother/infant interaction dialogue to people stuck in the first year (perlocutionary or early illocutionary) phases.

Assessment

The notion of affective communication, where the adult places meaning (e.g. like, dislike) on the infant's responses to the environment, is incorporated in the Affective Communication Assessment (ACA) by Coupe & Levy (1985). Three stages are involved. Stage one consists of observation: stimuli to which the child is already known to respond are presented in turn and any responses by the child noted. Stage two involves identification: an attempt is made to identify the child's strongest responses of like/dislike/want/reject, and the consistency of the behaviours checked. Stage three involves interaction, following upon identification of the child's repertoire of behaviours.

The Pre-verbal Communication Schedule (PVCS; Kiernan & Reid, 1987) similarly identifies the handicapped child's current communicative abilities. The PVCS covers needs, interests and preferences; the non-communicative expression of emotion and social interaction; the degree to which the child is socially and emotionally withdrawn or outgoing; the child's ability to sing or respond to music; infant and parent communication; and categories of communicative acts.

Such assessment tools as the ACA and PVCS enable the professional to get a picture of the communicative repertoire of the person with severe learning disorder.

Burford's "Communication through Movement" approach (Burford, 1988) is built on observations of infant/mother dialogue, and is applicable to interacting with profoundly handicapped children and adults. Again, the principle is that the subject 'calls the tune' rather than the adult, who must free himself from the natural tendency to set the agenda by verbal acts. The basic principles are to try to find out before starting some history of the person with a profound handicap (for example, what his preferred way of signalling is; what he finds enjoyable from adults), and then to watch and spot 'what's on offer' (that includes assuming intentionality: unless proved otherwise, every movement and every silence means something); and to be particularly sensitive to the pace or rhythm of interaction.

Mothers and infants have what appear to be universals of pace of interactions depending on the occasion and purpose. Nigerian and Scots mothers, for instance, have been found to share precisely the same 'mother song' rhythms (Trevarthen, 1986), and so do skilled interlocutors with people with profound handicaps. Burford (1988) identified five categories according to rate of 'action cycles', each cycle having its own communicative purpose.

It is essential that the psychiatrist can observe changes in interactions and communicative failures in care-givers, and help to remedy them.

Listening to crying

Mothers of normal children are fairly aware of their offspring's subjective states from the child's crying. There are three main aspects which influence the cry signal: the internal state of the infant; its age; and the situation in which it is involved.

A fourth factor – the clinical disorder from which the disabled child may be suffering – also has to be taken into account when the child has a learning disability.

The best future method for systematically studying cries is likely to be a combination of the spectrograph and the Cry Index (Pratt, 1981), which is calculated by multiplying two components together: amplitude and density. Amplitude is a measure of the loudness and density is a measure of the amount of time spent crying. The informal method that parents use is to use the child's cry as an alerting device, detecting a change in its causal characteristics. The child and the setting in which the crying is occurring are observed and examined to decide whether he is in pain and why. In people who have a learning disability the rough order of likely causes of pain are: locomotor discomfort; eyelash in eye; sore throat; sore ear; colic; oesophagitis; sphincter spasm; voluntary muscle spasm; joint pain; and so on.

The appearance of syntax and locutionary speech

At the end of the first year, the space between two sounds is split and in most languages, in much the same way throughout the world, 'mama' and 'dada' appear. These single though duplicated words are really one word sentences.

The normal child at around 18 months crosses a language watershed. The child starts to link objects and ideas together, and when he has developed the idea of the permanency of objects, so he can put on labels. Children develop a two-word stage where they employ only a small number of semantic operations – between eight and 15. The kind of meanings that are usually grammatically encoded are, in order of frequency nomination: recurrence; non-existence; agent and action; agent and object; agent and action and object; action and locative; entity and locative; possessor and possession; entity and demonstrative.

At about two years of age, personal pronouns start to appear, usually in the order of 'my', 'me', 'you' and 'I'. 'We' starts at about three years. The two-year-old learns words, and the three-year-old starts to use them. Now the normal child is a pattern learner. He tends at first to over-regularise rules, e.g. one sheep, two sheeps; but his mistakes tend to vanish by the age of seven years. The normal child extends control over the prosodic system, the grammatical system and the phonological system in a piecemeal fashion, bringing one aspect under control at a time. Prosody is under control early, by one year normally, but it may be eight or nine years before the child can cope with the more complex consonant clusters. The person with a learning disability may continue to make mistakes; he may obstinately make mistakes about plurals and pronouns and past tenses. When you press him, you realise that he often knows the rules – yet, showing impulsiveness in language, he seeks the easy way out. Normal adult competence (in some aspects of language) may never be reached.

Communication techniques

Professionals must be aware of and practice a variety of techniques in order to communicate with people who have severe learning disability. These are listed in Box 12.2.

Beveridge & Conti-Ramsden (1987) consider that with non- handicapped peers, children who have learning disabilities are non-assertive and deferential. Children with learning disabilities are particularly likely to experience problems in using language in social interactions with both their handicapped and non-handicapped peers. The experience of situations that present uncontrolled or aversive outcomes induces a psychological state of learned helplessness and a general disposition to avoid participation in certain types of problem situations.

Much faith is currently being placed in giving children who are learning disabled 'real world' experiences, but the recent moves to encourage persons with learning disabilities towards independent living within the community do not guarantee that full social integration will follow. The social world is, to quote Beveridge & Conti-Ramsden, "a baffling and problem-strewn battleground, even for many non-handicapped adults", and social integration requires the availability of a large number of methods and strategies for solving many of the problems. Unless people with learning disabilities can do this, they will remain on the fringe of society.

Autistic spectrum disorders

Almost all autistic children show retarded language development (very occasionally a child may have overcorrect grammar or normal verbal intelligence and yet have other features of autism, as may occur in Asperger's syndrome). Musical abilities are commonly preserved and other islets of competence such as visual short-term memory and memory for faces and topography, while impaired functions include auditory attention, auditory verbal memory, verbal reasoning and fluency. Autistic subjects often break phonological, syntactic and semantic constraints (pragmatic and situational rules are also often broken). Baltaxe (1980) has shown this most noticeably in the more able autistic individual, for example a switching from an inappropriate 'formal' code to an inappropriate

---

Box 12.2 Communication with people with severe learning disability

Make it enjoyable – practice where the person produces most (e.g. outings).
Do it regularly.
Do not cramp your style by too much formality.
Be an opportunist – sing, act, whistle, change your voice, gear and speech.
Use consistent labels.
Take small steps, and do not reach for a level too far beyond the person's development.
Remember to signal vigorously with your face and do not forget that the person may not signal back.
If he is not looking, he is not likely to be listening.
Give him time to answer.
Cue him by his name.
The onus is on you to ensure you are understood.
The behaviour of the person with a learning disability is the starting point.
Relate to the person's disability rather than their chronological age. (Note: this does not fit the normalisation philosophy of Wolfensberger.)
Always assume intentionality – that the behaviour, however strange, means something.

'informal' code. When autistic children of normal or near normal intelligence acquire adult speech, deviance is still noticeable. In addition to continuously breaking situational constraints and conventions of discourse, their prosody (by which is meant stress, rhythm and intonation) still remains quaint. Baltaxe has commented that their speech is improperly modulated, produced with overprecision. Their speech is flat and colourless. The communicative failure of a person with Asperger's syndrome can to all intents and purposes be regarded as that of a high functioning person with autism. The failure is largely due to a cognitive deficit rather than a primary semantic–pragmatic linguistic defect; that is, the problem is likely to be in the autistic person's lack of appreciation of the other person's perspective (see chapter 7). Children with a primary semantic–pragmatic linguistic defect are inappropriate in what they say and make grammatical errors similar to autistic children, but are usually friendly and biddable.

The poorly developed 'theory of mind' of the person with autism or Asperger's syndrome means that he may not be able to clearly transmit his intentions, and makes little or no self-repair of incomplete or 'fuzzy' unclear utterances. Sensitive help from a professional to clarify often obscure utterances may be necessary.

Mild learning disabilities

People with mild learning disabilities are recognised as unusual by the manner of their speech, but the causes are harder to pinpoint. Individuals with mild learning disabilities are deficient in a variety of cognitive abilities and in their knowledge of the world. Accordingly, their mastery of pragmatics may be patchy. They may have problems, for example, in taking turns: normally one speaker switches to the next without marked overlap or noticeable hesitation. They may be unable to produce or understand illocutionary acts: an illocutionary act is basically the function utterances are intended to perform in the communicative interaction. For example, "Could you help?" can function as a request for action or for information, but people with a learning disability may have difficulty fathoming out which (usually the intention is inferable from the information available). A person with a learning disability may have difficulty with conversational obligations; a participant in a communicative interaction often has the option to speak or not to speak, but sometimes in questions the listener is obliged to speak. He may have problems in selecting the content of his utterance. As a communicative exchange is more than a series of unrelated speaking turns, there is a logical progression and a competent listener keeps track of the topic to make an appropriate contribution. It is also important to establish reference: the listener must determine what an expression refers to and the speaker must ensure that the reference identification is possible. There must be an appropriate use of ties, i.e. linguistic devices such as 'this' or 'that', which make sentences coherent. A speaker must also ensure that when he is not understood, he repairs the situation and corrects any errors in his utterances. Such cognitive abilities as, for example, involvement in repair, are commonly referred to as 'metacognitive', i.e. the ability to reflect on one's cognitive processes. Reflection is not a strength of people with learning disabilities.

This creates distress in communicative interactions and anxiety states in the handicapped person, sometimes even phobic states, stemming from this inability to provide organised texts and to design information adequately in extended discourse. This failure to take into account the listener's state of mind is at its worst in people with Wing & Gould's (1979) triad of social impairment, but all who have learning disabilities are to some extent affected.

Leudar (1989) provides a useful framework for problems of pragmatics in the discourse of people with learning disability, that is, problems of *intentions*, *conventions* and *face*.

In problems of discernment of *intention*, one finds it difficult or impossible to discover, even in people with learning disabilities who have good syntax, what the point is.

Social workers, psychologists and doctors tend to rely on whoever accompanies the person with learning disability to acquire explanations. There is little research on how best to conduct such multiparty interactions to make this less humiliating for the handicapped person and more illuminating for the interviewer. Leudar has specified the problem of violating *conventions* of conversation: these are communicative maxims which audiences assume speakers are abiding by. His research has identified maxims that people who have mild learning disabilities are more likely to violate than members of the general population: the maxims of quality (what he says is likely to be backed by evidence); relevance (whether he picks up the topic and says what is relevant); manner (he does not explain himself in enough detail or tends to say more than is needed to be informative); disclosure (e.g. talks to strangers as if he knows them well); communality (pays no attention to the needs and interests of others).

Although unable to reflect on the causes of his communicative incompetence, the person with learning disabilities may be only too aware of his conversational limitations and inappropriateness, and will take steps to avoid situations in which this can occur. He may become fussed when conversations are too quick or he is out of his depth, so that steps have to be taken both by him and his audience to maintain *face*. Leudar has also pointed out that violations of certain maxims are characteristic of certain behaviour disturbances, and has shown a strong relationship between behaviour disturbance and the communicative environment. The Communicative Assessment Profile (CASP), which Van der Gaag

(1989) has developed, evaluates both the individual's linguistic ability and the communicative environment.

Consultation skills

The principles of communicating with people with more severe learning disabilities apply equally to those who have a mild learning disability. It is important to know something about the person first, what the problem is, what their likes and dislikes are, to make the interview interesting and enjoyable; to listen and look for what the person with the learning disability has to offer in communication and to wait for cues. Most psychiatric interview techniques need to be modified as they are designed for people of normal intelligence. Tully & Cahill (1984) and Flynn (1986) provide examples of interviewing techniques and guidelines.

The problem of third-party or multi-party interviewing is not resolved in any current interview techniques as there are no rules of ceremony for consultation with a third party. The participating role of a third person has to be clarified: is he an official listener, an overhearer/eavesdropper or a bystander? In criminal proceedings, the third party often invigilates suggestibility. It is worth remembering that most people with learning disabilities will score a maximum on Gudjonsson's Suggestibility Test (1984), so further tests of compliance are needed. Concessions have to be made for particular difficulties with explanatory discourse – backing statements with evidence. Duckworth *et al* (1993) piloted a rating scale with assessors familiar with examining clinical interview accents (i.e. speech therapy tutors) to ascertain how good psychiatrists were at interviewing people with mild mental handicaps. Experienced consultant psychiatrists with a special interest in learning disabilities were compared with young psychiatrists in training who had no experience of working with people who had learning disabilities. Component behaviours were analysed from each videotape. Ten adults with mild learning disabilities resident in a mental handicap hospital and their care-givers (nurses) took part in 15-minute video interviews. The topics involved general health questions. Agreement between the assessors was poor on non-verbal behaviour but it was possible for the best and the worst interviewers to be identified. The good interviewers showed more rapport and showed (or pretended to show) more knowledge of the patient. They adjusted their linguistic complexity. They also avoided patient acquiescence. The good interviewers were younger.

Messages and channels

It may be helpful to the reader to classify communications into messages and the channels utilised (Box 12.3).

Box 12.3 Communicative channels and messages

Channels
Extralinguistic: setting, dress, accent
Paralinguistic: vocal, non-vocal
Linguistic: phonology, grammar, vocabulary
Messages
Management: proxemics, sequency
Indexical items: emotional leakage, mental state, intelligence
Topics: relevance, coherence, sophistication

A participant almost instantaneously makes a series of appraisals of another's communication using multimodal channels to get messages on which to adjust his or her propositions (or maintenance of silence). The messages include the setting.

For example, a middle-aged lady in short white socks in hospital (*extralinguistic*) with a high pitched voice (*paralinguistic*) and the grammatical development of a four-year-old (*linguistic*) who comes far too close to strangers (*proxemics*) and whose voice 'breaks' with emotion, irrelevantly reintroducing the death of Elvis Presley many years ago (*indexical items*, *topics*, *intelligence*, *sophistication*) communicates a lot, including perhaps the chromosome defect (Cri-duchat syndrome?).

The overall message of this chapter is that even those who are most profoundly disabled do produce communicative acts, and that parents and care staff can be very skilled in reacting to often very opaque communications. The professional ought to be at least as skilled.

References

Austin, J. L. (1962) *How to Do Things with Words*. London: Oxford University Press.

Baltaxe, C. (1980) Prosodic abnormalities in autism. In *Frontiers of Research: Proceedings of the Vth IASSMD Conference* (ed. P. Mittler). Baltimore: University Park Press.

Beveridge, M. & Conti-Ramsden, G. (1987) Social cognition and problem solving in persons with mental retardation. *Australia and New Zealand Journal of Developmental Disabilities*, **13**, 99–106.

Burford, B. (1988) Action cycles: rhythmic actions for engagement with children and young adults with profound mental handicap. *European Journal of Special Needs Education*, **3**, 189–206.

Coupe, J. & Levy, D. (1985) The Object Related Scheme Assessment Procedure. *Mental Handicap*, **13**, 22–24.

Duckworth, M. S., Radhakrishnan, G., Nolan, M. E., *et al* (1993) Initial encounters between people with a mild mental handicap and psychiatrists: an evaluation of a method of evaluating interview skills. *Journal of Intellectual Deficiency Research*, **37**, 263–276.

Flynn, M. (1986) Adults who are mentally handicapped as consumers: Issues and guidelines for interviewing. *Journal of Mental Deficiency Research*, **30**, 369–377.

Gudjonsson, G. H. (1984) A new test of interrogative suggestibility. *Personal and Individual Differences*, **5**, 303–314.

Halliday, M. A. K. (1973) *Explorations in the Functions of Language*. London: Edward Arnold.

Kiernan, C. & Reid, B. (1987) *The Preverbal Communication Schedule (PVCS)*. Windsor: NFER/ Nelson.

Leudar, I. (1989) Communicative environments for mentally handicapped people. In *Language and Communication in Mentally Handicapped People* (eds M. Beveridge, G. Conti-Ramsden & I. Leudar), pp. 274–299. London: Chapman and Hall.

Mitchell, D. R. (1987) Parents' interactions with their developmentally disabled or autistic infants: a focus for intervention. *Australia and New Zealand Journal of Developmental Disabilities*, **13**, 73–82.

Pratt, C. (1981) Crying in normal infants. In *Communicating with Normal and Retarded Children* (eds W. Fraser & R. Grieve), pp 3–23. Bristol: John Wright.

Stansfield, J. (1991) Augmentative and alternative systems of communication. In *Caring for People with Mental Handicaps* (eds W. Fraser, A. Green & R. MacGillivray), pp. 76–86. Oxford: Butterworth.

Trevarthen, C. (1986) Development of intersubjective motor control in infants. In *Motor Development in Children: Aspects of Coordination and Control* (eds M. G. Wade & H T. A. Whiting), pp. 209–283. Dordrecht: Martinus Nijhoff.

Tully, B. & Cahill, D. (1984) *Police Interviewing of the Mentally Handicapped: An Experimental Study*. London: The Police Foundation.

Van der Gaag, A. (1989) *The Communication Assessment Profile for Adults with Learning Difficulties* (CASP). Speech Profiles Ltd.

Wing, L. & Gould, J. (1979) Severe impairments of social interaction and associated abnormalities in children: epidemiology and classification. *Journal of Autism and Developmental Disorders*, **9**, 11–29.

13 Philosophical and ethical issues

Joan Bicknell

History • Patterns of care • Consent • The adult with learning disabilities • Conclusion

---

The term healthcare ethics refers to the application of the principles of decision-making to dilemmas in health care. Healthcare workers have personal value systems and there are values held by professions and society which reflect a wide range of beliefs. All these may influence decision-making, which falls largely into two categories: decisions that feel innately good and those that are made to bring the best outcome to the greatest number. There are many phrases that illuminate decision-making; acting in good faith, acting in the person's best interest, showing a duty of care, the concepts of justice and fairness, doing good and not doing harm (Gillon, 1985c), the least restrictive alternative, and the avoidance of both negligence and battery. The shoulds and oughts in formulations are essentially ethical questions. Ethical issues are often reflected in both religion and the law, but the viewpoints are not always identical. A doctor who is ethically competent has the abilities outlined in Box 13.1.

History

Throughout history, those who cared for people with learning disabilities reflected, for good or bad, the philosophy of the day. When there was no welfare state, people with learning disabilities were cared for by the family or suffered the same fate as orphans, the poor, the elderly and the mentally ill. Dr Barnardo, struck by the plight of abandoned children, took boys and girls off the street and away from a merciless world of crime. The same sentiments caused philanthropists such as Dr Langdon-Down and Dr Andrew Reid to start institutions for those of low intellect. Institutionalisation, reaching its zenith in the early 1900s, was at least kinder than the neglect and ill-treatment that was the lot of many others.

In the early years of the 20th century there seems to have been a collective fear in so-called civilised society that low intellect was going to be spread, especially by those who had children who would themselves in due course contribute to the decline of the national intelligence (see Gould, 1981, for a discussion of these issues). Keeping people in detention until the risk of procreation was over was "acting in good faith". This was the predominant belief underpinning this theory of the spread of national degeneracy. As H. H. Goddard, one of the leaders of this movement, wrote:

> "If we are absolutely to prevent a feeble-minded person from becoming a parent, something must be done other than prohibiting them from marrying. To this end there are two proposals: the first is colonisation, the second is sterilisation." (Goddard, 1914)

Goddard did not oppose sterilisation but he regarded it as impractical. He preferred colonisation in institutions like his own at Vineland, New Jersey.

At several times in our history people with learning disabilities have been threatened by eradication in small or large numbers because they were considered to be inferior stock, poor germ plasm, or not worth the cost to keep alive. Some with major physical handicaps were shown in circuses, but were treated cruelly while offstage and often died young. While few would suggest that Hitler's atrocities could be called 'in good faith' (Institute of Medical Ethics Bulletin, 1989), there have been incidents when people with learning disabilities have been put at risk "for the good of others", such as in early trials of the measles vaccine.

Where people with learning disabilities are regarded as substandard or a threat in any way, various conclusions follow. Their living accommodation is poor, privacy non-existent, their sexuality denied and ordinary healthcare not made available. Impoverished lifestyles with carers inadequate in numbers and training become acceptable. Wolfensberger, the protagonist of 'normalisation' and 'social role valorisation', speaks of "death-making" and reminds us that we must remain vigilant as there is still the possibility that people with learning disabilities receive less than good medical and social care for no other reason than their low intellect (Wolfensberger, 1989).

Box 13.1 The abilities of the ethically competent doctor

Knows the various concepts and principles involved in caring for people with special needs, including those with learning disabilities.
Aware of emotional issues and the human rights argument.
Adequate medical knowledge.
Has the determination to act when required.
Aware of ethical principles and not afraid of measuring his decisions against them.

Even now, people with learning disabilities have little citizen power. When the vote was allowed to those in institutions, in the early 1980s, each vote was transmitted to that person's place of origin, thus ensuring that a group of individuals in an institution were of no local political interest.

In today's complex, rapidly changing service with confused expectations and with a recent past history of failure to meet even basic needs, it is not surprising that internecine quarrels may break out. Nurses feel their core 'hands-on' role is threatened, and day-care staff that residential care staff are inadequate; psychologists feel that their core skills are unappreciated and doctors may feel that they are being made responsible for the medical models of yesterday. Many of these issues may focus on a client who is almost too difficult to manage.

Patterns of care

Institutional life

The large institutions provided homes for thousands of people with learning disabilities, in particular for those whose handicap was mild. The Physician Superintendents were mindful of their dual role, firstly to free the community from such people who would otherwise be a danger and an embarrassment, and secondly to provide care, protection and some training for the inmates in an asexual environment. Some institutions emphasised the custodial element and others the training for work within the institution. All were detained and long-term care was the aim so that no-one, having lived under such a paternalistic umbrella, should go out the more vulnerable into an uncaring society.

In the 1950s the laws changed to allow many to leave as informal patients. For some left behind, ill-treatment and neglect were uncovered later and behaviour problems were often dealt with only by sedation and restriction. Acting in good faith, showing a duty of care and using least restrictive alternatives had been forgotten. Many inmates were held inappropriately against their will with no recourse to the law. All of this signalled the end of institutions but little was ready in the community to take their place (Ashton & Ward, 1992).

Some people with learning disabilities have unacceptable behavioural problems and a 'micro' hospital may remain on the campus, or the resident and his team of carers may be transferred to an ordinary house in isolation from others. Another group particularly difficult to place are those who are hepatitis carriers. Should they be transferred without declaration? Or is this unfair to new caring agencies who if they knew would probably not accept them?

However, the vast majority of residents moving out of institutions, of whatever age, are excited to be in the community, and some high quality networks of services are developing to offer whole lifestyles rather than only housing.

Case example

Tom and Vera had known each other for many years in an institution that was closing. They were offered a flat in accommodation for the elderly near the hospital as they had no connections with their places of origin. They went for a trial period and their key workers supported them by regular visiting. After some apprehension, they accepted the flat and improved their daily living skills so that they were almost self sufficient and supported by a daily friendly visit from the Warden. They were introduced to the local church by the hospital chaplain and joined the club for the elderly where they found they were much more intellectually able than the others. They were encouraged to write their life stories as a way of expressing both the positive and negative feelings about their experience.

Community care

As people with learning disabilities move from institutions into the community, they join a large group already there, living with families or substitute families or in well-established alternative accommodation provided by private, voluntary or statutory agencies. A few, the least dependent, will live in supervised lodgings, flats or co-residences, for example, sharing the accommodation with university students. Some will be married or living with a partner and may have children.

The aim to create a harmonious community for all people is worthy but requires work and trust. Many situations can strain the system. Decisions have to be made when a person with learning disabilities becomes behaviourally disturbed or mentally ill and, by his symptoms, threatens to disturb the equilibrium of the neighbourhood. Has he a right of access to all usual psychiatric services? If the institution will not readmit, the local psychiatric hospital is considered inappropriate, and the local services for people with learning disabilities have no suitable facilities, then the dilemma is often solved by superhuman care in his home setting, but others may suffer. In the end, the rights of the handicapped person to effective treatment may be balanced against the rights of the locality to be free from molestation. The should and ought questions may help to take appropriate action, but that will always be difficult in the face of inadequate services.

Some people have mixed feelings about next-door-neighbours who have learning disabilities and resent their intrusion on what they insist was hitherto a peaceful and dignified environment. That kind of resentment can only be challenged by showing that people with learning disabilities can contribute to and not detract from society. This requires daily living, personal and social skills and if possible skills in helping others. It is well known that people with learning disabilities need to be tidier, cleaner and more polite than someone brighter than themselves to rank as equally acceptable in the locality. While for many this is distasteful, experience dictates it is often the case (Bicknell & Conboy Hill, 1992).

Some planners favour opening homes 'by stealth', where neighbours find out and are pleasantly surprised that people with learning disabilities are living next door. Others favour planning 'by proclamation', where the neighbourhood is informed, debates are held and information given such that misunderstandings are dealt with before the residents arrive. Occasionally the house is speedily bought by someone else. Each arrangement has its drawbacks and situations must be dealt with individually so that justice and fairness can be maximised together with goodwill.

There have been some claims for compensation based on the belief that people with learning disabilities should not be in the community and that their presence has inadvertently caused an accident for someone. These legal cases often show the extremes of feeling which have developed about community care, but there are many more disagreements that do not reach the courts. If a genuine accident was the cause of the upset then it is unlikely that the case would proceed, but if it was deliberate, for example a person with learning disabilities pushes an old lady into the road, then the situation is far more difficult. Ashton & Ward (1992) provide a full discussion of the law as it relates to learning disabilities.

Those who work with people with learning disabilities may become so much an advocate for this client group that they fail to see other viewpoints. This happened when a coastal town in the southwest of England was visited by large numbers of people with learning disabilities for holidays, to the extent that other holiday-makers complained that the facilities were not available to them. The principles of justice and fairness remind us to think of all parties involved in any debate and that people with learning disabilities, when congregated in great numbers, pose a threat to those who would happily coexist if the numbers were smaller.

Unacceptable patterns of care

Substandard care was not only a feature of some institutions but may be found in any part of the service in the community where monitoring is more difficult. Families are not immune and may run into difficulties especially if one parent is mentally ill or there are major housing, financial or dependency problems and other children. Here, neglect may be severe but not deliberate. Sometimes the situation seems calculated, such as the use of girls with learning disabilities as prostitutes or as unwilling victims of incest in the home. Sometimes the ill-treatment is grotesque, such as a young man who was made to watch his goldfish boiled to death and a girl found with cigarette burns over much of her body. Gross overprotection can cause similar concerns. An adult woman had been kept in bed one week before, one week during and one week after menstruation for no good reason.

Such eccentric patterns of care may be changed usually after trust of the care-giver has been gained. In very serious situations, the National Assistance Act may be used to remove the handicapped person against the will of the so-called care-givers, but complex human rights issues loom large if this is done. Likewise, concerns are growing about the increasing numbers of people with learning disabilities in prisons and in the inner-city populations of homeless people.

Paternalism to autonomy

The traditional hospital style of care involved minimising risk and providing father-like support. For many hospitals this became stale, the regime was infantilising and rigid and became based on tradition and staffing needs rather than needs of the residents for personal growth. People with learning disabilities were expected to take no risks, nor were they allowed to feel the effects of small mistakes.

The principles of autonomy (Gillon, 1985a) and paternalism provide useful guidelines in such an exercise as closing an institution. A wide range of human rights need to be protected at this time. Choice-making by residents for their life outside of the institution may be helped by visits and discussions, and ultimately their decisions respected and implemented if possible. This may include a wish to move with friends who may not have similar addresses of origin. Those who cannot choose must have choices made for them by those who know them well and have an idea of what might suit them best. This is the ethical principle of substituted judgement. Others may be able to make simple choices and so exercise their autonomy in part at least. The aim will be for autonomy to be maximised and individual rights and wishes respected, but political and financial pressures may dictate a less sensitive procedure.

In the wake of so many years of paternalistic service, it is easy to see why the pendulum may sometimes swing too far in the other direction when setting up modern services for people with a learning disability. It is unfortunate that paternalism now implies something inappropriate and demeaning rather than something that can be necessary and creative. If all paternalism is abandoned then people with learning disabilities may not have the support they need.

Case example
Sarah has Down's syndrome and lives in a group home. She is 23 years old and comes from a loving and caring family. In the home she has been encouraged to make her own decisions, and has abandoned

her slimming diet and her daily bath. She is now grotesquely obese and smells and her hair is rarely washed. She seems unhappy but cannot say why. Her parents are distraught because they feel she needs more supervision and direction and are considering having her home again to live, which they accept is a backward step.

A fine balance needs to be struck between support that keeps a client unskilled and childlike, and help that is needed and offered in a dignified and adult way. Recently, the development of autonomy has achieved unhelpful prominence in some services where it has become a yardstick of staff excellence. This can lead to dishonest appraisals of people with learning disabilities.

Case example
Kim, a totally helpless child, sat shivering in her wheelchair in a bitter wind. This was explained to a visitor as "exercising her right to be cold" and could only have been untrue in the context of Kim's handicap.

Sometimes, a choice or a risk goes wrong although taken with the best of intentions and with a desire for autonomy in mind. In these settings the client may be hurt, the carer with the client often takes the punishment, and the most senior members of the hierarchy may face the media or the courts. It is easy to see the force of the counter-pressure to be cautious at all times, which may not be in the best interests of the client (Carson, 1990).

Case example
A woman with epilepsy and mild mental handicap always bathed alone at the Social Education Centre. An attendant stayed near, but one day went to fetch a towel and returned to find the woman dead in the bath. Despite the fact that her death was not due to epilepsy, there was a move to change the policy to compulsory attendance at bathing, which would have eroded privacy and dignity indiscriminately. Fortunately, by powerful advocacy, this was avoided.

Unfortunately, there may be conflict between home, school, and place of day-care or employment. Parents are frequently seen as overprotective, a judgement that is often prematurely made on little evidence, but staff often feel the need to prove that parents are holding back their offspring. One unacceptable way in which this is resolved is to keep information from the parents, thus reducing their power and their position in decision-making. The solution rests in working together in honesty with the parents and the person with learning disabilities as part of the team of decision-makers, where confrontation can happen and a compromise found if necessary (Nadesalingham, 1990). For the person with learning disabilities to exercise their autonomy, it is essential they are briefed, understand the issues and can communicate effectively.

It is easy to offer choices to those who have never learnt to make them, to offer difficult ones to those who can only manage simple choices, and to offer none at all when it is quicker and more expedient for someone else to take the decision. While the past generations of adults with learning disabilities have not had opportunities to learn about making choices from an early age, it is hoped that the current generation of children with special needs are having this chance and will grow up to be more autonomous.

An ordinary life

'An ordinary life' is a phrase much used to denote the need for and the right of access to ordinary facilities for those who have learning disabilities. The concept of ordinariness is a useful one to denote the degree to which services move away from segregation. However, even this concept is complicated and does not always bring people with learning disabilities into contact with the best service there might be. Many segregated services are poor and devalued (although dental services can be a notable exception; many families have had better services from specialised dental facilities than from ordinary dental services). Does ordinariness mean sharing services that are under-resourced and under strain? Are we right to strain them even further by the introduction of a group of people who need an ordinary life but who also need services that reduce their frustration and fear to a minimum?

Other issues are less contentious. Access to buildings such as libraries and public toilets will often already have been improved because of the efforts of people with a physical handicap. But it is not only access that is needed but a sense of comfort for all, which comes when people with learning disabilities are treated as ordinary people while at the same time their special needs are acknowledged.

Many people with learning disabilities will never be in open employment, because of high levels of unemployment, the increased use of technology and their own limitations. However, those who can are encouraged to seek opportunities in open competition with those who are breadwinners. Many schemes have been developed to give personal supervision at the beginning of 'open employment' to ensure that the person with learning disabilities does not fail because of poor timekeeping or social ineptitude. With this extra help, many make first-class employees and become highly valued members of a workforce. However, those for whom there are no such opportunities go to day centres which are now often seen as outdated, segregated and never to be repeated. Once more, enthusiasm for the opportunities for some to do well is often matched by a devaluation of the service and staff who care for those who are not so able. It will be a tragedy if the 'ordinary life' philosophy means poorer services for those who have no chance for integration at present.

Should people with learning disabilities be employed before those not so handicapped and probably with financial responsibilities? Such positive discrimination occurs in some schemes but might lead to envy and a move away from ordinariness which is so precious. Once more, ideology must be mixed with pragmatism.

Consent

The Law Commission are currently undertaking a major review of the law as it concerns people who cannot give informed consent because of their mental incapacity (Law Commission, 1991). Their recommendations have now been published as a Government White Paper on "Mental incapacity" (Law Commission, 1995), but the proposals have yet to be considered by Parliament and it may be some years before they reach the statute book. The main features include:

(a) Until the age of 16 years, consent for procedures for children with learning disabilities are dealt with in the same way as for any other child (Bicknell, 1989*a*). After 16 years almost every individual becomes responsible for their own decisions and signs their own consent forms for medical and dental procedures.

(b) There are groups of individuals, however, who may not be able to do this. Those who are unconscious, those who do not understand the language, those with severe mental illness, those who are demented, and some of those who have learning disabilities may fall into this category, known as 'legally incompetent'.

(c) The law provides a clear statement concerning consent for those who are legally incompetent – that there is no one who can sign a consent form on their behalf. This includes parents, guardians, advocates, nurses and doctors.

(d) If no one takes responsibility for medical decisions for those who are legally incompetent, many people with learning disabilities would be neglected and vital treatment withheld. Clearly a decision needs to be taken by proxy, i.e. on their behalf.

(e) Many people with learning disabilities are able to give consent for themselves and are therefore legally competent. This occurs in particular if they have had experience of choice-making in their lives and if the medical choices are put to them simply by someone they know and trust. Heavy persuasion for one or other choice is not appropriate, although guidance will be needed. If the person cannot write, a witnessed cross on the paper will do.

(f) No one should be barred from making a medical choice simply because they have learning disabilities or they cannot write. People with a substantial level of learning disability will need a lot of help with decision-making, or will only be able to make simple decisions, or will be able to make none at all.

(g) Common law helps in decision-making for those who give consent by proxy for legally incompetent adults by offering principles for guidance. These are outlined in Box 13.2.

Throughout the procedures for decision-making by proxy for those who are legally incompetent, adequate consultations with the multidisciplinary team, other doctors and family are essential, as is adequate documentation. In a very small number of situations where, for example, parents are at odds with other decision-makers, wider discussion is required until consensus is reached, or in the case of continuing disagreement, the legal profession may be contacted. The Mental Health Act Commission may also give helpful advice. If the situation is life-threatening then the doctor's views must prevail (Bicknell, 1989*b*).

Implied consent is something used all the time in work with people with learning disabilities. The medication tablet taken willingly or the arm offered for blood-taking are examples. Implied consent is good enough for most everyday procedures, but is insufficient for bigger decisions.

Occasionally the wrong decision is made by the person with learning disabilities, for example, refusing to have a broken arm put in plaster. Carers will need to override such decisions which are probably based on fear of immediate pain rather on the long-term outcome. A proxy decision to have the plaster, based on acting to preserve health, is the more appropriate.

Box 13.2 Common law guidance for those who give consent by proxy for legally incompetent adults

Acting in the patient's best interests. (This means that a responsible body of medical opinion is being followed or that more than 50% of doctors/nurses would make the same choice.)

Acting to preserve life, health and well-being.

Acting in good faith. (This means that the decision is honest.)

Showing a duty of care. (Our intended actions are within a professional caring role and we would be negligent if we did not proceed.)

Avoidance of both negligence (not caring properly), battery and assault (caring inappropriately).

Using the least restrictive alternative (e.g. heavy sedation and a locked door might both be appropriate but one less restrictive than the other).

Have cultural and religious factors been respected?

Cover-all consent forms (e.g. for any dental treatment) or prospective consent forms (for any treatment in the future) are bad practice and should not be used.

It is possible that people with learning disabilities will want to be blood or organ donors, take part in research, or be used for teaching for nursing and medical students. Their decisions on these matters can be valid but no one should be exploited because consent is not forthcoming. Implied consent is inappropriate in these situations.

The Mental Health Act (1983) does not help in the matter of consent except concerning psychiatric treatments in a small group of patients held on a Section of the Act.

In controversial interventions, such as sterilisation (Gillon, 1987), the medical profession must involve the legal profession in the decision-making process. Some publicity in the press may be expected.

Proposed reforms in the law

The Law Commission has published proposals for new legislation concerning the legal situation of all people deemed to be mentally incapacitated (Law Commission, 1995). When enacted these proposals should enable psychiatrists and other professionals to have a much clearer view of how consent may be given on behalf of the person with severe learning disabilities who cannot give informed consent. It is likely that the proposed reforms will result in new consent forms being introduced for those deemed legally incompetent. These should stop, for example, last minute requests from surgeons for a signature on the usual style of form where there is no one legally entitled to sign it.

The adult with learning disabilities

The adult with learning disabilities may, through his life span, repeat recent history in moving from a position of inappropriate dependence to one of appropriate independence. He may with varying degrees of help fulfil many functions of adulthood in the community. Perhaps the greatest challenge for carers lies with those with challenging behaviours and those who are profoundly and multiply handicapped, to help them to experience whatever is possible of adult awareness, adult mores and adult responsibilities.

In all their efforts to become full members of society, people with learning disabilities take on rights and responsibilities of any other person, and yet still events happen which do not happen to others.

Confidentiality is such an issue (Royal College of Psychiatrists, 1990). Names may be placed in registers for people with learning disabilities without their permission and with uncertain benefit. The multidisciplinary team may feel that respect for the privacy of an individual is inappropriate for the person with learning disabilities, and a long list of people seem to 'need to know' (Williams *et al*, 1987).

So long as these double standards continue within the community it is easy to understand why labels are objected to by those at risk from ambivalent attitudes. Labels such as 'the mentally handicapped' can separate and alienate and are particularly insulting when the humanity is subservient to the category. "Label jars not people" was an early plea of those in the self-advocacy movement, strong in the US initially and now in this country. Labels that put down, demean and exclude must be dropped in favour of either no label or those that describe but do not segregate.

When formal arrangements for citizen advocacy schemes were introduced in the UK in the early 1980s, starting in institutions, a shortage of suitable volunteers was found and many were discouraged by what they discovered in the institutions and by the battles that they lost. Self-advocacy, a movement fuelled by people with learning disabilities themselves, has made an impact and has given many the platform they were waiting for, but they cannot be expected to speak up for their more handicapped co-residents who are the most vulnerable to a denial of human rights (Dybwad & Bersani, 1996).

A small group of people with learning disabilities are now in open employment, not only in factory or supermarket posts but in other positions such as in clerical and receptionist work, on the railways and as trained carers of disabled people. Others have taken part in developing community projects such as bakeries, coffee shops and craft shops. Many steps are necessary to take on such work: learning to get up on time, cleanliness, tidiness and appropriate clothing, and for some, self-medication. Many who are successful in this way often reside in a home setting which has given support, guidance and creative 'parenting' to bring out their capabilities. The sense of achievement is undeniable for those, but for others, from equally supported backgrounds, their major achievement is to walk to the bus stop or cross a road alone.

One might argue that people with learning disabilities cannot have it all their way. They cannot expect not to be labelled and then remembered when extra help is needed. They cannot have ordinary living and positive discrimination when times are hard. They cannot have their sexual rights and then be allowed to neglect their child (Gillon, 1985*b*).

This ambivalence is also seen within the church. Some priests are doubtful about preparing a person with learning disabilities for the sacraments, such as confirmation and adult baptism. Absorption into church life is often felt as uncomfortable by the parishioners, and patronisation often keeps them at the periphery of the congregation.

Exploitation is always a major hazard and some might say that 'the right to be exploited' includes everyone. Others, however, would want to protect all those who are easily exploited because of their gullibility and their low intelligence.

Simple exploitation at the level of being given the wrong change or being sold faulty goods is partly dealt with by assertion training and by increasing verbal competence. Sexual exploitation is a major issue for women with learning disabilities as seen in prostitution, rape and incest. Some are exploited within the family; their pensions are misused, food, clothing and heating is inadequate, and cruelty, both physical and psychological, may occur (Williams, 1993, 1995; Sobsey, 1994; Brown *et al*, 1995)

Case example

Patricia lived at home, was regularly raped, received little food and did all the housework. Her pet cat was strangled in a row. Her pension was taken from her and used by others. Despite many offers for her to move out and live in a variety of pleasant situations, she refused to leave saying that she would be followed and killed.

Situations such as this must give rise to great concern, rare though they are. Does Patricia have the right to choose to live in squalor and refuse offers to move out? Is she not making a choice in the usual sense of the word? Does society have a responsibility to move her against her will because she has reduced intelligence?

Conclusion

Children and adults with learning disabilities are now facing new expectations from society. Asylum is a thing of the past and is replaced by community care. Fall-back positions in long-stay hospitals are no longer found and mini-institutions in the community are, it is hoped, to be prevented.

At the same time that services are changing, responsibility is shifting and new professions are taking up leading roles. Expectations of families are changing as well. No longer are parents and then siblings anticipating years of unsupported and unremitting care. Many clients, families and professionals will take these changes in their stride but some may not. There will be new problems such as homelessness, people with learning disabilities inappropriately placed in prison, and a greater number of elderly people with learning disabilities, all challenging interagency cooperation. There are those who may become isolated in the community because of a lack of civic competence, psychiatric illness or challenging behaviour. Great efforts will be required if all those with learning disabilities and additional problems are able to lead a fulfilling life with no one suffering as a consequence. Carers, whether family or professional, will need support that enhances and does not deskill so that burnout is prevented.

There will always be those in society who believe that the world would be a better place without those with learning disabilities. While the threat of euthanasia lurks behind such philosophical arguments, advocates will be needed to ensure fairness in opportunities and distribution of resources with limited positive discrimination, showing that people with learning disabilities, both children and adults, can take their place in society and have something to offer.

Working in services for people with learning disabilities is both immensely rewarding and also frustrating. Every day there will be a 'should' or 'ought' decision, the outcome of which may be to enable a family to be stronger, a human right to be recognised, or a person with learning disabilities empowered to be even more confident and fulfilled. There is also the opportunity to ensure that in new approaches to service development, the moral and ethical issues, some of which have been outlined in this chapter, can be fully debated for the best possible outcome.

> "We have to provide the highest possible culture, the best physical, moral, and intellectual training and to open out fresh realms of happiness for those who have the strongest claims on our sympathy." (John Langdon-Down, 1866)

References

Ashton, G. & Ward, A. (1992) *Mental Handicap and the Law*. London: Sweet and Maxwell.

Bicknell, D. J. (1989a) Consent for children and adolescents who have an intellectual handicap. *Archives of Disease in Childhood*, **64**, 1529–1532.

—— (1989b) Consent and people with mental handicap. *British Medical Journal*, *ii*, 1176–1177.

—— & Conboy-Hill, S. (1992) The deviancy career and people with a mental handicap. In *Psychotherapy and Mental Handicap* (eds A. Waitman & S. Conboy-Hill), pp. 117–131. London: Sage.

Brown, H. & Turk, V. (1992) Defining sexual abuse as it affects adults with learning disabilities. *Mental Handicap*, **20**, 44–55.

——, Stein, J. & Turk, V. (1995) The sexual abuse of adults with learning disabilities. *Mental Handicap Research*, **8**, 3–24.

Carson, D. (1990) *Professionals and the Courts: a Handbook for Expert Witnesses*. Birmingham: Venture Press.

Dybwad, G. & Bersani, H. (1996) *New Voices: Self-advocacy by People with Disabilities*. Cambridge, MA: Brookline Books.

Gillon, R. (1985a) Autonomy and the principle of respect for autonomy. *British Medical Journal*, **290**, 1806–1808.

—— (1985b) Rights. *British Medical Journal*, **290**, 1890–1891.

—— (1985c) Beneficence: doing good for others. *British Medical Journal*, **291**, 44–45.

—— (1987) On sterilising severely mentally handicapped people. *Journal of Medical Ethics*, **13**, 59–61.

Goddard, H. H. (1914) *Feeble-mindedness: its Causes and Consequences*. New York: Macmillan.

Gould, S. J. (1981) *The Mismeasure of Man*. New York: W.W. Norton.

Institute of Medical Ethics Bulletin (1989) Contemporary lessons from Nazi medicine, p.13.

Langdon-Down, H. J. (1866) Observations on an ethnic classification of idiots. *Clinical Lectures and Reports, London Hospital*, **3**, 259–262.

Law Commission (1991) *Mentally Handicapped Adults and Decision-making – An Overview*. London: HMSO.

—— (1995) *Mental Incapacity*. London: HMSO.

Nadesalingham, K. (1990) John as a utility and 'utility'. *Psychiatric Bulletin*, **14**, 601–603.

Royal College of Psychiatrists (1990) Position Statement on Confidentiality. *Psychiatric Bulletin*, **14**, 97–109.

Sobsey, D. (1994) *Violence and Abuse in the Lives of People with Disabilities – The End of Silent Acceptance*. Baltimore: Paul H. Brookes.

Williams, C. (1993) Vulnerable victims? A current awareness of the victimisation of people with learning difficulties. *Disability, Handicap and Society*, **8**, 161–172.

—— (1995) *Invisible Victims*. London: Jessica Kingsley.

Williams, R., Singh, T. H., Naish, J., *et al* (1987) Medical confidentiality and multidisciplinary work: child sexual abuse and mental handicap registers. *British Medical Journal*, **295**, 1315–1320.

Wolfensberger, W. (1989) The killing thought in the eugenic era and today: A commentary on Hollander's essay. *Mental Retardation*, **27**, 63–65.

Additional reading

Copelman, L. & Moskop, J. C. (1984) *Ethics and Mental Retardation*. Reidel Publishing Co.

Laura, R. S. & Ashman, A. F. (1985) *Moral Values in Mental Retardation*. Beckenham: Croom Helm.

Thompson, I. E. (1987) Fundamental ethical principles in health care. *British Medical Journal*, **295**, 1461–1465.

14 The use of psychotropic drugs

Stephen Tyrer

Clinical pharmacology ● *Use of drugs in specific disorders* ●
Conclusion

Over the past three decades the use of drugs that affect mental functioning
has increased considerably. The word psychotropic (psycho = mind,
tropos = turning) implies alteration of the mind, and all drugs that affect
the mind in any way could technically be regarded as psychotropic drugs.
In practice, the term is usually employed to describe drugs the principal
effects of which are on thought, activity, behaviour and sleep.

Psychotropic drugs are widely used in people with learning disabilities
and often with poor indications. Those with a learning disability may
suffer from the same mental illnesses as people of normal intelligence
and drug treatment is similar in both groups. However, in the former
these drugs are often used when there is no evidence of psychiatric or
medical illness. They are widely employed in patients who are
behaviourally disturbed in order to control aggression and self-injurious
behaviour (Baumeister *et al*, 1993; Kiernan *et al*, 1995). As these behaviours
can arise from a wide variety of causes, no one treatment, whether
pharmacological or otherwise, is appropriate for every individual.

Despite this, studies carried out in a number of hospitals throughout
the Western world show that the use of these drugs is widespread, and
up to 50% of residents in institutions for those with learning disabilities
take at least one psychotropic drug regularly, not including those required
for control of epilepsy (Rinck *et al*, 1989). A similar number receive anti-
epileptic drugs. The use of psychotropic drugs in community settings is
considerably less than in hospital (Clarke *et al*, 1990; Branford, 1994).
However, surveys have shown that when patients who have lived in
hospitals for long periods are discharged to community facilities, there
is little change in the number of drugs received or their dosages (Thinn
et al, 1990; Fleming *et al*, 1996).

The incidence of prescription of psychotropic drugs has altered in
frequency over the past three decades. Following the advent of neuroleptic
drugs in the late 1950s, these drugs became widely employed within a
short period. Nowadays, with the recognition of the hazards of these
agents, in particular tardive dyskinesia, the use of these drugs has been
discouraged and there are strong pressures on agencies dealing with
people with learning disabilities not to use medication. These inclinations

were enhanced by the 'Coldwater' studies in the 1980s in the US, in which it was shown that discontinuation of thioridazine, the most commonly employed neuroleptic drug in treating behavioural disturbance in those with learning disability, was associated with improvement in behaviour, alertness and cognitive functioning (Breuning *et al*, 1983). These studies were persuasive and in one state, Connecticut, the use of thioridazine was restricted. However, the results did not match with clinicians' experiences of discontinuation of this drug and it was later shown that the work carried out by the chief investigator concerned in the original investigations was fraudulent (Lock, 1988).

The use of these drugs in specific conditions with precise indications for their employment is now accepted in most facilities for people with learning disabilities, but they are still over-prescribed. When examining the prevalence of psychotropic drug use, a distinction needs to be drawn between those drugs that are used for psychiatric purposes, those for behavioural indications, and those primarily for physical reasons.

Drugs used for the symptomatic improvement of patients with psychiatric illnesses and for the control of behaviour disorder are included in the first group. Anticonvulsants and drugs used in neurological and movement disorders largely comprise the second group.

Among workers in the learning disability field there is a difference in attitude towards the use of drugs within these two groups. In patients with epilepsy and in those with clear neurological or medical problems the value of drugs is accepted. Conversely, there is antipathy by many working with people with learning disabilities, particularly younger people working in community settings, towards the use of antipsychotic drugs, which is sometimes generalised to the use of antidepressants, hypnotics and related drugs. The reasons for these beliefs are multiple and will not be discussed here, but the attitudes of those largely involved in the care of people with a learning disability should be considered when prescribing drugs and the reasons for using these agents should be explained to those closely involved with the individual. The rationale for the prescription of antipsychotic drugs in a patient with clear schizophrenic pathology is much more firmly based than the empirical use of these agents in controlling disturbed behaviour in a severely handicapped individual who is unable to express his needs clearly.

Clinical pharmacology

The use of psychotropic drugs for defined psychiatric illnesses in those with learning disabilities is not medically controversial. However, antipsychotic drugs are widely employed in the control of aggressive and disturbed behaviour, in reducing hyperactivity and in stereotypic behaviour as well as in schizophrenia (Wressell *et al*, 1990). Similarly, carbamazepine, an anticonvulsant drug that is frequently prescribed in the treatment of epilepsy, is also valuable in controlling mood disorder and hyperactivity. Because of this overlap, the use of psychotropic drugs in the treatment of particular syndromes will be described after a brief review of the main classes of drugs concerned. In all cases correct dosages, important side-effects and contraindications should be established from the current edition of the British National Formulary (British Medical Association, 1996).

Antipsychotic drugs

Antipsychotic drugs, otherwise known as major tranquillisers or neuroleptics, comprise several different families. The phenothiazines were the first to be synthesised in 1951, closely followed by the thioxanthenes and the butyrophenones. Derivatives of diphenylbutylpiperidines (e.g. pimozide) and the substituted benzamides (e.g. sulpiride) followed, together with clozapine and loxapine, drugs of the dibenzodiazepine family. A recent addition is risperidone, a benzisoxazole derivative that antagonises different receptors than other neuroleptics. Sertindole and olanzapine are newer licensed drugs.

The common characteristic of all these drugs is their ability to block dopamine D_2 receptors in the limbic system and the hypothalamus, although the dibenzodiazepines affect other dopamine receptors in addition. Risperidone blocks α_1-adrenoceptors and $5HT_2$ receptors. The other antipsychotic drugs also have effects on receptors that are concerned with other neurotransmitters. Their anticholinergic activity and degree of blockade of noradrenergic receptors relate to their degree of sedation (see Table 14.1) and may be more important in determining their value in behavioural control. With all these drugs the lowest possible dose should be given to control symptoms.

The majority of neuroleptics are administered by mouth but there is an important group of these drugs that are given parenterally, the depot preparations. Depot neuroleptic drugs are designed to ensure compliance with treatment. They are given by deep intramuscular injection, usually at two or three-weekly intervals, and are widely employed in the treatment of schizophrenia, and occasionally in bipolar affective disorder.

Antiparkinsonian drugs

In people with learning disabilities, antiparkinsonian drugs are widely employed to combat the side-effects of antipsychotic agents. These drugs should not be given routinely to those who receive antischizophrenic agents but only when extrapyramidal symptoms and signs are present. Concurrent administration of these drugs with antipsychotics reduces the effect of the latter, and the development of tardive dyskinesia is more

Table 14.1 Relative affinities of neuroleptic drugs for receptor sites in the brain

	Affinity for		
	Acetylcholine (Ach receptor)	α-Noradrenergic (NA) receptor	Histamine (H$_1$) receptor
Phenothiazines			
Chlorpromazine	++	+	+++
Thioridazine	+++	+	+++
Trifluoperazine	0	+	+
Fluphenazine	0	+	++
Thioxanthenes			
Flupenthixol	+	+	+
Zuclopenthixol	0	++	+++
Butyrophenones			
Haloperidol	0	++	+
Droperidol	0	+++	+++
Pimozide	+	+	0
Sulpiride	0	0	0
Clozapine	+++	++	+++
Risperidone	0	+++	+++

High affinity for Ach receptors: dry mouth, urinary retention, protection against extrapyramidal side-effects.
High affinity for NA receptors: postural hypotension, sedation.
High affinity for H$_1$ receptors: sedation.

likely if these drugs are given for long periods. Equivalent dosage of these drugs are procyclidine 5 mg b.d., orphenadrine 50 mg t.d.s. and benzhexol 2 mg b.d.

Antidepressant drugs

Antidepressant drugs are divided into four main classes: tricyclics (e.g. lofepramine, desipramine, dothiepin), monoamine oxidase inhibitors (MAOIs) (e.g. phenelzine, tranylcypromine, moclobemide), the selective serotonin reuptake inhibitors (SSRIs) (e.g. fluoxetine, paroxetine, sertraline), and others including venlafaxine, trazodone and mianserin.

Antimanic and anti-aggressive drugs

Although lithium and the phenothiazine group of drugs are usually employed in the treatment of mania, other drugs such as carbamazepine, sodium valproate, verapamil, clonazepam and clonidine have all been used in this illness with success. Some of these agents also have anti-aggressive effects (carbamazepine, sodium valproate, verapamil and clonidine) and have been employed for this purpose in people with learning disability.

Anti-androgen drugs

Cyproterone acetate, benperidol and goserelin have all been used in the treatment of young men who exhibit inappropriate sexual behaviour.

Central nervous stimulants

Central nervous stimulants sometimes have paradoxical calming effects on activity and mood in overactive mentally handicapped people, particularly younger individuals. They should only be rarely prescribed because of the dangers of dependence and misuse. They should not be given to people with schizophrenia because they are likely to exacerbate acute symptoms. Dexamphetamine inhibits the reuptake and stimulates the release of noradrenaline and dopamine. In patients who are overactive, it may increase attention span and reduce behavioural disturbance. The usual starting dose is 5 mg in the morning, increasing to a maximum of 20 mg daily, with the total dose given before 2 p.m. to avoid sleep disturbance. The drug acts rapidly. Magnesium pemoline is different from other central nervous system stimulants in having minimal sympatho-mimetic effects. In animals it is a dopamine agonist although it is not definite that its effects in humans are mediated through this action. Insomnia, anorexia and irritability have been recorded. The initial dosage is 20 mg daily with a maximum of 100 mg daily. There is less likelihood of dependence with pemoline than with the amphetamines.

Other drugs

Other drugs used include propranolol, fenfluramine and naltrexone, and are described in the section concerned with the illness described.

Use of drugs in specific disorders

Aggression

Aggressive and destructive behaviours in those with learning disabilities are frequently referred to the psychiatrist and there is a temptation to use pharmacological means of control. However, before prescribing drugs it is instructive to determine the antecedents of these behaviours, what actually happens at the time of the disturbed act and what are the consequences. People with learning problems have difficulties in communication and have poorer impulse control than those with normal intelligence. Aggressive or destructive behaviour is a means of communicating frustration or distress, and in many institutional settings is territorial in nature.

It is worth asking the question "why has this particular patient reacted in the way he has at this particular point in time?" Detailed recordings of aggressive acts over a period are useful in order to be able to answer this. Psychologists working with people with learning disabilities call this process functional analysis; the assessment concerned is described in more detail in chapter 11. Some individuals are aggressive when they are over-aroused or have too little space, whereas others engage in these behaviours because they are bored and under-stimulated.

If environmental factors are thought to contribute to the aggressive disturbance there should be manipulation of these to reduce the unwanted behaviours. The response of the carers to the aggressive behaviour may also need to be altered. Initially behavioural and psychological techniques should normally be used in aggressive individuals; it is only if these techniques are not effective or if the environment concerned cannot be altered in any major way that pharmacological treatments should normally be employed. Even when drug treatment is recommended there should be a continual search for factors precipitating aggression. For instance, many people who are unable to communicate are aggressive or self-injurious when they are in pain. Recurrent otitis media and dysmenorrhoea are both conditions in which aggressive or self-injurious behaviour have occurred in patients and which can be effectively treated by addressing the underlying medical cause.

Treatment of acute aggressive episodes

The pharmacological control of acute aggressive episodes involves different treatments than for chronic aggression. Drugs are used frequently in acute disturbances to prevent escalation of an aggressive or self-injurious incident and to avoid further injury to the patient or others. Those with milder degrees of learning disabilities recognise when they are becoming distressed or over-aroused and sometimes ask for emergency medication. Although requests of this nature are often not considered to be *de rigeur* by nursing staff, they may indicate a degree of insight by the patient which is of help in aborting aggressive acts.

The frequency of prescription of emergency medication within a hospital setting is widespread compared with community facilities. At Prudhoe Hospital, the largest hospital for the treatment of those with a learning difficulty in the north of England (almost 400 beds), emergency medication is given between 60 and 70 times a month. The drug most frequently used is droperidol, a butyrophenone that has a quicker onset of action than haloperidol. The onset of action when administered parenterally is between three and ten minutes after administration. In patients who are intolerant to the antipsychotic agents, quick-acting benzodiazepine drugs can be used. Lorazepam and midazolam are the preferred agents because of their relatively short half-lives and lack of respiratory depression. Both these drugs are usually given by intramuscular injection for immediate effect, but lorazepam can be given orally.

Paraldehyde was the mainstay of chemical restraint in the first half of this century. A large part of the drug is excreted in the breath, although liver function still needs to be adequate in order to be able to metabolise the drug completely. It is long-lasting and usually subdues the recipient for four to six hours. Lactic acidosis has been reported. Intramuscular injection should be avoided as far as possible because of the danger of abscess formation. Although this drug is not now widely used it can still be of value in people who do not respond well to alternative medication.

Drug treatment in chronic aggression

In people with learning disability aggressive acts are frequent and pharmacological methods may be needed to control behaviour. Before employing these agents it is important to exclude physical and psychiatric illness as a cause of aggression. Patients who have manic or paranoid schizophrenic illnesses are often hostile, and individuals with pervasive developmental disorder often react with aggression when their territorial space is invaded.

Confusional states and drug misuse are also associated with aggression. If there is evidence of a psychiatric illness it should be treated in its own right with the appropriate agents – it must always be remembered that aggression is a description of behaviour and rarely a diagnosis in its own right.

If there is evidence of recent or past mood disturbance, or if there is a periodic cycle of aggressive behaviour, lithium or carbamazepine should be given. There is no firm evidence that carbamazepine is valuable in treating aggression in those with learning disabilities unless there is an affective component, although lithium is effective in patients with no evidence of an affective illness (Wickham & Reed, 1987). Lithium is potentially a dangerous drug. Toxicity frequently occurs if serum lithium levels are above 1.5 mmol/l, but they can occur at lower serum levels. Toxic symptoms include ataxia, tremor, a feeling of being drugged, and the sufferer looks grey and ill. Lithium should be stopped immediately if toxicity is suspected. There is no disadvantage in missing out a dose in a 24-hour period and if there is any suspicion of toxicity this is an essential action to take. Although lithium leads to an increase in cardiovascular abnormalities in the foetus when given to the mother in pregnancy, recent work suggests that the hazards of lithium treatment during pregnancy have been over-rated (Jacobson *et al*, 1992).

Lithium is best prescribed in a single night-time dose. The precise dose required to maintain a given serum lithium level can be determined from a pre-existing nomogram (Tyrer & Shaw, 1982). Information sheets about lithium should be given to those involved in the care of the patient. Details of the monitoring of lithium treatment and adverse effects have been covered in a recent review (Ferrier *et al*, 1995).

If there are signs of high adrenergic β-receptor over-activity (e.g. tachycardia, tremor, palpitations or other somatic signs of over-arousal) then β-blocking drugs may be of value. Propranolol has been the most widely used drug of this group and can be effective at a dosage of 40–120 mg daily although the dose may need to be raised to three times this value. Nadolol at dosages of 80–160 mg has also been used, and oxprenolol may be helpful in this regard. All β-blocking drugs slow the heart and reduce myocardial contraction. They should not be given if the pulse falls below 48 beats per minute or if there are signs of heart failure or myocardial depression. They should never be used in patients with a recent history of obstructive airway disease or asthma.

Carbamazepine may help those with a quick-cycling affective disorder, i.e. more than four episodes a year. If there is a history of epilepsy or of any EEG abnormality, retrospective studies have suggested that carbamazepine is more effective than in those with normal EEGs (Langee, 1989).

If in addition to exhibiting disturbed behaviour the patient concerned is also hyperactive, benefit may result from antipsychotic drugs, carbamazepine, or from the central nervous system stimulants such as pemoline or amphetamine. The latter two drugs should be reserved for resistant cases who have clear evidence of distractibility and attention deficit.

Naltrexone, an opioid antagonist that affects all opioid receptors, is valuable in reducing self-injurious behaviour in severely and profoundly handicapped individuals. There is some evidence that naltrexone is effective in doses as low as 25 mg on alternate days, but the normal dosage is 25 mg or 50 mg at night. Contrary to what would be expected, it has been shown that patients who frequently injure themselves have lower β-endorphin levels than those without this behaviour (Willemsen-Swinkels *et al*, 1996).

Antidepressant drugs that increase the synaptic availability of serotonin (5-hydroxytryptamine; 5-HT) are valuable in the control of impulsive behaviour in those of normal intelligence. There is reason to suppose that these drugs should reduce impulsive aggressive behaviour in those with learning disability, although controlled double-blind trials have not been carried out. The SSRIs (e.g. fluoxetine, fluvoxamine) are the most frequently used drugs, although trazodone and the tricyclic antidepressant drugs (e.g. clomipramine) have been used to good effect. L-tryptophan, a precursor drug in the synthesis of 5-HT, is also helpful, although is now not generally available because of the occasional occurrence of the eosinophil-myalgia syndrome with use of this drug.

There have been encouraging reports of a new class of 5-HT$_{1A}$ agonists, called serenics, in reducing aggression in the developmentally disabled, the best known example of which is eltoprazine (De Koning *et al*, 1994). This drug is valuable in the short term but loses potency after a few weeks.

Other agents, including buspirone, tetrahydrobiopterin and amantadine have been successful in open trials. Combinations of the drugs described may be useful. For instance, it has been shown that some people with rapid-cycling affective disorder are more likely to respond to a combination of lithium and carbamazepine than to either drug alone.

The choice of drug in the treatment of chronic aggression depends on the type of aggression exhibited, whether there is epilepsy or an abnormal EEG, the degree of sympathetic over-arousal, the extent of hyperactivity and the age of the patient. A suggested flow-chart to aid the psychiatrist in choice of drug in treating aggression is shown in Fig. 14.1. This is only a guide and the choice of treatment is not as hierarchical as indicated in this figure. For instance, in a profoundly handicapped person with severe self-injurious behaviour it may be appropriate to give naltrexone even if there was, say, evidence of sympathetic overactivity.

In practice, the most frequently used agents in people with learning disability who have a history of chronic behavioural disturbance are the neuroleptic drugs (Manchester, 1993). These drugs have the advantage of an immediate sedative effect and were used for over 30 years when the newer agents described above were not available. Despite this, it is remarkable that no well-conducted trial has been published which indicates that antipsychotic drugs are more effective than other agents in the treatment of aggression, or even more effective than placebo (Baumeister *et al*, 1993). Comparative studies have shown that the thioxanthenes are superior to the butyrophenones. There is clear evidence that patients maintained on antipsychotic drugs for the treatment of behavioural disturbance in whom treatment is withdrawn show an increase in aggressive behaviour. It is not generally realised that sudden withdrawal of antipsychotic drugs, particularly those with pronounced anticholin-ergic effects, is associated with withdrawal symptoms, mainly nausea, anorexia, restlessness and painful muscles. These effects may contribute to aggressive behaviour in patients who cannot communicate in other ways.

The use of antipsychotic drugs in the control of chronic aggression should not be started lightly. These agents are known to cause tardive dyskinesia when given for long periods, particularly in patients with evidence of brain damage. The indications for starting these drugs when it is known there is a strong possibility of inducing a permanent, disfiguring, abnormal movement disorder should reduce the enthusiasm of the doctor who is impressed by the effectiveness of these drugs when given for acute aggressive disturbances.

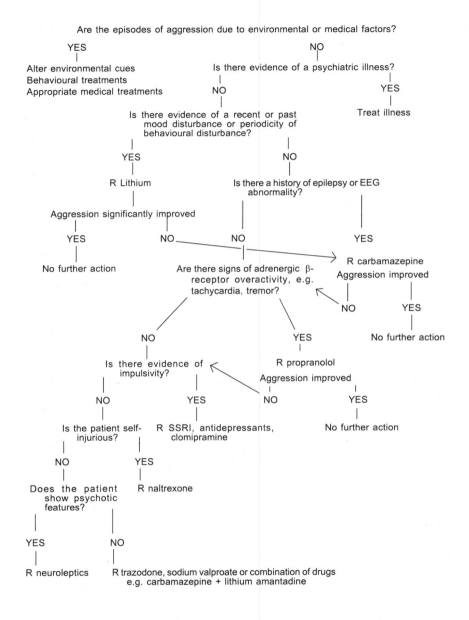

Fig. 14.1 Drug treatment in chronic aggression: recommended paths.

Schizophrenia

Restricted emotional response, withdrawal and stereotypical behaviour is common in this population and these signs do not indicate schizophrenia in this group. Notwithstanding this, those with moderate learning problems who have previously functioned normally, but who have become affectively remote and who now show incongruous behaviour, self-preoccupation or catatonic posturing, neuroleptic medication can have considerable and dramatic beneficial effects, suggesting that such syndromes are of schizophrenic origin.

There is no substantial difference between the pharmacological treatment of schizophrenia in people with learning disability and those of normal intelligence (see chapter 8, p. 117). It is wise to select a drug that has few side-effects, both acute and long-term. The phenothiazine group of drugs are now not so commonly used in schizophrenia because of their untoward side-effects; zuclopenthixol, pimozide and sulpiride have somewhat fewer side-effects and have more specific actions on the dopamine D_2 receptor. In addition, sulpiride acts at the pre-synaptic dopamine receptor and is reputed to cause fewer extrapyramidal side-effects in tardive dyskinesia than the older drugs.

Risperidone is a new neuroleptic drug that blocks dopamine D_2 receptors but also has antagonist actions at the 5-HT_2 receptor and at α_1 and α_2-adrenergic receptors. This drug is less likely to cause movement disorders and studies suggest that it may have advantages in patients who have negative symptoms.

The drug that is least likely to cause tardive dyskinesia and yet is unequivocally valuable in schizophrenia is clozapine, a tricyclic drug of the dibenzodiazepine family. Clozapine causes agranulocytosis in 3% of patients who receive it and because of this it can only be given to patients under carefully controlled conditions. The company manufacturing the drug only allows the use of clozapine if weekly blood counts are taken to check on white blood cell counts and the drug is immediately stopped if there is a fall in total white cell count to less than $3 \times 10^9/l$, total neutrophil count of less than $1.5 \times 10^9/l$ or platelet count below $100 \times 10^9/l$. Administration of this drug is rigidly controlled by the Clozaril Patient Monitoring Service. The incidence of agranulocytosis diminishes considerably after the drug has been taken for six months and blood samples can then be taken at less frequent intervals. In the UK clozapine is only licensed for use with treatment-resistant schizophrenia.

Psychiatrists using neuroleptic drugs in those with learning disabilities should be aware of the dangers of the older antipsychotic agents. A study has shown that 34% of those with a learning disability living in hospital receiving neuroleptic drugs had tardive dyskinesia (Sachdev, 1992). Compensation has been given to those with learning disability in the US who received neuroleptic drugs for long periods because of the resulting side-effects. Although the most disabling side-effect of these drugs is tardive dyskinesia, manifest by involuntary movements of the orofacial musculature and tongue, and akathisia, an irresistible desire to move the limbs associated with movement disorder, is frequently reported in those with learning disabilities.

Depot preparations are not widely used although their use is increasing. They are particularly valuable if compliance cannot be assured. Fluphenazine decanoate, zuclopenthixol decanoate, haloperidol decanoate and pipothiazine palmitate have all been used with success, although all are associated with the development of extrapyramidal side-effects and later tardive dyskinesia.

Autism

The fundamental abnormalities in the pervasive developmental disorders such as autism are impaired social interaction and communication (see chapter 7). There may be secondary behavioural difficulties which result from the handicaps of the autistic person. Although these are normally best treated by non-pharmacological means, the drugs indicated in the section on chronic aggression (above) may be appropriate for controlling aggressive and self-injurious behaviour. The drugs indicated below have been used for the treatment of core autistic symptoms.

Fenfluramine, a fluorinated amphetamine that does not have the stimulant properties of its parent drug and blocks serotonin receptors, was enthusiastically promoted for the treatment of autism following a report on three autistic boys. However, a later multicentre trial from California did not show major benefits and treatment successes were mainly related to reduction of hyperactivity and stereotypy. More promising results have been obtained using the SSRI fluoxetine (Cook *et al*, 1992) and the experimental 5-HT_{1A} agonist, eltoprazine (Tyrer & Moore, 1993).

In 1979 Panksepp proposed that symptoms of early childhood autism may result from excessive brain opioid activity. Although early work supported this theory, with higher cerebrospinal fluid β-endorphin concentrations being found in autistic children, these results have not been consistently reproduced. Naloxone, an opioid antagonist that can only be given by parenteral means, and naltrexone, which is longer acting and can be administered in tablet form, have been used in the treatment of autism on the basis of Panksepp's original hypothesis. Although early results were encouraging, recent controlled studies have not supported a positive effect of naltrexone in this condition (Campbell *et al*, 1993; Gillberg, 1995). β-blockers, pyridoxine, folic acid and tetrahydrobiopterin have been used in uncontrolled studies.

There is no one drug which is outstanding in the treatment of autism compared with any other. Most promise has been shown by the SSRIs and the 5-HT_{1A} agonists.

Affective disorder

The treatment of depression and mania in those with learning disabilities hardly differs from those without, certainly in the mild to moderate range. It has been shown that people with a learning disability who respond to antidepressants are more likely to present with symptoms of depression, psychosis or temper tantrums, whereas those with self-injurious behaviour are less likely to be helped. If there is persistent anhedonia and at least one vegetative symptom, patients should normally be given a tricyclic antidepressant, with the whole dose given one or two hours before going to bed. If there is no improvement after four weeks, with three weeks on the higher dosage, alternative strategies should be considered.

The diagnosis of depression at this time should be re-examined. If it continues to be supported, lithium should be added at a dosage of 400 mg nocte as long as the patient has normal creatinine and thyroid function. In a young healthy subject the dose should be increased to 800 mg after a few days and lithium continued for at least three weeks. Lithium has been shown to augment the effect of antidepressants.

If there is a risk of suicide, the tricyclic antidepressant lofepramine or a SSRI should be given. The latter should also be prescribed if there is undue sedation or major side-effects with the tricyclic antidepressants. If tricyclic antidepressants have failed to work the chances of an alternative antidepressant being effective is no more than 20% at most. Alternatives that might be considered to the SSRIs are moclobemide, trazodone or the MAOIs. If the latter group of drugs is used there should be an interval of at least ten days between stopping the tricyclic (five weeks with fluoxetine) and starting the MAOI. The MAOIs should not be given to individuals with learning disabilities unless the patient and carers are aware of the dangers of drug interactions with cheese, beer and prohibited foods.

If there is evidence of delusions or hallucinations electroconvulsive therapy (ECT) is usually the treatment of choice. Once a course of treatment is completed, maintenance drug treatment is required to prevent depression recurring.

The treatment of hypomania and mania in a learning disability setting does not differ from the management of this condition in patients with normal intelligence. Lithium is of advantage in hypomania, but in more severe illnesses haloperidol or other antipsychotic agents are likely to be required. Carbamazepine, sodium valproate, clonazepam and calcium channel blockers are useful second-line drugs. The combination of carbamazepine and lithium is sometimes of great assistance when either of these drugs used alone is ineffective.

Patients who have recurrent affective episodes should normally receive maintenance drug treatment. The indications for this are stronger in bipolar affective disorder than in unipolar illness. If the patient has had three or more episodes of depression or mania within a period of less than four years, maintenance drug therapy should be initiated. Lithium is the drug of choice for the control of bipolar illness, with carbamazepine as a second-line choice if lithium is either ineffective or cannot be given because of contraindications.

Lithium may be more valuable in rapid-cycling affective illness in individuals with learning disabilities than it is in people of normal intelligence. In patients who have had no history of manic episodes, either lithium or tricyclic antidepressants may be given prophylactically.

Anxiety

The use of drugs to control anxiety should be largely confined to the control of acute anxiety reactions. Even in these situations drug treatment is usually not required – reassurance and calming actions by others may be sufficient. The shorter-acting benzodiazepines such as lorazepam and oxazepam should be preferred to the longer-acting drugs like diazepam. Lorazepam has a particularly strong dependence potential and should not normally be given on more than four occasions in any one week.

Prolonged treatment for anxiety is not usually necessary. If this is envisaged, the benzodiazepines should not be given. Buspirone, an azaspirodecanedione, is a new anti-anxiety drug that has been used in those with learning disabilities to reduce anxiety and behavioural disturbance. The indications for its use are not certain and we need more information in these individuals. Propranolol and other β-blocking agents may be useful in patients who show sympathetic overactivity when emotionally aroused.

Sleep problems

As far as possible non-drug treatments should be used in those who complain of poor sleep. The benefits of exercise, avoidance of caffeine-containing drinks, substitution of a hot milk drink at night and prevention of sleeping during the day may render a previously poor sleeper somnolent at night. Behavioural programmes have been found to be of benefit if applied diligently and have been shown to be of particular advantage in children. If drugs are to be given they should be given for short periods only or intermittently. Short-acting benzodiazepines such as temazepam (10–20 mg nocte) are suitable. They are more effective if administered intermittently rather than every night, and as far as possible they should not be given for longer than two weeks because of the danger of dependence.

In patients who are receiving these drugs regularly over a period of more than three weeks, alternative treatment should normally be sought. The antihistamine trimeprazine at a dosage of 20–30 mg nocte is a useful drug and does not cause dependence, although there may be a hangover effect in the morning. Chloral hydrate or thioridazine may also be used alone or in combination with other drugs. Zopiclone is reputed to have less potential to cause dependence but has not been adequately tested in trials to prove this claim. The sedative antidepressants such as trimipramine and trazodone are helpful in sleep disorders, although their use long-term in patients without affective disturbance should probably be avoided.

Aberrant sexual behaviour

Sexual offences by those with learning disabilities are not infrequent and often lead to a request for psychiatric help. Many of those who commit sexual offences are not fully aware of what constitutes acceptable sexual practice. Sex education instruction packages are available and are valuable in determining gaps in the knowledge of patients and may also help to focus therapy. Psychological and behavioural treatments have a greater part to play than drug therapy in this condition. However, drugs may assist patients in avoiding sexual temptation. Before giving these drugs it is important to seek the consent of the patient or, if this is not possible, to consult with a close relative about the likely effects of the drugs to be administered.

The most widely used drug is cyproterone acetate. This drug decreases serum testosterone and open studies have reported its efficacy in reducing masturbation, indecent exposure and sexual offences in mentally retarded men (Clarke, 1989). Cyproterone is hepatotoxic if given in large doses and liver function tests should be performed on a regular basis if the drug is being given at a dosage of more than 200 mg daily.

Benperidol, which is an antipsychotic of the butyrophenone group, is also licensed for the control of deviant and antisocial sexual behaviour. Its use is supported by a wealth of uncontrolled trials, but the few double-blind investigations that have been performed do not suggest that it is an effective drug in reducing sexual desire. As benperidol does not affect the concentration of testosterone or leutenising hormone these results are not surprising. Other drugs that have been used include the progesterones such as medroxyprogesterone acetate, which is widely used in North America, and goserelin, a luteinizing hormone releasing factor analogue. Goserelin is not licensed for the reduction of male sexual drive but has been used for this purpose.

Cyproterone acetate should normally be the first drug of choice, although if this is ineffective, goserelin should be considered. Serum testosterone measurements are of value in determining how far cyproterone exhibits a pharmacological sexual suppressant effect. Goserelin does not come under the list of treatments under Section 57 of the Mental Health Act 1983 which require certification by a second-opinion doctor appointed by the Mental Health Commission.

Hyperactivity

It is not usually necessary to treat hyperactivity with drugs. If this is required, carbamazepine and the central nervous system stimulants have been found to be more effective than placebo. Comparisons between these treatments have not been made and for convenience, carbamazepine is probably the best first-line drug.

Stereotypies

There is good evidence that the antipsychotic drugs reduce stereotypies and that their effects are greatest in the most severely affected individuals. Clomipramine and lithium may also be of value.

Conclusion

The use of drugs in those with learning disabilities should be based on accurate diagnosis and sound pharmacological principles. When there is success with the prescribed agent a decision should be made as to how long to maintain treatment with this drug and whether the dose should be reduced. Above all, if there are unusual symptoms and signs patients should be examined to determine how far they are due to any drugs exhibited or to other factors. The psychiatrist prescribing psychotropic drugs has to be much more aware of the side-effects of these drugs when treating a population who, in the main, are not able to report side-effects accurately.

References

Baumeister, A. A., Todd, M. E. & Sevin, J. A. (1993) Efficacy and specificity of pharmacological therapies for behavioral disorders in persons with mental retardation. *Clinical Neuropharmacology*, **16**, 271–294.

Branford, D. (1994) A study of the prescribing for people with learning disabilities living in the community and in National Health Service care. *Journal of Inyellectual Disability Research*, **38**, 577–586.

Breuning, S. E., Ferguson, D. G., Davidson, N. A., *et al* (1983) Effects of thioridazine on the intellectual performance of mentally retarded drug responders and non-responders. *Archives of General Psychiatry*, **40**, 309–313.

Campbell, M., Anderson, I., Small, A., *et al* (1993) Naltrexone in autistic children: behavioral symptoms and attentional learning. *Journal of the American Academy of Child and Adolescent Psychiatry*, **32**, 1282–1291.

Clarke, D. J. (1989) Antilibidinal drugs and mental retardation: a review. *Medical Science and Law*, **29**, 136–146.

——, Kelley, S., Thinn, K. K., *et al* (1990) Psychotropic drugs and mental retardation: disabilities and the prescription of drugs for behaviour and for epilepsy in three residential settings. *Journal of Mental Deficiency Research*, **34**, 385–395.

Cook, E. H., Rowlatt, R., Jaselskis, C., *et al* (1992) Fluoxetine treatment of children and adults with autistic disorder and mental retardation. *Journal of the American Academy of Child and Adolescent Psychiatry*, **31**, 739–745.

De Koning, P., Mak, M., De Vries, M. H., *et al* (1994) Eltoprazine in aggressive mentally handicapped patients: a double-blind placebo and baseline-controlled multi-centre study. *International Clinical Psychopharmacology*, **9**, 187–194.

Ferrier, I. N., Tyrer, S. P. & Bell, A. (1995) Lithium therapy. *Advances in Psychiatric Treatment*, **1**, 102–110.

Fleming, I., Caine, A., Ahmed, S., *et al* (1996) Aspects of psychoactive medication among people with intellectual disabilities who have been resettled from long stay hospitals into dispersed housing. *Journal of Applied Research in Intellectual Disabilities*, **9**, 194–205.

Gillberg, C. (1995) Endogenous opioids and opiate antagonists in autism: brief review of empirical findings and implications for clinicians. *Developmental Medicine and Child Neurology*, **37**, 239–245.

Jacobson, S. J., Jones, K. K., Johnson, K., *et al* (1992) Prospective multi-centre study of pregnancy outcome after lithium exposure during first trimester. *Lancet*, **339**, 530–533.

Kiernan, C., Reeves, D. & Alborz, A. (1995) The use of antipsychotic drugs with adults with learning disabilities and challenging behaviour. *Journal of Mental Deficiency Research*, **39**, 263–274.

Langee, H. R. (1989) A retrospective study of mentally retarded patients with behavioral disorders who were treated with carbamazepine. *American Journal on Mental Retardation*, **93**, 640–643. (See also Laminack, I., letter, *American Journal on Mental Retardation*, **94**, 563–564.)

Lock, S. (1988) Fraud in medicine. *British Medical Journal*, **296**, 376–377.

Manchester, D. (1993) Neuroleptics, learning disability and the community: some history and mystery. *British Medical Journal*, **307**, 184–187.

Panksepp, J. (1979) A neurochemical theory of autism. *Trends in Neurosciences*, **2**, 174–177.

Rinck, C., Guidry, J. & Calkins, C. F. (1989) Review of states' practices on the use of psychotropic medication. *American Journal on Mental Retardation*, **93**, 657–668.

Sachdev, P. (1992) Drug-induced movement disorders in institutionalised adults with mental retardation. *Australian and New Zealand Journal of Psychiatry*, **26**, 242–248.

Thinn, K., Clarke, D. J. & Corbett, J. A. (1990) Psychotropic drugs and mental retardation; a comparison of psychoactive drug use before and after discharge from hospital to community. *Journal of Mental Deficiency Research*, **34**, 397–407.

Tyrer, S. & Shaw, D. M. (1982) Lithium carbonate. In *Drugs in Psychiatric Practice* (ed. P. J. Tyrer), p. 284. London: Butterworths.

—— & Moore, P. B. (1993) Eltoprazine improves autistic symptoms in self-injurious mentally handicapped patients. *European Neuropsychopharmacology*, **3**, 384.

Wickham, E. A. & Reed, J. V. (1987) Lithium for the control of aggressive and self-mutilating behaviour. *International Clinical Psychopharmacology*, **2**, 181–190.

Willemsen-Swinkels, S. H. N., Buitelaar, J. K., Weijnem, F. G., *et al* (1996) Plasma ß-endorphin concentrations in mentally retarded subjects with self-injurious and/or autistic behaviour. *British Journal of Psychiatry*, **168**, 105–109.

Wressell, S. E., Tyrer, S. P. & Berney, T. P. (1990) Reduction in antipsychotic drug dosage in mentally handicapped patients: a hospital study. *British Journal of Psychiatry*, **157**, 101–106.

Additional reading

Aman, M. G. (1987) Overview of pharmacotherapy. Current status and future directions. *Journal of Mental Deficiency Research*, **31**, 121–130.

Day, K. (1994) Male mentally handicapped sex offenders. *British Journal of Psychiatry*, **165**, 630–639.

Deb, S. & Fraser, W. (1994) The use of psychotropic medication in people with learning disability: towards rational prescribing. *Human Psychopharmacology*, **9**, 259–272.

Lapierre, Y. D. & Reesal, R. (1986) Pharmacologic management of aggressivity and self-mutilation in the mentally retarded. *Psychiatric Clinics of North America*, **9**, 745–754.

Sovner, R. (1990) Developments in the use of psychotropic drugs. *Current Opinion in Psychiatry*, **3**, 606–612.

Tyrer, S. P. (1994) Lithium and treatment of aggressive behaviour. *European Neuropsychopharmacology*, **4**, 234–236.

15 Epilepsy and learning disabilities

Jonathan Bird

Epidemiology ● *Aetiology* ● *Diagnosis* ● *Psychiatric aspects* ●
Management of epilepsy

The double misfortune of suffering from epilepsy and a learning disability results in a difficult management problem, often requiring considerable expertise in both areas for optimal control. Sadly, there are too few places where the specialised treatment of epilepsy in people with learning disabilities can be carried out, and it is important that all those involved in the care of people with such problems should have knowledge and understanding of epilepsy, its diagnosis and management. Thankfully, new methods of treatment which may be especially relevant to this combination of factors have recently emerged.

Epidemiology

In general, the more severe the degree of learning disability, the more likely it is that epilepsy will be present and the more severe that epilepsy is likely to be. The normal rate of 'active' epilepsy in the general population is 0.5%. In those with an IQ of 50–75 the rate is 5%, but an IQ of less than 50 results in a 30% risk of developing epilepsy, and an IQ of less than 20 is related to a 50% risk of having seizures. At the age of 22, if a person with a severe learning disability has seizures, there is a 40% chance that he or she has had them for over ten years. This indicates how chronic epilepsy can be in people with learning disabilities. The relationship between a learning disability and epilepsy may be explained in a variety of ways, as detailed in Box 15.1.

Aetiology

Certain causes of learning disability are especially likely to be related to the development of chronic epilepsy from childhood, others are less likely or are associated with the later development of epilepsy in adolescents, and some, such as the development of dementia in Down's syndrome, may be associated with the later development of seizures.

Box 15.1 The relationship between learning disability and epilepsy

Risk of active epilepsy
Normal population   0.5%
IQ 50–70   4.0%
IQ 20–50   30%
IQ less than 20   50%

Causes
Brain abnormality leads to a learning disability and to epilepsy, e.g. perinatal trauma, encephalopathy, non-accidental injury, head injury, neuro-migrational defects.
Seizures may (rarely) cause reduced IQ, e.g. febrile status, hypsarrhythmia.
Treatment of epilepsy may lower IQ, e.g. surgery, sedating drugs.
People with a learning disability and epilepsy are more 'noticeable'.
Certain deteriorating conditions result in reduced IQ and epilepsy, e.g. lipoidoses, Sturge–Weber syndrome, tuberous sclerosis, disintegrative psychosis.
Beware of partial complex and petit-mal status looking like low IQ.

Inborn errors of metabolism

Many of the inborn errors of metabolism are associated with epilepsy. Most are very rare but some are treatable. Severe seizures at or even before birth may be due to pyridoxine deficiency, which is eminently treatable with intravenous pyridoxine if detected very early. The amino acid disorders and adrenoleucodystrophy are associated with a non-specific seizure pattern.

If myoclonic seizures are a major feature of the epilepsy, this may suggest, along with the EEG pattern, that one of a group of inborn errors is present. These are detailed in Table 15.1. If progressive myoclonic epilepsy develops in adolescence, this is usually associated with a severe prognosis in general and may be due to one of the 'juvenile' forms of these disorders (e.g. Gaucher's disease, Lafora's disease, the Ceroid-Lipofuscinoses).

Developmental causes

The commonest cause of most epilepsy in people with a learning disability is almost certainly developmental. An understanding of the stages of brain development is therefore required. The brain passes through four main stages after the dorsal and ventral inductions of the embryonic neural plate:

(a) *Neuronal proliferation*, which is at its peak at two to four months after conception. Abnormalities in neuronal proliferation may result in microcephaly and macrocephaly and may underlie the abnormalities of (for example) tuberous sclerosis.

(b) *Migration* of nerves takes place during the first six months of gestation. In order to form the layered cortex and the subcortical nuclei, the neurones migrate inwards and across the surface of the cortex. Abnormalities of nerve migration are often associated with both epilepsy and learning disabilities. Areas of abnormal migration may be shown by pachygyria (few, broad gyri) or polymicrogyria (excessive numbers of small gyri). Generalised or focal abnormalities may occur in this way. Heterotopia is the least severe form of abnormal migration, in which nerves migrate to the wrong site. Such abnormalities may be found in a wide variety of severe and less severe specific and generalised learning difficulties. Agenesis of the corpus callosum may be the result of abnormal migration and is often associated with other disorders of neuronal migration.

(c) *Organisation* of the nerves takes place from six months of gestation to several years postnatally. Orientation, layering, ramification and synaptic proliferation take place. Abnormalities at this stage may well be major causes of a learning disability. They may result from rubella, phenylketonuria and Down's syndrome. They are seen as a cause of severe epilepsy in West syndrome. Perinatal insults of various kinds may interfere with neuronal organisation.

(d) *Myelination* occurs from three months of gestation to maturity. Various of the inborn errors of metabolism may cause abnormalities of myelination. Other causes include infection, toxins, alcohol, hypoxia and hypoglycaemia.

Diagnosis

Classification

As yet, there is no fully satisfactory and entirely agreed classification of the epilepsies. An internationally accepted classification of individual seizure types does exist (Box 15.2). However, this has its drawbacks and, in particular, the distinctions between simple and complex seizures based on the presence or absence of full consciousness during a seizure is contentious and not easily definable. It is, perhaps, preferable simply to define seizures according to: (a) whether they are generalised or partial (focal) in origin, and (b) what form of generalised or partial seizure takes place.

It is of vital importance to take a history that enables precise diagnosis of the form or forms of seizure which an individual shows. This is in order that appropriate treatment planning can take place.

Table 15.1 Some special problems of epilepsy

	Epilepsy	West's syndrome	Lennox–Gastaut syndrome	Epilepsy with onset in later childhood or adolescence
Perinatal brain injury	+		+	
Metabolic abnormalities				
Phenylketonuria	+	+	+	
Maple Syrup urine disease	+	+		
Hyperornithaemia	+	+		
Isovaleric acidaemia	+	+		
Non-ketotic hyperglycaemia	+	+		
Pyridoxine dependency	+	+		
Leucine-sensitive hypoglycaemia		+	+	+
Tay-Sachs disease	+	+		
Lipoidosis GM 1 & GM 3	+		+	
Metachromatic leucodystrophy	+		+	+
Homocysteinuria			+	
Dysplastic conditions				
Tuberous sclerosis	+	+	+	+
Sturge–Weber syndrome	+	+	+	+
Megalencephaly	+		+	
Other cerebral malformations	+	+	+	
Aicardi syndrome	+	+		
Prenatal infections				
Cytomegalovirus	+	+		
Syphilis	+	+		
Toxoplasmosis	+	+		
Postnatal infections				
Purulent meningitis	+		+	+
Acute encephalitis	+		+	+
Subacute sclerosing panencephalitis	+		+	
Postimmunisation encephalopathy	+	+		
Post-traumatic	+			+
Chromosomal abnormalities				
Down's syndrome		+		
Autistic syndromes	+	+		+
Others				
Rett syndrome	+			+

The term 'psychomotor epilepsy' is no longer widely used, since it has little specificity either in terms of symptomatology or of anatomical focus. The term 'temporal lobe seizures' should be confined to those seizures that definitely arise in the temporal lobes. About 75% of partial complex seizures do arise in the temporal lobes, but about 20% arise in the frontal lobes.

In classifying seizures, it is important also to recognise that an 'aura' or 'warning' (either to patient or observers) is actually part of the seizure. An aura is, in fact, a partial seizure. This may well progress to a generalised, tonic-clonic attack but it clearly indicates a focal origin for the seizure, which is then defined as a partial complex seizure, with secondary generalisation.

Generalised seizures

Grand mal – tonic-clonic

The typical primary generalised tonic-clonic seizure starts with no warning (hence primary). A sudden cry, total muscular rigidity, falling and then

---

Box 15.2 Classification of seizures (ILAE)

Partial seizures (beginning locally)
a. Simple partial seizures (consciousness not impaired)
    i.   With motor signs ('Jacksonian')
    ii. With somatosensory or special sensory symptoms
    iii. With autonomic symptoms
    iv. With psychic symptoms (e.g. perceptual or mood changes)
b. Complex partial seizures (with impaired consciousness)
    i.   Beginning as simple partial ('aura') and progressing to impaired consciousness
    ii. With impaired consciousness at onset – either alone or with automatisms ('psychomotor attacks')
c. Partial seizures secondarily generalised (to tonic-clonic)

Generalised seizures (bilaterally symmetrical, no local onset)
a. Absence seizures ('petit-mal')
    Atypical absence seizures ('petit-mal variant')
b. Myoclonic seizures
c. Clonic seizures
d. Tonic seizures
e. Tonic-clonic seizures ('grand-mal')
f. Atonic seizures ('drop attacks')

Unclassified

powerful clonic movements of all four limbs are seen. Such attacks usually last in the acute phase for less than two minutes and are followed by unresponsive coma for a few more minutes. Emptying of the bladder, biting of the tongue and other injuries may occur.

Absences (petit-mal) attacks

'Generalised absences' is a term which should probably be reserved for typical 'petit-mal' seizures in which three per second spike-and-wave EEG changes are seen. Such attacks are rare in adulthood. The seizure involves a brief (usually less than 45 seconds and often less than 10 seconds) lapse of consciousness; usually the child is motionless but eyelid-blinking may be observed and more complex automatisms, myoclonus or drop attacks have been described. The onset and cessation are abrupt. Rarely, petit-mal status may occur and is prolonged and there may be some subsequent confusion.

'Atypical absences' may appear similar but have 1–2.5 per second spikes or polyspikes and waves and carry a very much worse prognosis. They are usually found with other forms of generalised seizure.

Myoclonic seizures

Stereotyped clonic jerking of all four limbs, or of just upper or lower limbs, with or without head-jerking, is regarded as a generalised epilepsy although such seizures may only involve the deep subcortical or brain-stem structures. On occasions spinal myoclonus may be present alone. The scalp EEG during a myoclonic jerk may well be entirely normal. Careful back-averaging of a series of jerks may even demonstrate a cortical spike occurring after the jerk, presumably secondary to earlier subcortical paroxysmal activity.

Myoclonic epilepsies are particularly associated with learning disabilities and, in severe epilepsy in people with intellectual disabilities, often occur in conjunction with other forms of seizure. Myoclonic seizures may be particularly difficult to control.

Atonic seizures

Sudden loss of postural tone resulting in a 'drop attack' can be severely damaging. The head may fall forward alone, often resulting in severe injury to the face. If uncontrollable (as they may be in people with learning disabilities who have severe epilepsy) they are, perhaps, one of the few acceptable reasons to use a protective helmet for the patient.

Partial (focal) seizures

Simple partial seizures

Simple partial seizures are those which do not involve disturbance of consciousness. These are rather rare and, even if a seizure starts without disturbance of consciousness, it very often progresses to at least some impairment. The commonest form of simple partial seizure involves the motor cortex and consists of focal tonic spasm of a muscle group which may spread to nearby groups (Jacksonian epilepsy). If the left hemisphere is involved, expressive speech may be impaired. The seizure may be followed by a period of paralysis of the affected muscle group (Todd's paralysis), and in adults this is often associated with some structural lesion, although in children this may not be the case. Adversive seizures (head-turning) were regarded as demonstrating that there was a focus in the frontal region opposite to the direction of turning; however, recent work has shown that this is not an entirely reliable localising sign.

Sensory seizures are more rare and are usually associated with motor phenomena. A sensation of numbness or pins and needles is the most common form of attack. Ill-formed visual hallucinations may arise from the occipital lobe, while well-formed and complex visual hallucinations may arise from the temporal lobes but are rare. Other sensory phenomena include gustatory and olfactory auras, ill-formed auditory hallucinations, dizziness and visceral sensations – all of which may arise in the temporal lobes and are usually followed by a complex partial seizure. The typical aura of a temporal lobe seizure is of an unpleasant rising epigastric sensation which may be very difficult for the patient to describe.

Complex partial seizures

Most partial seizures involve psychic phenomena, if not actual disturbance of consciousness. A wide variety of such phenomena may be seen and offer one of the fascinations of the study of epilepsy. An epileptic aura is a demonstration of the brain in action and gives the opportunity to study the localised functioning of brain areas. Careful history-taking (including witness reports) at this stage will be most rewarding to those interested in how the brain works. Automatisms of various kinds usually occur; these may vary from simple chewing, lip-smacking and fumbling to more complex and prolonged, apparently semi-purposive behaviour including walking, undressing or perseveration of previously initiated behaviour. Usually such behaviour is brief, less than five minutes in 80% of cases. Very rarely does a true automatism last more than an hour, although complex partial status epilepticus is becoming increasingly recognised as ambulatory monitoring is more widely used. This condition may occur more commonly in people with a learning disability.

Automatisms may also merge into post-ictal twilight states and fugue states on occasion. These poorly understood and rather rare phenomena fall on the borderlands of neurology and psychiatry and are, perhaps, forms of hysterical phenomena released by the seizure. Twilight states are those in which altered consciousness, alertness and perception are prominent, while fugues are those in which abnormal behaviour (particularly running) predominate. However, there is no clear distinction between these two forms.

Investigation

The basis of the diagnosis and classification of epilepsy is a combination of meticulous history-taking (including witness reports) with proper electroencephalogram (EEG) investigation. In those with a learning disability, both may be difficult to clarify. Specific difficulties in the differential diagnosis of seizures in people with a learning disability are created by the increased prevalence of tics, motor stereotypies, associated neurological abnormalities and movement disorders of various kinds, as well as a tendency for atypical presentations of psychiatric disorders. Careful history-taking from family and carers, as well as the patient, is vital. The hallmark of the epileptic phenomenon is the paroxysmal nature of the disorder – brief, episodic changes are looked for.

The EEG is invariably abnormal during a true epileptic seizure. Such abnormalities may, rarely, be very localised and not detectable in the routine scalp EEG since they can only be seen in cortical or depth EEG recordings. However, in the vast majority of seizures, an EEG taken at the time will confirm the diagnosis by showing paroxysmal discharges. This is a seizure – paroxysmal EEG changes at the same time as altered brain function.

However, if a seizure is not occurring when the EEG is being carried out, the presence of epileptiform EEG activity does not necessarily indicate a tendency to epilepsy. In a normal, random population the incidence of such changes is only 2 per 1000. However, in populations with learning disabilities but without epilepsy, as many as 40% may show some evidence of epileptiform abnormalities. On the other hand, 15% of people who have definite epilepsy repeatedly have normal interictal EEGs.

The routine EEG can, therefore, give some idea of the likelihood of epilepsy being present, but requires careful and cautious interpretation.

Ambulatory EEG monitoring accompanied by careful observation is to be preferred if seizures are occurring frequently (preferably at least two or three times each week). In people with learning disabilities, severely disturbed behaviour may preclude the use of ambulatory monitoring because of the risk of damage to the equipment. However, it is vital that at least one routine EEG be carried out and there is no major objection to using light or even heavy sedation in these circumstances, as allowances can be made for the effects of medication. Sleep and sleep-induced EEGs are in fact a useful diagnostic tool. Promethazine is a useful sedative in this respect, but quinalbarbitone and chloral hydrate are also used. Prior sleep deprivation is useful in those who do not have learning disabilities but may not be practicable otherwise. Anticonvulsant withdrawal may be appropriate in order to provoke focal discharges, but generalised and photosensitive discharges may simply be due to the withdrawal and are not necessarily evidence of epilepsy.

The chief uses of the EEG in epilepsy are:

(a) To assist in diagnosis – remembering that epilepsy is a clinical not an EEG diagnosis in most cases (unless the seizure occurs during recording, in which case it is a combination of clinical and EEG diagnosis).

(b) To indicate whether the origin of the seizures is likely to be generalised or focal, and if focal, where the focus might be or if there is more than one focus. In particular, this is useful if surgery is to be considered as a treatment. The definitive diagnosis of petit-mal (absence) epilepsy is made with the EEG.

(c) To assist in the diagnosis of the underlying cause – for instance if a tumour or generalised toxic or metabolic dysfunction is present.

(d) To assist in assessing prognosis – after a first seizure an abnormal EEG significantly raises the likelihood of repeat seizures from 40% (with a normal EEG) to 80%.

The CT and MRI scan may be of importance and it can be argued that all patients with partial seizures or with EEG evidence of focal abnormalities should have a CT scan in order to exclude a tumour as the cause. The yield of abnormalities on CT scanning varies depending upon the population. Patients with primary generalised seizures (particularly true petit-mal) and without focal neurological signs are very unlikely to have any treatable abnormality on CT scan, certainly less than 5%. However, patients over the age of 55 with onset of focal seizures have a 35% risk of having a tumour. It has been argued that in the elderly (aged over 65), the onset of epilepsy, as long as progressive neurological signs are not present, is not a reason to carry out a CT scan. This is because most will be caused by small infarcts which would not be treated.

In people with learning disabilities, carrying out a CT scan may be very difficult because of failure to cooperate with the procedure. It may also prove difficult to interpret, even if movement artefact is not present. This is because a variety of developmental brain abnormalities may be present and their relevance, or otherwise, to the development of epilepsy may be doubtful. However, certain diagnoses (such as tuberous sclerosis) may be confirmed with the CT scan.

The MRI scan will supply far more detailed anatomical information. Areas of heterotopia may be clearly demonstrated. However, this may be of only academic interest and the procedure of having an MRI scan could be very frightening for a person with a learning disability; cooperation by lying still is essential. If vital, both CT scans and MRI scans can be performed under a general anaesthetic.

Neuropsychological assessment may be useful in determining whether selective cognitive deficits are present and likely to be associated with a focus of brain dysfunction and a source of epilepsy. Serial neuropsychological assessments will be essential in determining whether intellectual decline is taking place, as will be the case in a number of the degenerating conditions associated with epilepsy in people with learning disabilities (such as dementia in Down's syndrome).

Other investigations will be appropriate to screen for the causes of the learning disability.

Specific epileptic syndromes presenting in childhood and associated with learning disabilities

Although most people with learning disabilities who have epilepsy do not have any specific epileptic syndrome, there are certain groups of epileptic phenomena which are most likely to be seen in patients who have a learning disability, or in babies and children who will develop a learning disability. The myoclonic epilepsies, usually arising in early childhood, are particularly associated with the development of severe learning disabilities since they are usually associated with severe cerebral disturbance.

Early infantile myoclonus

The development of myoclonus, tonic infantile spasms and partial motor seizures in the neonatal or early infancy period (before three months) carries a grave prognosis for future development. Confusing and inconsistent classification of these rather rare disorders have been developed but are at present of little real clinical usefulness. These disorders are associated with many of the inborn errors of metabolism but may also be due to perinatal damage, developmental abnormalities and, often, with no biochemical or pathological diagnosis. Nevertheless, a full metabolic work-up is indicated as treatable causes (e.g. pyridoxine deficiency) may be found.

The EEG in early infantile myoclonus will be abnormal and may be characteristic. A pattern of 'burst-suppression' may be seen, in which bursts of complex spike and sharp wave activity occur over both hemispheres (and may occur over localised areas as well), but in between these bursts, the background activity is of very low voltage. By about six months this will usually change to a completely disorganised hypsarrhythmia pattern or show multifocal paroxysmal activity.

The prognosis for these conditions is very poor, most are very severely disabled and many die in the first two years of life. No treatment has yet been found to be consistently effective, but corticosteroids, ACTH and, recently, lamotrigine may be helpful.

West syndrome

This form of infantile spasm was first described by W. J. West in 1841; he described the condition in his own child. There are three elements to the diagnosis:

(a) Infantile spasms – flexor (salaam) and extensor myoclonic spasms of neck, trunk and limbs.
(b) Severe learning disability.
(c) Hypsarrhythmia – an EEG pattern of a chaotic mixture of high amplitude slow waves with variable spikes and sharp waves.

To these a fourth might be added:

(d) Onset at less than one year old (usually at 3–7 months).

This condition results from a variety of causes and complete (including postmortem) investigations usually reveal some pathology. West syndrome is the final common pathway of a number of disorders which grossly disrupt cerebral functioning. Tuberous sclerosis is one of the more common causes. Other congenital brain malformations may be identified. Down's syndrome, leucodystrophy, phenylketonuria and various inborn errors of metabolism may cause West syndrome. Prenatal infections may result in this disorder. However, the most common identified cause is perinatal hypoxia. Postnatal events rarely cause West syndrome.

Treatment is difficult and many of the standard anticonvulsants have no effect – phenobarbitone, phenytoin and carbamazepine do not work. Some control may be achieved with ACTH or corticosteroids, which are usually the first line of treatment. There is some evidence that early control reduces the later severity of the learning disability, but it is also likely that the more easily controlled cases are likely to be less retarded in any case. Sodium valproate may be effective and the benzodiazepines (clonazepam and nitrazepam) can be initially effective in as many as 50%, but tolerance usually develops. Vigabatrin has recently been shown to have a significantly beneficial effect in some patients.

Prognosis is poor but depends on the underlying condition. Only 20% will make a complete recovery; the good prognostic features include 'primary' aetiology (normal development, no identifiable cause), late onset (after six months) and rapid control of the seizures. The other 80% are left with permanent neurological and/or mental deficits, usually severe mental handicap and continuing severe epilepsy.

Lennox–Gastaut syndrome

This syndrome was first described clinically by Lennox and Davies in 1950 and more clearly defined in 1966 by Gastaut. It is an important cause of severe epilepsy in people with a learning disability, especially important since the new anticonvulsant lamotrigine seems to be remarkably effective in a proportion of cases.
The triad of clinical features are:

(a) A combination of generalised seizures – with atypical absences, tonic seizures, atonic (drop) attacks and myoclonic seizures.
(b) An EEG showing interictal diffuse slow (2–3 Hz) spike and wave changes with bursts of fast activity (10 Hz) during sleep. The ictal EEG depends on the form of seizures.
(c) Slow mental development, even if a severe intellectual disability does not ensue, major learning difficulties are almost always present and may be progressive.

The age of onset is over one year, but usually between three and five years. There is a predominance of males. There is no clear-cut aetiology, although non-specific neurological abnormalities often pre-date the onset of the epilepsy and there may be some form of generalised cerebral disorder (referred to imprecisely as 'encephalopathy') at the onset of the syndrome. The disorder may be preceded by West syndrome.

The seizures are usually tonic initially; they may be focal or axial. Atypical absence attacks with partial or complete loss of consciousness then become part of the clinical picture. Myoclonic and atonic attacks may then develop. Status epilepticus or serial seizures develop in up to two-thirds of cases and may be recurrent and resistant to medication.

Treatment until recently has been with sodium valproate and the benzodiazepines (clonazepam and nitrazepam). However, the new anticonvulsant lamotrigine may be dramatically successful in some cases. Other anticonvulsants, particularly vigabatrin, phenytoin and carbamazepine may make the myoclonus very much worse.

If the condition is very severe and unresponsive, a ketogenic diet may be tried. This is a diet in which the intake of lipids is very high relative to the protein and carbohydrate content. The mechanism of action is unclear, but such diets alter cerebral hydration, energy metabolism, sodium concentration and other biochemical indices.

The prognosis is usually severe, with the development of intractable epilepsy and mental deterioration. Bad prognostic indicators include early onset (under three years), high frequency of fits and status, onset after West syndrome, and an EEG with a marked excess of slow wave and focal abnormalities. However, the use of lamotrigine may alter the prognosis for some.

Seizures presenting after childhood in people with learning disabilities

Most of the seizures associated with learning disabilities start in childhood, but some specific associations occur between severe intellectual disability and epilepsy starting in adolescence. These include epilepsy associated with autism, post-traumatic epilepsy and progressive cognitive deterioration associated with epilepsy. Epilepsy due to tuberous sclerosis may start in adolescence. Epilepsy in Down's syndrome may develop as a late complication associated with dementia.

Autism

Autism is a final common pathway presentation of a variety of abnormalities of brain development and dysfunction. During adolescence, a third of patients with autism develop epilepsy, although no specific epileptic syndrome is evident. The other specific causes of epilepsy which may be complicated by the onset in adolescence or late childhood, include metachromatic leucodystrophy (due to deficiency of aryl sulphatase A), tuberous sclerosis, Sturge–Weber syndrome, Rett syndrome, and juvenile forms of Lafora's and Gaucher's diseases. Progressive myoclonic epilepsy developing in late childhood or adolescence is usually due to a 'juvenile' form of one of the inborn errors of metabolism and is usually associated with a very poor prognosis.

Post-traumatic epilepsy

Post-traumatic epilepsy due to head injury, anoxic damage and vascular damage may result in the development of severe intellectual disability and epilepsy. The risk factors for development of epilepsy after head injury all relate to focal cortical damage (as with a missile injury, dural tear, depressed fracture or intracranial bleed). The risk of developing epilepsy in such cases is 30% if prophylactic anticonvulsants are not used. If such focal damage is present and accompanied by a post-traumatic amnesia of more than 24 hours and a seizure within the first week, the risk of developing epilepsy rises to 60%. On the other hand, if there have been none of these factors present the risk is about 2%. In 60% of those developing seizures after head injuries, the onset is within the first year and in 85% within the first two years. After five years the risk drops almost to that of the normal population.

Progressive cognitive deterioration

A very small group of people with epilepsy undergo progressive cognitive deterioration, although the reason for this is not clear. It tends to occur in those with more severe epilepsy and with pre-existing brain damage. It may be that the developmental abnormality which produced the epilepsy is progressive and an expanding reactive gliosis may be found in some cases. The effects of repeated seizures and of sedating anticonvulsant medication may also be responsible for the intellectual deterioration.

Epilepsy and Down's syndrome

The early writers on Down's syndrome, including Langdon Down himself, rarely mentioned epilepsy and clearly did not regard it as a complication of the syndrome. This was perhaps because epilepsy may not be as common in Down's syndrome as in many other causes of learning disability. However, over the last 20 years it has increasingly been recognised that there are several interesting relationships between epilepsy and Down's syndrome, some of which may help to increase our broader understanding of the causation of epilepsy. The awareness of an increased incidence of epilepsy in Down's syndrome has probably come about because of the very much increased life expectancy for people with Down's syndrome in recent years.

Approximately 10% of a population of adults with Down's syndrome have epilepsy (McVicker *et al*, 1994), however this rises to 40% of those over the age of 40 and to 80% in those with Alzheimer's disease. It is therefore clear that Alzheimer's disease is a very significant cause of epilepsy in Down's syndrome – far more so than in the general population, for reasons which are not clear but which will be discussed shortly.

However, there are two further peaks in the incidence of epilepsy in Down's syndrome; these are early infancy and the third decade of life.

In early childhood there is a particular association with West syndrome, but this tends to be more benign, more easily controlled and with a greater tendency to myoclonic seizures than in West syndrome without Down's syndrome. It is of great theoretical interest that the gene for a rare familial progressive myoclonic epilepsy (Unverricht-Lundborg disease) has recently been identified on the distal long arm of chromosome 21, within the critical Down's syndrome region.

The second period of increased epilepsy incidence is in the 20s. This is not associated with the onset of dementia and may well be equivalent to the increased incidence of partial epilepsies in adolescence in individuals without learning disabilities. This is thought to be related, in a neurodevelopmental fashion, to the myelination and proliferation of a sufficient bulk of nerves and synapses in order to connect abnormal areas of brain and allow paroxysmal spread.

The final peak of incidence of epilepsy in Down's syndrome comes with the development of Alzheimer's disease over the age of 40. Seizures start after the clinical onset of dementia in 60%. The seizures are usually tonic-clonic in type but, interestingly, myoclonic seizures are again particularly prominent. Inter-ictal EEGs often only show non-specific slow wave changes.

In addition to these increased incidences of epilepsy, it should be commented that there are certain epilepsies which are less common than might be expected, particularly febrile convulsions (in spite of a very significantly increased incidence of infections in infancy) and Lennox–Gastaut syndrome (which clearly is associated with learning disability generally). These anomalies may assist our understanding both of Down's syndrome and of epilepsy generally.

The mechanisms of production of epilepsy are as imperfectly understood in Down's syndrome as elsewhere. However, again, testing hypotheses about how epilepsy is produced here may assist our general understanding of epilepsy. The brains of people with Down's syndrome are small and show abnormal neocortical cytoarchitecture, there are reduced granule cells (possibly the inhibitor GABA cells), and the neurones and dendrites show abnormal morphology which may enhance excitability. There may also be altered neuronal physiology and membrane reactivity as well as a number of neurotransmitter abnormalities (particularly 5HT and glutamate).

Finally, it must at all times be remembered that there are a wide variety of causes of 'funny turns' in Down's syndrome (such as breath-holding, behavioural abnormalities, heart dysrhythmias, sleep disorders and a large number of undiagnosable episodes). Thus careful assessment, with observation, EEG and scanning, is vital. However, if epilepsy is diagnosed treatment is often very effective and rewarding.

Psychiatric aspects

There is a significant association between epilepsy and nearly all forms of psychiatric disorder. The prevalence of anxiety, depression, suicide, schizophrenia and dementia are all raised in epilepsy. However, this section will deal with those psychiatric aspects of epilepsy seen as especially relevant in people with learning disabilities. These are dyscontrol syndromes, pseudoepileptic seizures and self-induced seizures.

Episodic dyscontrol syndrome

The relationship between epilepsy and aggressive behaviour is fraught with controversy. The majority of people with epilepsy are no more aggressive than the general population. However, there does seem to be an increased prevalence of violent behaviour in people with epilepsy; this is likely to result from a number of causes which are situational and cultural and not part of the discussion here. The question of whether epilepsy itself, or something akin to it, gives rise to aggressive loss of control is unclear.

Initial investigation by Heath in the 1950s using studies of depth electrode recordings, and followed up by Mark and Ervin in the 1960s, suggested that aggressive feelings and violent outbursts could be associated with paroxysmal activity particularly in the amygdala, a brain structure which is known to have a close relationship to aggressive behaviour in various animal studies. However, an extensive study of 5400 seizures by Delgato-Escueta *et al* (1981) found only 13 cases of violent behaviour. As Fenwick, in his useful survey of aggression and epilepsy (1986), pointed out, this study took place in a video-monitored epilepsy laboratory and not in the real world, which is where aggression occurs.

In the person who has a learning disability there are, perhaps, still more reasons to react violently than in others who have seizures. They may be less likely to understand and be understood as they recover, they may be in more restricted environments, and with others who may be more frightened or frightening, than a person who is not disabled. However, it is the common experience of the staff in mental handicap hospitals that in the prodromal period the person with epilepsy may become much more irritable, and after the seizure they may be more settled.

True episodic dyscontrol syndrome (if it exists) occurs in people who may have some other evidence of developmental delays and 'soft' neurological signs. The episode is quite out of character, the individual has little or no memory for the event and is remorseful afterwards. Some EEG changes may be present. Occasionally such events are clearly post-ictal phenomena, but in Gunn's study (1979) of offenders with epilepsy, only two out of 158 showed evidence of the crime being carried out as part of a seizure (post-ictal).

Inter-ictal violence may be more prominent in people with epilepsy, but this may be because of a number of sociocultural factors. A review by Rutter (1982) suggests that the relationships between poor impulse control and epilepsy lies in the fact that both may arise from brain damage.

Non-epileptic attack disorder (NEAD)

There is no clear evidence that NEAD (pseudo-epileptic seizures, 'hysterical seizures') occurs more commonly in those with a learning disability than in the general population of people with epilepsy. However, there is a suggestion that, on the one hand, people with limited communication skills may be more likely to express emotional conflicts in this fashion, especially if there is some underlying tendency to organic brain disorder, and on the other hand, people with a learning disability may be more suggestible as well as more likely to have witnessed seizures and their effect on staff than are the general population.

Most medical studies have drawn up lists distinguishing between true and non-epileptic attacks (see Box 15.3). However, it must be recalled that cases exist which are at the very borderlands of epilepsy and hysteria, in which it seems impossible to distinguish "real" from "pseudo" epilepsy, and Landouzy's term "hystero-epilepsy" is the only appropriate diagnosis. It is also important to remember that real and non-epileptic seizures may well occur in the same individual.

Self-induced seizures

It is well known that seizures may be precipitated, in those vulnerable to epilepsy, by a variety of external or mental stimuli. In a recent study (Antebi & Bird, 1992), 92% of patients with epilepsy felt that some emotional factor could increase the frequency of their seizures. However, it has been regarded as extremely rare for individuals actively to induce their own seizures by some act of will. A review of this subject in 1962 reported only 51 cases worldwide. The 'typical' case was reported to be female with an average age of 11, of a moderate degree of intellectual disability, and suffering from frequent photosensitive petit-mal seizures. The typical method of evoking these fits was by oscillating the hand in front of the eyes so that sunlight would flicker onto the eyes. By 1980 Binnie *et al* had estimated that 27% of people with photosensitive epilepsy evoked their own seizures on occasion (an estimated 1.2% of the total population with epilepsy), and a study at the Maudsley Hospital found that as many as 20% of patients admitted to occasional self-induction. This was, no doubt, an unusual population, but it is probably true that far more people induce seizures than has been realised. This may particularly be so in people with a learning disability, although this problem can certainly arise in people with epilepsy who have normal and above normal intellectual abilities. The reasons for self-induction may be unclear but include avoidance of stress, pleasurable auras, attention-seeking and obtaining a sense of control over the seizures. The management of such seizures must involve behavioural and psycho-therapeutic approaches, since medication alone is unlikely to be successful.

Management of epilepsy

The principles of the management of epilepsy in people with learning disabilities are the same as for anyone else. Good care of a person with epilepsy involves careful and sympathetic listening and examination, taking time, supporting the individual, the family and the carers, as well as appropriate and well-monitored use of medication and consideration

---

**Box 15.3 Non-epileptic attack disorder ('hysterical fits',
pseudoseizures)**

Twenty per cent of patients with severe, intractible 'epilepsy' have
   non-epileptic attacks (± true fits).
But patients with true epilepsy are the most likely to have
   pseudoseizures. Distinguishing features are listed below.

The attack
   May be emotional precipitant, primary and secondary gain.
   Wide range of often bizarre events and behaviour, talking,
   screaming, laughing, random struggling.
   Often gradual onset, possibly with prolonged 'warning'.
   Varied, non-stereotyped attack pattern.
   No true tonic-clonic movements, although it may resemble them.
   May be suggestible.
   Tongue-biting, incontinence, nocturnal occurrence and injury are
   rare, but may occur.
   Highly directed violent behaviour is occasionally seen, often at
   home and with others present.
   Pupillary responses present.
Post-ictally
   Confusion is rare.
   May smile or laugh – often not unpleasant feelings.
   May recall events in detailed fashion.

EEG normal (with artefacts) during and after seizure.
Serum prolactin normal.

---

of the wider issues of education, work and social activities. It is very clear
that stress and anxiety can exacerbate epilepsy (Antebi & Bird, 1992) and
appropriate counselling should be given to avoid these provoking factors.
Other provoking factors may include menstruation, which may further
complicate the issue of sexuality which the person with a learning disability
and her family can find particularly difficult to deal with.

Gross parental (or care-staff) overprotection, with vigilant focusing on
symptoms, obsessional attention to medication and side-effects
(sometimes complicated by over- or under-dosing by the family) and
major, unnecessary restrictions of lifestyle can occur. Working with the
family in these circumstances may be difficult but can be very rewarding
in the long run.

The attitudes of families and carers, both to epilepsy and to learning
disabilities, may be negative, as may the attitudes of doctors (general
practitioners and neurologists). As Craig & Oxley (1988) pointed out, the

ideal approach to epilepsy is a combination of expertise, enthusiasm and empathy, perhaps along with the time to deal properly with the complex problems of people with learning disabilities and epilepsy. The fact that busy neurology clinics may only have a few minutes to sort out the complex problems of the person with a learning disability who has chronic, difficult epilepsy means that all those involved in the care of people with learning disabilities should build up a good working knowledge of modern approaches to the management of epilepsy.

Psychological management

Although psychological methods are very rarely adequate in themselves to control epilepsy, they can improve the control obtained with medication as well as improving the general well-being of the patient and family.

Simple, non-specific relaxation techniques may prove surprisingly effective, especially if associated with attention to environmental and intrapsychic factors causing anxiety and unhappiness. Careful management of changes in the individual's environment is important. The avoidance of boredom can be a key factor, since the inactive brain is likely to be more prone to seizures.

Specific behavioural methods may be used, in which very careful study of the circumstances of seizures is undertaken, followed by the use of operant conditioning techniques to reduce the frequency of seizures. Biofeedback techniques of various kinds have been used, often with some EEG phenomenon as the biological parameter being used. These specific techniques require a high intensity of effort and expertise on the part of the therapists and, as a result, are too rarely tried.

Anticonvulsant medication

The principles of treating epilepsy in people with learning disabilities are no different from those in the general population, but sticking to them may be more difficult.

The main principles of initiating treatment are:

(a) Ensure, as far as possible that the patient has epilepsy – take a careful history, hear witness reports, assess the EEG sensibly, possibly monitor the EEG.
(b) Assess the risks and benefits of drug treatment – a single fit has an 80% chance of recurrence. At the other end of the scale, in severe epilepsy which has not responded to anticonvulsants, it may be appropriate to stop all drugs. All treatment is a trade-off between therapeutic and adverse effects.
(c) Always start with a single anticonvulsant in the lowest effective dose. Consider the choice of drug carefully (see Box 15.4).

(d) Explain and discuss the reasons for taking the drug, and potential side-effects, with the patient and family. Discuss also the possible length of treatment. Allow time and discussion in order for the patient and family to come to terms with the diagnosis and need for medication.

(e) Introduce the drug very slowly whenever possible; adverse effects of all kinds are very significantly reduced by doing this.

(f) Monitor the drug with serum assays *where appropriate* (largely for phenytoin only).

Box 15.4 Choice of drug in epilepsy

Generalised seizures
    Childhood petit-mal
        1. Sodium valproate
        2. Lamotrigine
        3. Ethosuximide
        NOT phenytoin (aggravates)
    Adult tonic-clonic
        1. Sodium valproate
        2. Lamotrigine
        3. Carbamazepine
        4. Topiramate
        5. Gabapeutin
        6. Vigabatrin
        7. Phenytoin
    Myoclonic/atonic
        1. Valproate
        2. Lamotrigine
        3. Clobazam
        4. Gabapeutin
        5. Topiramate
        (Vigabatrin may exacerbate myoclonus)
Partial seizures (simple or complex)
        1. Carbamazepine
        2. Valproate
        3. Lamotrigine
        4. Gabapeutin
        5. Topiramate
        6. Vigabatrin
        7. Phenytoin

Primidone and phenobarbitone are not first-choice drugs (in any case they are probably the same thing). There is no point in using them together.

(g) Inform all appropriate carers (general practitioner, community psychiatric nurse, hostel careworkers) of the treatment.

(h) Record all seizures carefully on a standard chart, along with all changes in medication.

If the epilepsy has become apparently intractable, the following principles apply:

(a) Assess compliance, the lack of which is a major cause of 'uncontrolled' epilepsy.

(b) Assess for non-epileptic seizures, which occur in 20% of 'uncontrolled' epilepsy.

(c) Reassess the cause of the seizures – a focal lesion may have been missed, do a CT scan.

(d) Assess the importance of emotional or other precipitants and stresses.

(e) Ensure that one drug (e.g. carbamazepine for partial seizures or valproate for generalised seizures) has been tried at the maximum tolerated dose, whatever the blood level.

(f) Alter drug therapy to a *different* drug first, not simply adding an additional drug. However, manage the changeover in an overlapping fashion.

(g) Consider adjuncts – e.g. clobazam, acetazolamide.

(h) Use one of the new anticonvulsants, particularly lamotrigine for generalised epilepsy (e.g. Lennox–Gastaut).

(i) Consider suitability for surgery – excision of localised lesion, lobectomy or selective amygdalo-hippocampectomy for temporal lobe seizures, callosotomy for generalised seizures, hemispherectomy for severe hemiatrophy with epilepsy.

The use of a single drug is to be encouraged wherever possible, but in severe epilepsy this may not be the ideal situation. Clearly there has been excessive use of combined anticonvulsants, resulting in various interactions and a worsening of control. However, slavish adherence to a programme of single drug use may be equally inappropriate. Careful recording of seizure frequency must be used to assess any changes.

References

Antebi, D. & Bird, J. M. (1992) The facilitation and evocation of seizures. *British Journal of Psychiatry*, **160**, 154–164.

Binnie, C. D., Darby, C. E., DeKorte, R. A., *et al* (1980) Self-induction of epileptic seizures by eye-closure. *Journal of Neurology, Neurosurgery and Psychiatry*, **43**, 386–389.

Craig, A. & Oxley, J. (1988) Social aspects of epilepsy. In *A Textbook of Epilepsy* (eds J. Laidlaw, A. Richens & J. Oxley). Edinburgh: Churchill Livingstone.

Delgato-Escueta, A., Mattson, R. & King, L. (1981) The nature of aggression during epileptic seizures. *New England Journal of Medicine*, **305**, 711–716.

Fenwick, P. (1986) Aggression and epilepsy. In *Aspects of Epilepsy and Psychiatry* (eds M. R. Trimble & T. G Bolwig), pp. 31–60. Chichester: John Wiley.

Gunn, J. (1979) Forensic psychiatry. In *Recent Advances in Clinical Psychiatry* (ed. K. Granville-Grossman). Edinburgh: Churchill Livingstone.

McVicker, R. W., Shanks, O. E. P. & McClelland, R. J. (1994) Prevalence and associated features of epilepsy in adults with Down's syndrome. *British Journal of Psychiatry*, **164**, 528–532.

Rutter, M. (1982) Concepts, issues and prospects in developmental psychiatry. *Journal of Clinical Neuropsychology*, **4**, 91–115.

Additional reading

Deb, S. & Hunter, D. (1991) Psychopathology of people with mental handicap and epilepsy. *British Journal of Psychiatry*, **159**, 822–834.

Laidlaw, J., Rickens, A. & Oxley, J. (eds) (1988) *A Textbook of Epilepsy* (3rd edn). Edinburgh: Churchill Livingstone.

Stafstrom, C. E. (1993) Epilepsy in Down's syndrome: clinical aspects and possible mechanisms. *American Journal on Mental Retardation*, **98** (suppl.), 12–26.

16 Counselling and psychotherapy

Sheila Hollins

Assessment ● *Communication* ● *Preconceptions and misconceptions*
● *Therapeutic aims* ● *Disability and dependence* ● *Sexuality* ●
Bereavement and loss ● *Different therapeutic approaches* ●
Conclusion

The ideal psychotherapy candidate is said to be young, intelligent, attractive and articulate – not a description which fits usual images of people with learning disabilities. One of the challenges facing the therapist of such supposed ideal patients is the need to examine the intellectual defences they use to avoid getting in touch with their own feelings. Their skills with language may be used to try to distract and divert the therapist from the patients' real conflicts. But just as psychotherapists working with very young children do not work primarily through language, nor do therapists working with articulate adults. In all psychodynamic work, from the very first session, therapeutic use is made of the transference and countertransference feelings in the relationship between therapist and patient, or patients. The therapist has to learn to listen with her eyes and her feelings as well as her ears; to listen to what is not said as well as to what is spoken.

Assessment

One misconception about people with learning disabilities is that their limited intellect will preclude them from a treatment which seeks to increase affective understanding. But what is required to engage in therapy is emotional contact between patient and therapist, and the belief by the therapist that the patient has even a limited ability to make object relationships. Part of the assessment interview must be an honest appraisal by the therapist of her own feelings and reactions to the patient. It is customary for the therapist to make trial interpretations in the assessment interview to see how the patient responds. Is the patient going to be able to take any risks? Will he give any sign of his understanding? I would like to suggest that the therapist must also take some risks at this first meeting. Other people's, and even one's own, assumptions may need to be confronted (McConachie & Sinason, 1989).

For example, when I met George for the first time after referral for help with his difficult behaviour, his mother advised me not to sit close to him as he would surely hit me. This was said in front of George who was angrily thrashing around. He had athetoid cerebral palsy and his movements were rather inaccurate and exhausting. I replied that it was not me he wanted to hit and sat on a chair next to him. His body stilled and he turned to look at me. Counselling someone without speech who is not responding conventionally can lead one to feel rather foolish for trusting one's instinct and/or interpretation of his communicative attempts as intentional, especially when other people may not agree with your interpretation (Leudar, 1989). What is important is your ability to make a relationship with the person who is seeking help, and to provide an opportunity for trust to develop so that he dares to show something of his real self.

If we believe that children and adults without good intellect, even without speech, may have feelings, may have feelings about other people, may experience comfort in warm loving relationships, and experience the loss of important people, places and events; then a psychodynamic approach to imagining and understanding such a person's experience of life seems both possible and important.

Finally, part of the assessment is to determine the level of psychotherapy which is appropriate, given the needs of the individual and the qualifications and experience of the therapist. This will be explored further in the section on therapeutic aims

Communication

Effective counselling is dependent on well-developed and appropriate communication skills in the counsellor. Effective communication involves at least two people, each of whom has two roles. Turn-taking by the participants requires and allows each person to move from one role (e.g. listening and observing) to another role (e.g. talking or signing).

The members of the partnership must move at the same speed, and thus the counsellor has to judge how long to pause to allow time for her partner to respond. People who have autistic features or avoidant personalities offer a major challenge to the counsellor. Their discomfort with eye contact and difficulty in making object relationships will interfere with attempts to turn-take. An example was a middle-aged and institution-alised woman I tried to counsel before her move from hospital to a group home. Staff were concerned that she showed no apparent understanding of the move, and would not engage in the group's preparations for the move. I found her in a corner of the dining room on her own with a large pile of pieces of paper or card, most of which had been scribbled on with the same symmetrical but meaningless 'writing'. She was sorting the papers and re-sorting them, with her head bowed, and my entrance provoked no flicker of recognition that anyone had entered. I paused for a while to see if a delayed response would emerge and then tried some different ways of making contact. The comment which finally broke the ice was my question about the colour of her eyes. "With your head down like that I cannot see the colour of your eyes – are they blue like mine?" This woman, who had never met me before, responded: "Your eyes are grey, not blue". Counselling such a person is arduous. and without occasional gems of feedback such as the one described, can leave the therapist feeling very unsure about the impact of her attempts to communicate.

The medium of communication does not necessarily involve spoken language but always includes an enormous amount of body language (Morris, 1987). In addition, signed or written language and even drawings may be important. Cultural influences on communication roles must be taken into account – an aspect of communicating which is highlighted when working in a multiracial community. Counselling and psychotherapy with people with learning disabilities requires a holistic approach to communication in which the above aspects apply. In addition, psychodynamic principles underlie the approach used in this chapter.

Therapy is likely to be complicated by conceptual and communication difficulties, and another medium may need to be used as an added channel for communication, for example art, sand, music or drama. This can lead to idiosyncratic ways of working.

Preconceptions and misconceptions

While some adults with learning disabilities may be at an early developmental level emotionally, comparisons with therapeutic work with children should be used cautiously. The range of life experiences of the adult must be remembered, even if therapy is focusing on pre-oedipal relationships. Increasing doubt is now being thrown on previous assumptions about the lack of understanding of people with profound learning disabilities (Crossley, 1980). Participation in infant observation seminars may help to increase our skills in understanding the communication attempts of some of the people in this group. Appropriate and full use of communication aids should also be explored.

Another misconception is that psychoanalytical psychotherapy is about cure. The debate about learning disability and psychoanalysis in the past tended to revolve around the hope that analytical techniques would cure the child or adult of the primary impairment, for example, the cause of the learning disability or the autistic behaviour. If the impairment could not be cured, therefore, it was said nothing could be done. In this country psychodynamic theories about the causation of autism have largely been discredited. Sinason (1986) has written about the way in which secondary mental handicap can be a defence against trauma experienced by the individual. Sometimes learning disabilities turn out to be less severe than originally thought when emotional conflicts have been resolved and the person acquires the freedom to think. Usually where organic brain damage is present, such emotional release does not result in major cognitive gains. Considerable effort is now turning to understanding the nature and remediation of the emotional and communication disorders which lead bystanders to assume either that an inability to express one's thoughts is synonymous with impaired intelligence, or that emotional intelligence is linked to an ability to articulate one's feelings.

In many instances of severe learning disability the brain is damaged permanently. A request for therapy may be misunderstood as a denial of the reality of this damage; as a search for another diagnostic exploration which might uncover a remedial cause. But realistic requests for therapy might arise from a wish to come to terms with the internal and external experiences of the individual who has such damage. To understand this further demands knowledge of the features which are often seen in the psychological adjustments of disabled people and of families who have a member with a disability. This will be explored in more detail in the next section.

Therapeutic aims

People with learning disabilities will benefit from counselling or psychotherapy in the same way and for similar reasons as people without learning disabilities. Relationship or adjustment and personality difficulties are common presenting problems.

Cawley (1977) described several levels of psychotherapy of increasing depth and complexity, and the therapist must decide on the appropriate level and aim for each individual.

Thus, providing relief, support and counselling are part of the repertoire of any good doctor or social worker. Sharing one's problems with a sympathetic impartial listener can put things in clearer perspective. Such supportive counselling may include the need to provide information or education, for example on sexual matters. The main aim is either to restore the status quo in someone whose equilibrium is temporarily impaired by a crisis such as a bereavement, or to build up the strength of the person with a severe personality disorder in order to achieve the best possible adjustment. Exploring the inner world of such people is unnecessary and may be contraindicated in someone whose defences are precarious.

Intermediate levels of psychotherapy aim to clarify problems within a deepening relationship. The therapist confronts the defence mechanisms used by the patient, and interprets the way he or she relates to the therapist. At deeper levels more active psychodynamic work explores earlier traumas and conflicts in an attempt to reconstruct an individual's inner world, and allow him or her to relinquish disabling symptoms. At this level the aim is to achieve change in personality functioning and an increase in maturity. Advice is withheld, and emotional regression within the sessions is encouraged. Medication is discouraged. Anxiety is expected to occur and may be necessary to enable the working through of past conflicts.

Thus although support is part and parcel of all psychotherapies, exploration is not, and is reserved for the deeper levels as practised by suitably qualified and experienced clinicians (Box 16.1).

The focus of psychotherapeutic work depends on the stage reached in the life cycle of an individual or family and on any recent or unresolved life events. Themes which seem to be common at several different stages have been described elsewhere as the three secrets (Hollins & Grimer, 1988). These are the secrets of disability and dependence, of each person's sexuality, and of their own and their parents' mortality. In fact these are universally difficult issues for us to understand and adjust to, and all three are taboo subjects to a greater or lesser extent in different cultures and ages. People with learning disabilities are often subjected to a conspiracy of silence about these areas, over and above any conventional reticence.

Disability and dependence

When the diagnosis of a handicapping medical condition is made either at birth or after a later traumatic event, the shocked family members experience the loss of their normal healthy child (Bicknell, 1983). Their bereavement reaction is similar to the reaction of parents whose child

---

Box 16.1 Cawley's levels of psychotherapy

Outer (support and counselling)
1. Unburdening of problems to sympathetic listener
2. Ventilation of feelings within supportive relationship
3. Discussion of current problems with non-judgmental helper

Intermediate
4. Clarification of problems, their nature and origins, within deepening relationship
5. Confrontation of defences
6. Interpretation of unconscious motives and transference phenomena

Deeper (exploration and analysis)
7. Repetition, remembering, and reconstruction of past
8. Regression to less adult and less rational functioning
9. Resolution of conflicts by re-experiencing and working them through

has died. Their loss is compounded by the daily reminder their surviving damaged child provides for them.

We can only surmise about the experience for such an individual of being a disappointment to parents. Each person will have feelings and attitudes about their own limitations and their effect upon the family. Vanier (1985) suggests that every human being is to some extent a disappointment to parents and to self.

Attachment relationships in infancy may have been interfered with for a number of reasons; perhaps because of the emotional work involved in coming to terms with a child's difference, because of enforced separation from a sickly child, or because of a primary impairment in the responsiveness of the child. The achievement of satisfactory separation in adulthood depends on these early relationships developing more or less normally.

The aims of therapy here will be to come to terms with difference and disappointment. It is appropriate for the therapist(s) to be able to share the reality of the disability: to be able to feel the hopelessness and the sense of disappointment and even panic which the disabled individual with some insight may have about himself, or which his parents feel on his behalf.

People with learning disabilities sometimes comment on their own inadequacies, which a carer in attendance might quickly contradict: "You're not stupid"... "There's nothing wrong with the way you talk"... Such social convention which expects one to ignore the person's handicap may be quite inappropriate. The counsellor or therapist has an opportunity to respond differently by acknowledging the patient's insight. For example, the therapist might say she agrees with him and wonders if it feels upsetting to look or sound different.

Is not the family denial of disability an attempt to hide the painful 'secret' of disability from each other and from the affected individual? Such confusion leads to fear and loneliness.

Sexuality

Physical sexual development is not delayed in people with learning disabilities, although emotional maturity usually is. The arrival of puberty can be an unwelcome reminder of approaching adulthood. Parental fears about their adolescent child's naïvety and vulnerability may well be justified. Likewise parents may have fears about their child's inappropriate sexual behaviour, perhaps leading to embarrassing situations in the neighbourhood, or even to a conviction for a sexual offence. Infantilising attitudes which see people with learning disabilities as eternal children may contribute to a tendency in parents to want to protect their children from the possible consequences of their sexuality. Vulnerability to sexual abuse is high, and secondary emotional handicaps caused by such trauma may present with difficult behaviours such as eye-poking or other self-injury (Sinason, 1988, 1992).

As is so often the case when counselling people with learning disabilities, there is likely to be an educational aspect to the task. Personal relationship and sex education classes are not as available for children in special schools as for those in mainstream education. Nothing can be assumed in terms of the extent or accuracy of any factual knowledge about sexual matters.

> **Case example**
> Moses was 18 years old when arrested for indecent exposure. He had mild learning disabilities and a very smart and pleasant appearance. The police officer questioning him asked him if he was responsible for about 20 other minor sexual offences in the area. He told me the officer seemed pleased when he said 'yes' so he said 'yes' lots of times so that he could go home sooner. When I asked him to explain the charges against him he did not know the meaning of several key words including indecent exposure, guilty and not guilty. Moses lived with his parents in a two bedroom council flat and shared a bedroom with an older brother. He had been told that masturbation was wrong. No one had talked to him about the sexual feelings he was experiencing, especially at work where his manager had pictures of nude women on the wall. In some ways it seemed that Moses was expected to cope with adolescent sexuality rather better than average, with less help.

Bereavement and loss

Loss frequently looms large in the recent history of referrals of people with learning disabilities referred for psychiatric assessment. A relative inability to take control of one's own life seems to make one more vulnerable to loss.

For example, a person may not have been told about an important change or loss. Secondly, their feelings about loss and change may be difficult to articulate and their reaction may be misunderstood or ignored. Thirdly, their ability to make contact with a peer or carer who has moved may be precluded by an inability to write or phone or drive a car. Similarly, after the death of someone important, their need to look for the person who has died, to check out whether they have gone for ever, to visit places which remind them of that person, are all likely to be forgotten by carers.

The death of a parent may be the start of a chain of losses. Admission to residential care may be inevitable, possibly some distance away from home, resulting in a change of daily activities and the loss of friends and familiar staff. The bereaved person may be worried about who is feeding the cats or bringing in the post – tasks which perhaps had been theirs for years. Even the milkman will be different. None of the old familiar routines will be experienced again, and it is not unknown for the family home to be disposed of without the handicapped individual ever going back. David Cook's novel *Walter* movingly describes a similar sequence of events which sadly still occur in the 1990s (Cook, 1978). Therapeutic aims will focus on accurate information, perhaps including death education, and on the healthy resolution of grief (Conboy-Hill, 1992).

Different therapeutic approaches

Individual, group and family work all have a place depending on the identified needs at any particular stage. Counselling or therapy might focus on a life event which has occurred and on the consequences within the individual or family or caring group. Parent counselling, family therapy and bereavement counselling will all be considered briefly here; for information on individual and group analytical therapy see Symington (1981), Hollins & Evered (1990), Hollins (1992) and Hollins *et al* (1994).

Parent counselling

The first task is to break the news of suspected disability to parents. The consensus is that it should be told to both parents together, sensitively and honestly, as soon as there is any doubt – even if the doctor has to answer their questions with "I don't know". The conveyor of bad news will always be unpopular but despite this, he or she should offer further appointments to help the parents to express their feelings and to increase their shared understanding. Such essential counselling may be better done by a trusted family doctor, an experienced hospital social worker or a member of the community team for people with learning disabilities or child development team. Sometimes it will be appropriate for the psychiatrist to be the counsellor.

Work with parents at this early stage should reap dividends later, as parents who grieve together are more likely to work well together as parents. In fact, engaging fathers in such counselling is not easy and mothers traditionally become full-time carers of disabled children, with fathers having less chance of playing a normal parenting role. There is a tendency for the attachment bond with the mother to be so strong that normal sharing in a family triad is not possible.

Unless the father is involved right from the beginning, his wife may find it difficult to let him gradually introduce their child to the outside world. It is not difficult to imagine the consequences of such distorted relationships in later adult life. If separation in infancy is difficult, separation in adulthood will be even harder (Richardson & Ritchie, 1989).

'Letting go' groups for middle-aged or elderly parents, whose handicapped sons and daughters are still very dependent on them, are a valued way of introducing change into a family system. Often it is the death of a spouse which leads the surviving parent to seek help in planning for the future.

In my experience when parents are brought together, whether in formal or informal settings, they talk endlessly and honestly about experiences which they have in common. Other parents can be an invaluable support to grieving struggling parents.

Child development units to which most parents are referred are not, by and large, services to which parents take their own problems.

Case example
Carole, the mother of Robin, a 7-year-old boy with cerebral palsy and uncontrolled epilepsy, said the appointments with the paediatrician offered the only possibility of a cure and she wouldn't waste a moment of that precious time talking of her own suicidal ideation. The paediatrician described this mother as a wonderful, down-to-earth woman who coped marvellously and certainly didn't need any involvement with child psychiatry. At her first meeting with me, requested only after a serious overdose, she asked how long her son would live. He had already been in intensive care twice in status epilepticus and the prognosis was very poor. We talked about her realistic fear of finding him dead in the morning. At our next meeting she told me that facing up to the severity of his handicap had enabled her to have her son christened, and she had made renewed efforts to get her family rehoused to improve the quality of their lives while Robin was still alive to enjoy it.

Family therapy

Family therapy is a more specialist and scarce resource which can encourage better coping strategies. It should not be a last resort but should be considered early on if signs of stress in any family member are causing anxiety. Working with family groups when there is an adult handicapped member is also appropriate. For example, it may be useful when issues of dependence and fear about what will happen when parents die have led to more complex patterns of behaviour.

Case example
Charlie was 27 years old and his weight had dropped to below six stone when his parents finally agreed to psychiatric intervention. After several family therapy interviews all three were able to agree to, and cooperate with, an admission to a unit for people with anorexia nervosa. Confrontation about separation and dependency issues was carefully avoided, and gradually all three began to explore how they could negotiate a permanent separation for Charlie without anyone feeling rejected.

The needs of siblings may also emerge in family therapy. Often parents omit to explain to their other children anything about their sibling's disability, or they fail to update such explanations as each child's understanding develops. The subject of handicap may become a taboo at home, with siblings having to face insensitive questioning or comment from children in the playground.

Making a family tree at a first family interview can help to elucidate who knows what about loss and illness in different members. In a family with two children, the older of whom had serious communication and behavioural difficulties, it emerged that the 8-year-old daughter had completely misunderstood explanations about her brother's disability. He had been diagnosed as having fragile X, and she had had a chromosomal analysis herself two years earlier. Her mother had explained to her that her test was fine and that her children would not have the same condition as her brother. Two years later her understanding of this was that she herself would gradually lose skills and become disabled like her brother.

Clarifying difficult or taboo areas in a supportive setting such as this can help families to improve communication at home (Wilkins, 1992).

Bereavement counselling

The task here is to help with the work of mourning. On occasion the counsellor will find that the bereaved person has not been told of their loss. It is still commonplace for people with learning disabilities to be excluded from the funeral. Yet these are practical ways in which someone can be helped to understand the finality of their loss; joining in the funeral rituals, and experiencing the loss through seeing and hearing and touching. Helping someone to say goodbye may involve the counsellor in revisiting the grave or the home of the deceased person with him or her, and in looking at photographs or other mementoes with them. The bereaved person may need permission to express negative feelings about their dead relative: feelings about being let down or deserted. The counsellor is in a position to understand how normal such feelings are, whereas a carer may discourage an individual in her care from speaking ill of the dead. A guided mourning approach is very appropriate (Sireling *et al*, 1988).

Bereavement counselling is available to many people through an individual's church, through voluntary organisations such as CRUSE – Bereavement Care, or through health and social service agencies. For people with learning disabilities such counselling may be withheld for a variety of reasons. Counsellors may have little experience of being with people with learning disabilities and may feel de-skilled when their ordinary communication skills appear inadequate.

Trying to understand and to explain and comfort are vital. Perhaps a genuine and sustained attempt to communicate and share will convey enough emotionally. Two books telling the story of the death of a parent in pictures have been published to assist the counsellor (Hollins & Sireling, 1994). An intellectual understanding of the permanence of a loss is less important than an emotional awareness of what has happened. Senses of sight and hearing and touch will reinforce the realisation of loss. The person is not here, the bed is empty, as is the place at table. At the funeral service the coffin and the flowers are seen and perhaps touched. The funeral music and singing is heard, as are subdued voices of the mourners.

Looking more closely, the following responses are described by people who have been bereaved: feelings of fear and panic, feelings of disbelief about what has happened, feelings of remorse, feeling out of control, being under or over-active, losing an appetite for food, being unable to sleep, having a poor memory, hearing the voice of the dead person, wanting to talk to them, forgetting they have died, being cross with other people, crying a lot, being unable to think or work.

For someone with a learning disability the same reactions may be expressed behaviourally rather than through speech. Disturbances of sleep and appetite are relatively easy to notice. Denial of the death or a failure to understand its finality may lead to searching behaviour. Unexplained anger towards objects or people or episodes of self-injury may be harder to understand. A loss of intellect or other skills, and the loss of bladder control may seem completely unrelated. Our difficulty is in recognising the behavioural manifestations of grief – especially if the apparent response to the death is one of indifference.

Bereavement counselling can be very effective in small groups where some of the learning emerges through sharing experiences. The counsellor may find an active approach is most effective. This might include visits to places which remind the bereaved person of the deceased and to the cemetery. The bereaved person should be encouraged to bring a photograph to the session to enable clear communication about the deceased person and as a measure of the extent to which the person is avoiding reminders of their loss. Hopefully therapy will continue until the person is able to look at the photo and talk about their deceased relative or friend in a realistic and positive manner.

Assessment for any psychotherapeutic intervention must consider the availability of an appropriate venue. The requirements may be straight-forward and simply include a quiet and private place easily accessible to the patient. On the other hand the therapist may require some art or play materials which cannot be readily transported. I lost my ability to communicate with one young man when he moved from the hustle and bustle of his parents' home to the quiet and rather sterile environment of a local authority hostel. No longer could he eye-point to the photo of his sister's wedding, to the telephone, or to the toys belonging to his nephews. No longer could he strain to hear the content of his parents conversation in the kitchen. Without these clues I was lost for a 'way in' to his current concerns.

The ability to make full use of the traditional 50-minute hour in a bare office must be questionable for many individuals whose communication relies so much on visual and aural stimuli. Well-meaning escorts or carers may unwittingly undermine the patient/therapist relationship by cancelling sessions or arriving late, by trying to talk to the therapist between sessions, by failing to respect confidentiality, by interrupting the session to see how things are going or to offer the therapist a cup of tea! Careful thought must be given about whether to offer treatment in the patient's own home, as such interruptions are more likely in the family home.

Establishing clear boundaries for therapy is essential, and it is advisable to ensure that another worker is available and willing to work with the carer and to deal with any practical arrangements or other needs which emerge for the patient during treatment.

Conclusion

Why is there often a reluctance by psychiatrists and psychotherapists to work with individuals or groups who have learning disabilities or with their families? Is it a reflection of the relative inability of us all to sort out our feelings about the incurability of chronic disability? Do we avoid the experience of handicap in order to avoid the acknowledgement of our own limitations? Even within the counselling or therapeutic relationship the therapist may have difficulty acknowledging his or her own negative feelings. Skilled supervision is strongly advised so that issues such as this are properly examined.

In working psychotherapeutically we must be prepared to tolerate the fact that there is no cure for our patient's disabilities. The best we can hope for is that secondary social and emotional handicaps are not added to their burden.

A psychodynamic understanding of the impact on the individual, his family and other social groups of his learning disability is long overdue. If we do not take into account the unconscious of the individual and the people he relates to, we will run the risk of misunderstanding.

Throughout the clinical examples given above, it will be apparent that misunderstandings readily occur, and that at no point can emotional and intellectual understanding and acceptance be complete. Life is a dynamic process of achievement, loss and adjustment. Counselling psychotherapeutic interventions can be carefully targeted to release blocks, to enable systems to interact dynamically and to allow reorganisation to take place.

References

Bicknell, D. J. (1983) Inaugural lecture: the psychopathology of handicap. *British Journal of Medical Psychology*, **56**, 167–178.

Cawley, R. H. (1977) The teaching of psychotherapy. *Association of University Teachers of Psychiatry Newsletter*, January, 19–36.

Conboy-Hill, S. (1992) Grief, loss and people with learning disabilities. In *Psychotherapy and Mental Handicap* (eds A. Waitman & S. Conboy-Hill). London: Sage.

Cook, D. (1978) *Walter*. Harmondsworth: Penguin.

Crossley, R. (1980) *Annie's Coming Out*. Harmondsworth: Penguin.

Cunningham, C. & Davis, H. (1985) Early intervention for the child. In *Mental Handicap. A Multi-Disciplinary Approach* (eds M. Craft, J. Bicknell & S. Hollins), pp. 209–228. London: Baillière Tindall.

Hollins, S. (1992) Group analytic therapy for people with a mental handicap. In *Psychotherapy and Mental Handicap* (eds A. Waitman & S. Conboy-Hill), pp. 139–149. London: Sage.

—— & Grimer, M. (1988) *Going Somewhere: People with Mental Handicaps and their Pastoral Care*. London: SPCK.

—— & Evered, C. (1990) Group process and content: the challenge of mental handicap. *Group Analysis*, **23**, 55–67.

—— & Sireling, L. (1991) *When Dad Died. Working through Loss with People who have Learning Disabilities*. Windsor: NFER-Nelson.

—— & —— (1994) *When Mum/Dad Died* (2nd edn). London: Gaskell.

——, Sinason, V. & Thompson, S. (1994) Individual, group and family therapy. In *Mental Health in Mental Retardation* (ed. N. Bouras). Cambridge: Cambridge University Press.

Leudar, I. (1989) Communicative environments for mentally handicapped people. In *Language and Communication in Mentally Handicapped People* (eds M. Beveridge, G. Conti-Ramsden & I. Leudar), pp. 274–300. London: Chapman and Hall.

McConachie, H. & Sinason, V. (1989) The emotional experience of multiple handicap – issues in assessment. *Child Care: Health and Development*, **15**, 75–78.

Morris, D. (1987) *Man Watching*. London: Grafton Books.

Richardson, A. & Ritchie, J. (1989) *Letting Go*. Milton Keynes: Open University Press.

Sinason, V. (1986) Secondary mental handicap and its relationship to trauma. *Psychoanalytic Psychotherapy*, **2**, 31–154.

—— (1988) Richard III, Hephaestus and Echo: sexuality and mental/multiple handicap. *Journal of Child Psychotherapy*, **14**, 93–105.

—— (1992) *Mental Handicap the Human Condition: New Approaches from the Tavistock*. London: Free Association Books.

Sireling, L., Cohen, D. & Marks, I. (1988) Guided mourning for morbid grief: a controlled replication. *Behavior Therapy*, **19**, 121–132.

Symington, N. (1981) The psychotherapy of a subnormal patient. *British Journal of Medical Psychology*, **54**, 187–199.

Vanier, J. (1985) *Man and Woman He Made Them*. London: Darton, Longman and Todd.

Wilkins, R. (1992) Psychotherapy with the siblings of mentally handicapped children.In *Psychotherapy and Mental Handicap* (eds A. Waitman & S. Conboy-Hill). London: Sage.

Additional reading

Depression in People with Learning Disability. A Help is at Hand leaflet, Defeat Depression Campaign, Royal College of Psychiatrists.

Waitman, A. & Conboy-Hill, S. (eds) (1992) *Psychotherapy and Mental Handicap*. London: Sage.

17 Forensic psychiatry and learning disability

Tony Holland

Historical background ● *Offending behaviour and intellectual development* ● *From arrest to conviction* ● *Assessment and treatment of offending behaviour*

People who have an impairment of their intellectual development are potentially vulnerable and, in particular circumstances, may require protection or some special provision (Williams, 1995). In childhood normal development and the acquisition of social and living skills is delayed, and at school the presence of a learning difficulty, if not already apparent, becomes so. Some children may also be socially impaired, having the characteristics of the autistic spectrum of disorders, and others may have additional physical disabilities and sensory impairments. As a group they are also more prone to developing additional behavioural problems and/or psychiatric disorders, and those with more severe disabilities have an increased risk of epilepsy. In adult life many of these problems become even more pronounced for a variety of reasons, including the lack of appropriate services, the fact that difficult behaviour becomes even more unacceptable, and there is likely to be less understanding and tolerance of the problems of social impairment.

An offence may occur in the context of pre-existing behaviour problems. For people with severe or profound levels of learning disabilities prosecution may be unlikely as court proceedings, for less herious offences such as criminal damage or public order offences, are rarely seen to be in the public interest. However, prosecution for more serious offences is likely, and people with lesser degrees of disability may well be charged and come to trial if their behaviour is against the law (see Ashton & Ward, 1992, for a summary of current legislation).

This chapter discusses the different psychiatric aspects which may have to be considered when a person with a learning disability has been charged with an offence. The criminal justice system is concerned ultimately with seeing that the guilty are brought to justice where this is in the public interest and, whatever the intervention (prison, probation order, admission to hospital), that the public are adequately protected, particularly in the case of serious crime.

259

Historical background

For hundreds of years there has been special legal provision for people with learning disabilities who break the law, in the form of pardons from the Monarch. Early in this century the Mental Deficiency Act (1913) allowed for the detention of people in institutions who had "arrested or incomplete development of mind". The criteria required for detention were broad and largely depended on the presence of what was perceived of as problem behaviour. Unlike the 1959 and 1983 Mental Health Acts, 'subnormality of intelligence and social functioning' was not an essential criterion for detention. People who would not now be considered as having a learning disability, and would not meet the criteria for 'mental impairment' or 'severe mental impairment' as defined in the 1983 Mental Health Act (MHA), were compulsorily detained in hospital, some for long periods.

In the early 1900s people with learning disabilities, who had previously been seen as in need of care and attention, were now seen as a threat to society. "Arrested or incomplete development of mind" (the phrase used in the Mental Deficiency Act) was thought to play a "fearful role" in the "... production of vice, crime and delinquency ..." It was stated that "not all criminals were feeble-minded but all feeble-minded were potential criminals". The effects of the ideas of the Eugenic movement was that segregation was seen to be the only solution to the social problems of this group of people and the myth was perpetuated of the link between crime and 'feeble-mindedness'.

Following the Percy Commission some of the problems of definition in the Mental Deficiency Act were corrected in the 1959 Mental Health Act. It became necessary to have "significant or severe impairment of intelligence and social functioning" to meet the criteria for mental subnormality or severe mental subnormality, respectively. With the development of new treatments for mental illness, the emphasis of this Act was on medical intervention and not judicial certification. The major thrust of the 1959 MHA was the right to treatment with the possibility of ultimate discharge from hospital. However, particularly for those detained under categories other than mental illness, and, in the absence of any alternative, 'treatment' was reduced to long-term residential care. The 1983 MHA gave rise to a further change in terminology and also in definitions. The terms used became 'mental impairment' and 'severe mental impairment' instead of 'mental subnormality'. These changes were primarily to avoid situations whereby people with learning disabilities, in the absence of additional mental health needs, could be compulsorily admitted to hospital under the MHA for extended periods. However, the 1983 MHA still allows admission for 28 days (Section 2) for assessment for people with a mental disorder (any other disorder or disability of mind) who may not necessarily meet the criteria for one of the four named mental disorders.

Changing attitudes concerning the care of people with learning disabilities has rightly emphasised the need for "an ordinary life" (Blunden & Allen, 1987). Supporting those people who present with additional problem behaviour also requires that community and hospital-based services are available to allow for the assessment of such behaviour and to institute appropriate treatments. This is particularly so for those who offend (see Home Office Circular 66/90; and Department of Health, 1994).

Offending behaviour and intellectual development

The assumed link between the propensity to crime and 'mental deficiency' had been based on a circular argument. Definitions of 'idiot', 'imbecile' and 'feeble-minded' in the 1913 Mental Deficiency Act did not specifically require intelligence to be assessed, and at the time IQ tests were only beginning to be developed. Attempts at assessing ability were not standardised and the results were likely to be influenced by the level of education available. Problem behaviour itself was the main criteria for hospitalisation.

There is little evidence to suggest that the presence of a learning disability predisposes to criminal behaviour. In fact, some offences which require an income or at least average intellectual ability, such as counterfeiting, tax evasion and motoring offences, are likely to be under-represented. Furthermore, any possible association can only be examined on the basis of the numbers convicted and, with some crimes, as few as 10% of crimes committed result in conviction. It is therefore impossible to identify the characteristics of those who have committed crimes but who have never been apprehended. MacEachron (1979) reviewed the studies which have reported very different prevalence rates for 'mental retardation' in prisons in the US (2.6% to 39.6%). She put forward a number of explanations to account for these differences, which included the types of psychological tests used, the circumstances surrounding the test administration, differing parole conditions and problems of definition. Her own study of convicted prisoners in two northeastern states found evidence of only a slight overrepresentation of people with IQs in the learning disabilities range, and comparisons between offenders with IQs below 70 and those with IQs in the borderline range (70–84) suggested that there were social factors the two groups had in common.

In the UK, annual prison and Home Office statistics do not give details on intellectual ability. Surveys of convicted prisoners have not found an overrepresentation of people with IQs below 70 in the prison population (Craft, 1985; Murphy *et al*, 1995). Furthermore the fourfold increase in indictable offences reported between 1955–1975 was not related to any appreciable increase in the number of people with learning disabilities living in the community (Robertson, 1981), as might have been expected if the presence of a learning disability was an important cause of criminal behaviour. In contrast a recent population-based cohort study in Sweden suggested that mental disorder, including intellectual disability, increases the likelihood of committing and being convicted of a criminal offence (Hodgins, 1992). Similarly, two studies in the UK have found that people with a learning disability are over-represented among those arrested and taken to two London (Gudjonsson *et al*, 1993) and one city police stations (Lyall *et al*, 1995*a*).

Although a clear relationship between learning disabilities and criminal behaviour has been discounted, it continues to be argued that people with learning disabilities are overrepresented among those convicted of arson or sexual offences. Walker & McCabe (1973), in their study of men and women receiving hospital orders, found about half of the offences of arson were committed by the third of people who had been detained under the category of mental subnormality. However, it is not possible to verify whether or not those detained under this category had 'significant impairment of intelligence' as no psychometric data, or information regarding schooling, were given. A later study suggests that those convicted of fire-setting offences may be of below average intelligence and have a history of special schooling or limited education (Bradford, 1982).

Similar observations have also been made regarding those convicted of sex offences, based initially on observations from Walker & McCabe's study (1973) which reported that people classified as 'mentally subnormal' were over-represented among those admitted under Hospital Orders after committing sexual offences. More recent studies suggest that this is not the case (Gostason, 1985; Swanson & Garwick, 1990). There is now some evidence that people with a learning disability may themselves be more prone to sexual abuse, possibly because of their social isolation and acquiescence. This might in turn increase their own propensity to inappropriate sexual behaviour, if abusing situations have been the only experience they have had of intimate sexual relationship.

From the commission of an offence to conviction there are a number of factors which may influence the outcome. For example, a person with a learning disability may be more likely to be caught, and may more readily confess regardless of whether or not they committed the offence; the police may, in the case of a person with more severe and obvious handicaps, choose not to proceed with prosecution (Lyall *et al*, 1995*b*). These factors will alter the observed rates of conviction for people with learning disabilities, making them an unreliable measure of the true relationship between offending and learning disabilities.

From arrest to conviction

The police are responsible for investigating a possible criminal offence, arresting the suspect and assembling the evidence which will aid the

Crown Prosecution Service in deciding whether the suspect should be brought to trial. At the trial the evidence is placed before a jury, the prosecution and defence counsel presenting the two sides of the case. This whole process is set within a framework of procedures, the purpose of which is to ensure that the defendant has a fair trial and that justice is done. This process is summarised in Fig. 17.1.

It is recognised that people with a mental disorder who commit offences may be vulnerable at particular points within the criminal justice process. In 1975 the Court of Appeal quashed the conviction of a man with mild learning disabilities who had been convicted of arson and manslaughter on the grounds that the conviction was unsafe. The subsequent Parliamentary Inquiry concluded that the questioning of the suspect had not been appropriate to his mental age and therefore the confession evidence could not be relied upon. The acquiescence of people with learning disabilities as well as their suggestibility are now recognised as important, particularly in the context of police questioning (Bull, 1994; Clare & Gudjonnson, 1995; Williams, 1995). Specific Acts of Parliament have been enacted to provide for such eventualities. In court, psychiatric and/or psychological evidence may be called to advise the court as to whether the defendant does or does not have a mental disorder, what form it takes and whether the presence of the mental disorder may be of importance in any specific way. Within this context the following legislation includes special provision for people with learning disabilities.

Police and Criminal Evidence Act 1984

At the time of arrest the police have a responsibility to inform the suspect of his or her rights. This is in the form of the 'caution' and the 'Notice to detained persons' which gives details of individual rights, for example, to consult a solicitor. If the police have reason to believe that a person has a mental disorder, for example, they are mentally handicapped and have significant impairment of intelligence and social functioning, this Act requires, among other things, that the police stop interviewing and arrange for a third party to be present, usually a social worker. The person acting as third party has the responsibility to support the suspect and to ensure that he or she understands his or her rights and is not placed under undue pressure. If these guidelines are not adhered to the defence can ask the judge, at the time of the trial, to rule that part of the evidence, for example a confession, is inadmissible. The police themselves have limited training to help them recognise if a person has a mental disorder, but some observations make it evident that the person may have a learning disability, for example, by the nature of the individual's behaviour, whether they can read and write, or if they are known to have been in a psychiatric or mental handicap hospital or to live in a hostel or group home for

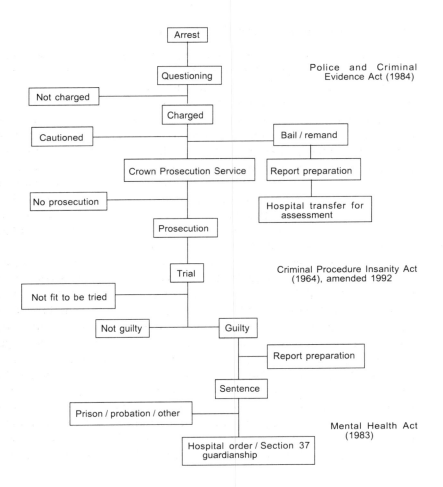

Fig. 17.1 Some of the stages during the criminal justice process from the time of arrest to sentence. Points at which psychiatric assessment might be requested are indicated and the names of relevant Acts of Parliament are given at the stages in this process when they may be of relevance. This diagram is not a comprehensive guide to all the possible options at the different stages in the criminal justice system. For further details consult the text, and in individual cases if in doubt seek further psychiatric or legal advice.

people with mental health problems. The safeguards in the Act relate to all aspects of detention and interrogation.

Criminal Procedure (Insanity) Act 1964

This Act of Parliament was intended to protect those recognised as being 'unfit to plead' by reason of disability from the distress of trial. Under this Act those found unfit to plead or not guilty by reason of insanity had to be detained indefinitely in hospital, without trial and therefore without the facts of the case being determined. The person may of course have been innocent of the offence, and there have been much publicised cases in which people have been detained for prolonged periods of time. For those who were mentally ill at the time, treatment may well result in them becoming fit to plead and stand trial and a trial could then take place. However, for those found unfit due to 'arrested or incomplete development of mind', the likelihood of marked change was small. Furthermore, the criteria for being unfit were such that many, regardless of intellectual level, could be considered unfit.

The problems created by this Act have led to the use of 'unfit to plead' being avoided if at all possible. The Act was amended as a result of a Private Member's Bill and became law on 1 January 1992. It is now possible for a trial of the facts to take place and the person, if found unfit to plead, will not automatically have to be detained in hospital. Other options will range from the equivalent of a restriction order to absolute discharge. The psychiatrist, if consulted by the court or by the defence, has a responsibility to assess whether the person concerned understands the concept of being 'guilty' or 'not guilty', can follow the proceedings in court, can instruct his or her lawyers and challenge a jury. If because of the presence of a significant learning disability the person may have limited understanding, the defence may choose to raise the question of fitness to plead, expert evidence may be called and the jury asked to decide.

Mental Health Act 1983

The fact that people may, against their will, require treatment in hospital for a mental disorder is well-recognised, and the Mental Deficiency Act (1913) and subsequent Mental Health Acts (1959, 1983) enabled compulsory detention in hospital or a registered mental nursing home to take place. Under such circumstances there is a delicate balance between the right of choice and the right to treatment, and for this reason since the 1983 MHA there has appropriately been the right of appeal to a mental health review tribunal (MHRT) against detention. Part III of the MHA is concerned with those who may have or do have a mental disorder and have committed a criminal offence. In this Act 'mental disorder' is broadly defined and includes 'arrested or incomplete development of mind', 'mental illness', 'psychopathic disorder' and 'any other disorder or disability of mind'. For assessment orders, 'reason to suspect' that a person may have a defined mental disorder is acceptable but for treatment orders, if the person is to be detained, he/she must have one of the four named mental disorders (mental illness, mental impairment, severe mental impairment or psychopathic disorder) as well as meeting other criteria.

The definitions of mental impairment and severe mental impairment are given in the MHA and include four particular points: arrested or incomplete development of mind, significant (severe) impairment of intelligence and social functioning, and that this is associated with abnormally aggressive or seriously irresponsible conduct on the part of the person concerned. In order to make a diagnosis of mental impairment, information is therefore required on the person's early development, the acquisition of living and social skills, a standardised measure of intelligence and information on the individual's behaviour. The British Psychological Society recommend that 'significant impairment of intelligence' should be taken to mean an IQ score of less than 70 using an established IQ test. The 'behaviour' clause was inserted in the 1983 MHA to make the point that detention under the MHA for treatment is only appropriate if a person with 'arrested or incomplete development of mind' has an additional mental health problem which may require admission. How this phrase should be interpreted is open to question, but there needs to be definite evidence of significant problem behaviour which may include a conviction so that, at least, the facts have been judged in a court of law. Admission to hospital for treatment can take place under this category if the mental impairment is "of a nature or degree which makes it appropriate for him to receive medical treatment in a hospital" and, in the case of mental impairment (and psychopathic disorder), "treatment is likely to alleviate or prevent a deterioration of his condition and it is necessary for the health or safety of the patient or for the protection of other persons that he should receive such treatment and it cannot be provided unless he is detained under this section".

The four named mental disorders in the MHA are not mutually exclusive and if a person with a learning disability has a mental illness and requires treatment in hospital, detention under that category may be the most appropriate. An improvement or not in the person's mental state will be the best guide to the need for continuing detention. The problems created by the term 'mental impairment' and by compulsory detention in hospital under this category are discussed further below.

Options available to the court

At different stages throughout the criminal justice process the person with a learning disability may have special problems which may result in inappropriate conviction, or, if convicted, inappropriate disposal. Expert psychiatric and/or psychological evidence may be requested to advise on fitness to plead, whether the person does or does not have a mental disorder, and the reliability of, for example, a confession statement. At some point the court or the defence may request advice about possible sentencing options. This may be requested in the knowledge that the defendant is pleading guilty, in anticipation of a possible guilty verdict, or courts, having reached a guilty verdict, may adjourn to seek advice before sentence is passed. For those found not guilty of the offence, the court no longer has any power to decide what should happen.

Under such circumstances the psychiatrist will be expected to present to the court a report which sets out the facts as he or she sees them as well as answers to the questions asked by the court or defence solicitors and which are pertinent to the stage the defendant has reached in the criminal justice process. This may include discussing the circumstances surrounding the offence, whether the person does or does not have a mental disorder, and if so whether detention in hospital is appropriate, or whether the court might consider a number of other options, for example, the possibility of a probation order with conditions of treatment, or a Section 37 Guardianship Order. Where none of these are appropriate, the court relies on the usual options, such as fines or imprisonment. Even if a psychiatric report does not recommend any specific option, it may help the court to arrive at a decision (see case example 1).

> **Case example 1**
>
> Mr Phillips is a 36-year-old man who has always lived at home. His mother is now 75, and his father died two years ago. He went to a special school because of moderate learning difficulties. His numeracy and literacy skills are poor but his living skills are adequate. He was charged with indecent exposure having allegedly shown his penis to two young children who live next door. He has no regular day-time occupation apart from doing some local shopping for his mother and he spends all his leisure time at home. On mental state examination he was anxious because of the court proceedings but there was no other abnormality of note. He pleaded guilty to the offence and the court accepted that he had a learning disability, he was very socially isolated and had had no opportunity to make friends. He was conditionally discharged in the knowledge that the local Community Mental Handicap Team had become involved and were working with him and his mother to help increase the opportunities available to him.

In the case of a person who is mentally ill, the advice to the court is usually that the person requires treatment in hospital and a Section 37 order may well apply. In this case a mental disorder (mental illness) is identified which has a specific treatment, and improvement can be monitored by regular mental state examinations. Furthermore, if the person was to receive a prison sentence it is likely that his or her mental state would deteriorate further, and therefore the potential benefits of transfer from the criminal justice system into the health service clearly outweigh any possible disadvantages.

For those who have a learning disability and are not obviously mentally ill, the judgement as to whether transfer to hospital is either possible or appropriate is not always as easy. Under these circumstances there are powers available to the court to remand the person to hospital for assessment (Sections 35, 36). This allows 28 days, renewable for two further periods of 28 days, to determine whether the person has a specified mental disorder, whether it is of a nature or degree requiring treatment in hospital, and in particular whether treatment will prevent deterioration or bring about an improvement in the person's condition. Treatment is defined very broadly in the MHA and may mean no more than on-going care in hospital, but it should no longer be considered to be just residential care but should be for specific purposes. Under the circumstances where an offence has been committed the role of a hospital is clearly to assess the problem, treat where possible and/or devise an appropriate management strategy and to help the person concerned to return to more normal life outside a hospital setting. A recommendation to the court should recognise that this group of people are likely to have lifelong social and health needs, and admission to hospital should only be considered if it is necessary for the purposes of assessment and/or treatment, and should only then be considered in the context of a longer term plan of resettlement outside a hospital setting. It is often advisable that these issues are addressed during the court process, so that if necessary the managers of the appropriate local authority or health district can advise the court as to how support will be offered in the longer term, as would be required under Section 117 (after-care) of the MHA if the person was to be admitted compulsorily to hospital.

Initial assessment may indicate that further treatment is necessary and that admission to hospital is appropriate. The problem may then arise as to where the person should be admitted. District health authorities have the responsibility to provide the means whereby a person can receive treatment and local services need to plan for this. Increasingly, district-based psychiatrists who specialise in learning disabilities have access to local psychiatric beds. Regionally based secure units or more specialist services for people with learning disabilities may be available. These more specialist services have different models; evaluation of such services is required (Day, 1988; Murphy *et al*, 1991). For those people who have been convicted of serious offences there are national special hospitals now administered by the Special Hospitals Health Authority. These hospitals offer high levels of security and admission is limited to those considered to be a 'grave and immediate danger'. The nature of the offence and the likelihood of further offending and thus the level of security required have to be considered. The decision to offer admission to a special hospital now lies with an admission panel rather than any one psychiatrist, and only those who require the high level of security offered by special hospitals are likely to be offered admission.

Within any given district it is likely that a number of possible options need to be available should someone within the service offend. In the past there has been a focus on hospital-based services but, for those who offend and who, for example, meet the criteria for mental impairment or severe mental impairment, the legal framework of a Section 37 Guardianship Order may be sufficient to allow for the safe management of that person within a community setting. This may be of particular relevance when the offence has taken place in the context of limited support being available to the person and a lack of any structure to the person's life. The local authority have to agree such an order; it allows them to determine where the person lives, and the person can be returned there if they leave. There is generally little experience concerning the use of guardianship (whether as a civil order or through the courts) but it may provide a useful framework to build a package of care around and by doing so reduce the risk of future offending.

Assessment and treatment of offending behaviour

The principles of psychiatric assessment are essentially similar in the context of an offence as in any other situation, the difference being that the power to proceed in any given direction lies with the court. One of the major concerns will be to obtain some idea as to the factor(s) contributing to the offending behaviour and how they might be modified in order that the likelihood of further offending is reduced.

Offending behaviour may well be the consequence of existing problem behaviour. A survey of residential establishments for people with learning disabilities in one health district found that there was a distinct lack of operational policies relating to alleged offending. Whether challenging behaviour was also considered offending behaviour and the involvement of the police was arbitrary (Lyall *et al*, 1995). Psychological and psychiatric assessment has the task of attempting to answer the questions: what is the best way of understanding the index behaviour, and what factor(s) increase or decrease the propensity to such behaviour and how can they be modified? The commission of an offence may give rise to the opportunity to address these issues in a systematic way. Obtaining the facts as far as possible and a thorough mental state examination are crucial. Much of the literature on offenders with learning disabilities has been based on those who have been admitted to specialist in-patient services. Little is known about the characteristics of people with learning disabilities whose offence does not lead to hospital admission. The former group, however, have been reported by Day (1988) to have high rates of additional psychopathology. Thirty per cent of 20 people followed up by him from a secure unit had had additional mental illness, and nearly 60% had come from deprived social circumstances. The experience of the Mental Impairment Evaluation and Treatment Service, a regional assessment service, has been similar (Murphy *et al*, 1991). Sixty per cent of the first 40 people seen by the service had suffered from additional psychiatric illness. In the majority of cases it seemed likely that a disordered mental state had contributed to their offending behaviour, and the likelihood of future offending would at least partly depend on the effective treatment of the mental illness together with the provision of appropriate support.

The presence of a learning disability, however, separates this population from those seen in the mainstream forensic services. As has already been argued, there appears to be little relationship between intellectual impairment and criminal behaviour. However, the level of social development may be important in understanding the offending and in the subsequent management of the person. Those people who fall within the autistic spectrum of disorders, including those with Asperger's syndrome, have very particular difficulties which markedly impair their understanding of the social world (Baron-Cohen, 1990), and they may be more prone to problem behaviour and therefore to offending. Those with Asperger's syndrome may be particularly vulnerable as their disability may not be obvious initially. Identifying the presence of the disorder and helping the individual, family and/or care staff to understand the nature of the disability is likely to change peoples' perceptions of the difficulties and to bring about more appropriate help for the person concerned.

The psychiatrist's role is to contribute a particular perspective to the understanding of the offending behaviour. The complexities of some of the problems are such that a variety of different perspectives and approaches are frequently required. This is particularly the case when trying to make some assessment of the risk of future offending.

Assessment of risk

One of the major criticisms, particularly of special hospitals, but also of hospital-based assessment services, is that assessing the likelihood of further offending is difficult if someone is held in conditions of security. This is clearly crucial as the decision, for example, to discharge someone from their section may well depend on this. The propensity to offend is not fixed but very likely to be influenced by a variety of factors which vary over time. Psychiatric and psychological models of problem behaviour are very different but they complement each other when assessing risk. The diagnostic psychiatric model and the resultant formulation focuses, for example, on such issues as the presence of additional mental illness, epilepsy, the cause of the person's learning disabilities, and the relationship between these factors and the offending behaviour. The psychological functional model is concerned with the antecedents to, and the consequences of the behaviour, and the 'setting' events which make the index behaviour more likely (see Holland & Murphy, 1990, for review).

The complexities of a given problem may require a logical and hypothesis-testing approach. Case example 2 illustrates how a number of factors were thought to have contributed to the propensity to offend: some could be treated, others required understanding and a sensible and informed management strategy. Such an approach does not expect that the person's learning disability can be cured, but rather identifies the factors which may have contributed to the offending and looks for appropriate interventions. These may include, for example, treatment of a mental illness, psychological strategies such as anger management training, individual or family counselling, improving the opportunities in their lives, or helping the person to develop new skills which may allow them to cope in situations which had previously led to problem behaviour. An example of how very different factors might have contributed to fire-setting by a particular person and the very different interventions which followed the identification of these factors is well illustrated in a case report by Clare *et al* (1992).

Case example 2

Mr Brown is 24 years old. He was admitted to a private psychiatric hospital under Section 37 of the MHA having been found guilty of stealing a motor vehicle. The local authority had been concerned about his behaviour for many years and by the fact that he regularly expressed an interest in children. His early developmental history was characteristic of Asperger's syndrome and he had a history since childhood of abnormal speech development and intense interest in particular subjects. On admission to a specialist assessment service he talked about wishing to touch children and was distressed by his persistent and intrusive thoughts about them. Over several weeks his mental state fluctuated between periods of agitation, pressure of speech and intense preoccupations to, at other times, being more relaxed and less preoccupied. Detailed observation supported the diagnosis of a bipolar mood disorder and it was possible to demonstrate that when his mood was stable (on lithium carbonate medication) his obsessions were less intrusive and he was in control of them. On these occasions he was also willing to accept sexual counselling and would participate in other aspects of his treatment programme.

Many people with a learning disability who have offended are likely to have life-long social and emotional needs. The successful support of this group of people within a community setting will require a long-term commitment from both health and social services. Providing the right level of support, understanding the nature of the person's disability, and where appropriate treating additional problems, may help to decrease the likelihood of re-offending. This is a complex task and requires good case management and multidisciplinary team work.

References

Ashton, G. & Ward, A. (1992) *Mental Handicap and the Law*. London: Sweet & Maxwell.

Baron-Cohen, S. (1990) Autism: a specific cognitive disorder of 'mind-blindness'. *International Review of Psychiatry*, **2**, 81–90.

Blunden, R. & Allen, D. (eds) (1987) *Facing the Challenge: an Ordinary Life for People with Learning Difficulties and Challenging Behaviour*. London: King's Fund.

Bradford, J. (1982) Arson: a clinical study. *Canadian Journal of Psychiatry*, **27**, 188–192.

Bull, R. (1994) Interviewing people with communicative disabilities. In *Handbook of Psychology in Legal Contexts* (eds R. Bull & D. Carson). Chichester: John Wiley.

Clare, I. C. H., Murphy, G. H., Cox, D., *et al* (1992) Assessment and treatment of firesetting: a single case investigation using a cognitive behavioural model. *Criminal Behaviour and Mental Health*, **2**, 253–268.

—— & Gudjonsson, G. H. (1995) The vulnerability of suspects with intellectual disabilities during police interviews: a review and experimental study of decision-making. *Mental Handicap Research*, **8**, 110–128.

Day, K. (1988) A hospital-based treatment programme for male mentally handicapped offenders. *British Journal of Psychiatry*, **153**, 635–644.

Department of Health (1994) *Review of Health and Social Services for Mentally Disordered Offenders and Others Requiring Similar Services. Vol. 7. People with Learning Disabilities (Mental Handicap) or with Autism*. London: HMSO.

Gostason, R. (1985) Psychiatric illness among the mentally retarded. *Acta Psychiatrica Scandinavica*, **17** (suppl. 318), 1–117.

Gudjonsson, G. H., Clare, I. C. H., Rutters, S., *et al* (1993) *Persons at Risk during Interview in Police Custody: the Identification of Vulnerabilities*. The Royal Commission on Criminal Justice, Research Study No. 12. London: HMSO.

Hodgins, S. (1992) Mental disorder, intellectual deficiency and crime. *Archives of General Psychiatry*, **49**, 476–483.

Holland, A. J. & Murphy, G. (1990) Behavioural and psychiatric disorder in adults with mild learning difficulties. *International Review of Psychiatry*, **2**, 117–136.

Home Office (1990) *Provision for Mentally Disordered Offenders*. Home Office Circular 66/90. London: Home Office.

Lyall, I., Holland, A. J., Collins, S., *et al* (1995a) Incidence of persons with a learning disability detained in Police custody: A needs assessment for service development. *Medicine, Science and the Law*, **35**, 61–71.

——, —— & —— (1995b) Offending by adults with learning disabilities and the attitudes of staff to offending behaviour: implications for service development. *Journal of Intellectual Disability Research*, **39**, 501–508.

MacEachron, A. E. (1979) Mentally retarded offenders: prevalence and characteristics. *American Journal of Mental Deficiency*, **84**, 165–176.

Murphy, G., Holland, A. J., Fowler, P., *et al* (1991) MIETS (Mental Impairment Evaluation and Treatment Service): a service option for people with mild learning difficulties and challenging behaviour or psychiatric problems. 1. The philosophy, the service and the clients. *Mental Handicap Research*, **4**, 41–66.

——, Harnett, H. & Holland, A. J. (1995) A survey of intellectual disabilities amongst men on remand in prison. *Mental Handicap Research*, **8**, 81–98.

Robertson, G. (1981) The extent and pattern of crime among mentally handicapped offenders. *Apex (Journal of the British Institute of Mental Handicap)*, 100–103.

Swanson, C. K & Garwick, G. B. (1990) Treatment for low functioning sex offenders: group therapy and inter-agency co-ordination. *Mental Retardation*, **28**, 155–161.

Walker, N. & McCabe, S. (1973) *Crime and Insanity in England*, vol. 2. Edinburgh: Edinburgh University Press.

Williams, C. (1995) *Invisible Victims; Crime and Abuse against People with Learning Difficulties*. London: Jessica Kingsley.

Index

Compiled by Linda English